CULTURE AND NATIONALITY

CULTURE
AND
NATIONALITY

ESSAYS BY
A. G. BAILEY

ALFRED
GOLDSWORTHY
BAILEY

The Carleton Library No. 58

McClelland and Stewart Limited
Toronto/Montreal

The Canadian Publisher
McClelland and Stewart Limited
25 Hollinger Road, Toronto 374

Printed and bound in Canada by
T. H. Best Printing Company Limited

THE CARLETON LIBRARY

A series of Canadian reprints and new collections of source material relating to Canada, issued under the editorial supervision of the Institute of Canadian Studies of Carleton University, Ottawa.

Table of Contents

Preface

When I was asked to say how I happened to write these essays, I was glad to do so as it gave me an opportunity to trace the development of my thinking over the period represented by the collection and to express my thanks to a number of persons for help and encouragement in the course of my academic life. I thought that I might very well begin with the summer of 1927, since at that time I had just graduated from the University of New Brunswick and was thinking of entering a graduate school for further study. It was at that juncture that I met an old acquaintance, Captain Horace Hume VanWart, who urged me to seek admission to the University of Toronto's School of Graduate Studies. I decided to do so on little more than impulse as I knew very little about Toronto, and hardly anyone who had ever been there. I had spent most of my boyhood in Fredericton, and in Quebec, which was my birthplace, in a community whose contacts were mostly with England and which was at that time strongly imperialistic in sentiment and outlook.[1]

On arriving at the University of Toronto I found there a spirit of Canadian nationalism which was new to me and which manifested itself in a number of ways. For one thing the paintings of the Group of Seven were everywhere in evidence and were clearly regarded as representing the first authentic expres-

[1] In 1914, and after, the streets were filled with soldiers. Fleets of transports stood at their moorings in gray anonymity below the Dufferin Terrace, waiting to take the First Contingent of the Canadian Expeditionary Force, numbering 32,000 men, to Europe. Among them we recognized the *Empress of Japan* from her clipper bow. We were often in cadet uniform marching and drilling, or in Boy Scout outfit at camps and rallies. The air was filled with the sound of bugles and kettledrums. One evening Colonel William Wood came to say goodbye to us, on leaving to join Jellicoe's flagship as Official Eye-Witness and, as it turned out, to take part in the Battle of Jutland. Nothing so aptly epitomizes the era described by Carl Berger in his *A Sense of Power*. (Toronto, 1970), pp. 238, 246-8.

sion of a Canadian spirit as distinct from the works of older painters, such as Krieghoff, which I was used to seeing in the homes of English Quebecers, and which were much publicized in Toronto as derivative of a particular European school. Almost the first person whom I met at the University was the Librarian, the late William Stewart Wallace, in whose graduate seminar in Canadian history I was urged to enrol. I was grateful for the advice as Major Wallace remained a good friend to me ever afterwards. He had just published an important work on the growth of Canadian national feeling and I soon discovered that both he and the other students in the seminar regarded Canadian history as having a significance beyond its intrinsic interest, an attitude which I came to share and which I have never lost, as would be evident to anyone who might happen to glance at the table of contents of the present volume.

It would be noted also that there is a good deal of emphasis in these pages on social and cultural history. During that first year in Toronto I shared a library study with James J. Talman who had become absorbed in investigations into the social development of Upper Canada, in part at least as a result of having been a student with Fred Landon at the University of Western Ontario. I caught something of his enthusiasm for this approach to the study of history, having, I believe, been predisposed in that direction by courses in sociology given at the University of New Brunswick by Wilfred Currier Keirstead, different as sociology and social history may be in both nature and aim.

It was perhaps natural that all the while I should have kept casting back to my early surroundings in Quebec, and in the village of Tadoussac, one hundred and thirty miles to the northeastward, where I had spent much of my early life. To have lived during one's most impressionable years in the visible presence of history had effects that would have been difficult to eradicate had one attempted to do so. The windows of our country home looked down on the place where the Huguenot fur trader, Pierre Chauvin, in 1600 built the first house in Canada; and across the shifting currents of the Saguenay lay the long wooded promontory, Pointe des Allouettes, where in 1603 Champlain found the Montagnais and their allies celebrating a victory over their Iroquois enemies.[2] My earliest memories

<hr>

[2]W. J. Wintemberg believed the site of the Iroquoian village of Stadacona to be within an arrow's flight of the house, at 37 Ste. Ursule Street, in which I was born and which had been built by a military engineer, Richard Goldsworthy, a great great grandfather

were of Quebec itself during the tercentenary celebrations of the founding of the city by de Monts and Champlain, watching a parade from the top of the city wall, and ships of the Royal Navy firing salutes from their big guns in honour of the occasion. I found, however, that no graduate course in the history of New France was being offered in the University of Toronto when I went there, and it was only through the kindness of Professor Ralph Flenley that I was able to add a course on the French regime to my syllabus. It had been the social and institutional aspects that had interested me most, and later, after a short interval in journalism, when I went back to study for the doctorate, Chester Martin, the new head of the department, suggested a field requiring a combination of historical with anthropological studies. This was the beginning of a long and happy association with the leading professor of anthropology in the University, the late T. F. McIlwraith, who henceforeward became the principal director of my studies. The upshot was that I embarked on a work that today would be referred to as interdisciplinary, and which was certainly a departure from the strictly departmentalized approach to the humanities and social sciences prevailing at that time. Although George Henry Lane-Fox Pitt-Rivers had produced an important work on European contacts with the peoples of the Pacific, there was very little else of a scientific nature in the field of cross-cultural relationships. My task was to bring what anthropological insights I could muster to bear on the relations of the French and English, on the one hand, with the tribes of the eastern woodland in the sixteenth and seventeeth centuries. Harold Innis, not yet head of the great composite department that he was soon to develop, had just published his history of the fur trade[3] that was in some ways to revolutionize the study of Canadian history, and I was more than fortunate in finding him interested in the work that I was proposing to undertake.

It was necessary for me to try to account for the disappearance of Iroquoian peoples from the St. Lawrence in the six-

on my mother's side, who came from Cornwall after the Conquest to assist in rebuilding the fortifications of Quebec. It remained in the family until 1952 although rented for a few years to Mrs. M. M. Chaplin who painted the picture of it reproduced by Marius Barbeau in *I Have Seen Quebec*, (Toronto, 1957). He was thus altogether mistaken in describing the Goldsworthy house as the home of Madame de la Peltrie.

[3]H. A. Innis, *The Fur Trade in Canada; an introduction to Canadian economic history* (New Haven, 1930).

teenth century. Innis thought the results to be worth publishing, and arranged to have them presented to the Royal Society of Canada.[4] Although the paper was not included in the edition of my book on the Eastern Algonkians, which had been sponsored by the New Brunswick Museum in 1937 on the recommendation of William Francis Ganong and John Clarence Webster, the subject had to be looked into again when a second edition was undertaken by the University of Toronto Press in 1969. The first study in the present volume represents a completely new treatment of the subject. The second essay was omitted from the original work, though published separately.[5]

II

In the course of the above-mentioned study I had become increasingly interested in problems of a general or perhaps, one might say, of a philosophical nature, and an opportunity to read widely in the fields of sociology, and in the works of the philosophers of history from Vico to Marx and Toynbee, was made possible in 1934 through the award of a post-doctoral fellowship by the Royal Society of Canada which took me to the University of London where I came under the influence of Morris Ginsberg. He had succeeded, in the Chair of Sociology, the eminent scholar L. T. Hobhouse whose works I had read as an undergraduate at the University of New Brunswick. Ginsberg had gathered about him a number of leading scholars, some of them, such as Karl Mannheim, who were refugees from the Nazi persecution. In Ginsberg's seminar race theories were subjected to a searching analysis, and questions concerning the causes of the uneven contributions of different peoples to the advancement of civilization were raised, and answers sought. The subject was clearly related to the whole problem of cultural efflorescences and involved an assessment on a wide scale of the

[4]A. G. Bailey, "The significance of the identity and disappearance of the Laurentian Iroquois." *Transactions and Proceedings of the Royal Society of Canada*, vol. 27, section 2 (1933), pp. 97-108.

[5]The essay published here as "The Ordeal of the Eastern Algonkians" was originally "Social Revolution in Early Eastern Canada", *Canadian Historical Review*, Volume XIX, 1938, pp. 264-276. It was to have been the concluding chapter of *The Conflict of European and Eastern Algonkian Cultures, 1504-1700, A Study in Canadian Civilization* (Monograph 2, The New Brunswick Museum, Saint John, N.B., 1937) but was omitted from that work, as well as from the second edition published in 1969.

role of diffusion through drift as well as the contact of diverse peoples such as I had studied in Canada. Ginsberg arranged for me to see Arnold Toynbee and set me to reading the first volumes of the great historian's *A Study of History* which had just appeared, and which had such an important bearing on the problems with which I had become concerned. He directed me also to a truly remarkable work by G. Spiller entitled *The Origin and Nature of Man*[6] which served to deepen one's understanding of the processes and patterns of what, after Sir Edward Tylor, anthropologists always referred to as "culture".

The acquisition by man as a member of society of all those traits of a material and spiritual nature which go to make up the cultural heritage was seen to be characterized more by imitation by many peoples of what were often unique discoveries and inventions made elsewhere in the world by individuals or groups more opportunely situated. Indeed the progress of research had eventuated in a reduction of the number of traits believed to have been independently created. The degree of originality of the human mind was clearly minimal, and was seen to be in large measure a function of the sociocultural environment. Studies of primitive culture-areas by Clark Wissler, R. B. Dixon, and many others had indicated that the creative process was likely to be more pronounced and of greater frequency at the centres or nuclei of such areas than on their peripheries. While this fact had been amply demonstrated in ethnological literature, the method had not been applied to any extent to the processes at work in civilized societies. When studying cultural contacts in colonial America one had come upon traits that were clearly the result of the interaction of peoples of diverse culture, such as the French and the Indians, and therefore newly formed. No better illustration could be found than the craft which we called the North Shore canoe, in which I had spent so much of my youth on the lower St. Lawrence, and which represented a fusion of a Montagnais canoe and a European keeled boat. It nevertheless remained true that the great creative acts that had carried civilization on its upward course had occurred in the metropolitan centres rather than at the outposts and margins of civilization, and that the people in colonial areas derived almost all their material resources, their values and inspirations from such centres of creativity. Later while teaching courses in anthropology and Canadian history I

[6]Gustav Spiller, *Origin and Nature of Man; an enquiry into fundamentals, reconciling man's proud achievements with man's humble descent.* (London, 1931).

began to speculate on the possibilities of applying the culture-area concept to the development of literature and the arts in the Canadian provinces. Curiosity concerning causes operative in the history of the arts had been aroused while a student in art and archeology under C. T. Currelly, director of the Royal Ontario Museum, at one time an associate of Sir Flinders Petrie; during further studies in 1935 at the British Museum and the Victoria and Albert; and later still while holding the office of curator of the Department of Arts and Industries in the New Brunswick Museum. The result was a rather lengthy study only a portion of which has been included in the present volume under the title "Evidences of Culture Considered as Colonial."

Both before and during the time in the mid-forties, when I was engaged in this work, besides teaching courses in history and anthropology, I came more and more to the acceptance of what A. L. Kroeber called the superorganic as explicable in its own terms and characterized by style-patterns, the growth and exhaustion of which had been the subject of one of that scholar's principal works[7]. I found myself endeavouring to apply this concept to the various fields with which I was concerned, especially the development of literary expression in the Maritime Provinces. I had been familiar from childhood with the poetry of Bliss Carman who had been one of my father's teachers at the Old Park Barracks School in Fredericton. My father might be heard reciting poems by his friend, Theodore Goodridge Roberts, at any time of day. It is essential to mention here that the Baileys, and their Marshall-d'Avray forebears, had been close friends of the families of Sir Charles G. D. Roberts and Bliss Carman for several generations. The Baileys were in fact connected with them through the Bliss's and Emersons back in Concord in the Massachusetts Bay Colony; and my great grandfather, d'Avray,[8] had numbered among his students at the University of New Brunswick the father of Sir Charles Roberts as well as George R. Parkin, later Sir George, both of whom were to play a crucial part in the emergence of a school

[7]A. L. Kroeber, *Configurations of Cultural Growth* (Berkeley, 1944).

[8]Joseph Marshall de Brett, 2nd Baron d'Avray, Professor of Modern Language and Literature in the University of New Brunswick, 1848-1871, son of the Physician Extraordinary to King Ferdinand and Queen Maria Carolina of Naples, and a participant in the events leading to the downfall of Napoleon and the Restoration of the Bourbons to the French Throne.

of Romantic poetry in Fredericton. When it is born in mind that all these families were intimate with the descendants of Jonathan Odell, the Tory poet of the American Revolutionary War, and a founder of Fredericton, no further evidence should be required to prove that there existed in this place a literary tradition which has persisted to the present day, whatever anyone may say to the contrary. When in the spring of 1949 I was asked by my colleague, Desmond Pacey, to prepare a paper on this subject for a regional conference of the Humanities Research Council of Canada shortly to be held in Halifax, I was glad to comply, with the first of the two essays included in the present volume in the section called "Provincial Efflorescences."

I had already had occasion to work in the field of Maritime history at a time when New Brunswick was passing through one of its recurrent phases of retrospective assessment of the effects of Confederation on the regional economy. I had returned to the Province from abroad in the summer of 1935 to accept a position with the New Brunswick Museum and not long afterwards an appointment to the newly established Chair of History in my old University. The view was widespread that the Maritime area had been wrenched out of the international and oceanic context, within which it had come to a measure of maturity, and that it had been forced into a continental framework that was incompatible with its needs and welfare. George Wilson had published in the *Canadian Historical Review*[9] a fine paper on New Brunswick's entrance into Confederation, but I was determined to enquire into the way in which the people of the time regarded the matter, especially the economic issues involved. Three of the papers concerned with aspects of this subject, and written at the time, are included in the present volume. In view of the evident strength of anti-Confederation sentiment, it is somewhat surprising to discover the degree to which Roberts and his father had become, not long after 1867, imbued with the spirit of Canadian nationalism. Whatever its source there seemed little doubt that it had served as something of a stimulus to literary developments in Fredericton, and I was anxious to find out whether the contemporary literary and nationalist ferment in Toronto had had something to do with it. The opportunity came in 1955 when I was asked to accept the Innis Visiting Professorship in the University of Toronto. I felt

[9]G. E. Wilson, "New Brunswick's entrance into Confederation", *Canadian Historical Review,* Vol. 9, No. 1. (March, 1928).

particularly honoured to be offered this appointment to a professorship established in memory of my old professor and friend, and I hoped to be able to extend to other areas the approach taken in the Maritime literary study, mentioned above, which the late J. B. Brebner believed to have opened up a new and fruitful line of investigation. When I told Dr. W. S. Wallace, then in retirement, of my interest in the nationalist movement that had sprung up in Ontario in the era of Confederation, he put me on to the fact that there were papers in the possession of Mr. Harold Foster relating to his father, W. A. Foster, the founder of Canada First, which had apparently never been made accessible to scholars. While examining them, through the kindness of Mr. Foster, who put them fully at my disposal, I came to feel that they should be available to students and arranged to have a microfilm made of the portion which I called the Canada First Scrapbook. I came to the conclusion that Foster and his associates had become confirmed nationalists long before the Ottawa meetings of 1868 and in the essays included in this volume I laid less stress on those meetings than had been customary. A number of unpublished Goldwin Smith letters enabled me to define his relationship, I believe more clearly than hitherto, with the nationalist movement. Relatively mild though it was, I found the racism of some of the members repellent, and it was, in any case, quite contrary to all that one had learned in the course of one's anthropological studies. It was in the hope of correcting false conceptions of race, current in Canada and elsewhere, that I wrote the essay that appears last in this collection. I always appreciated Arthur Lower's attempt to understand, and present in a fair light, the other Canada. Nationalities were often regarded as divided by factors of biological heredity, and misunderstandings between such peoples as the French and English were undoubtedly accentuated by this illusion. It is true that many French and English in Quebec mingled amicably, especially the well-to-do, and that intermarriages were by no means infrequent, thus accounting for many Irish and Scottish names among the French Canadians (the word Québecois was never used in those days, not in its present sense). One encountered daily numerous persons, among them some who were one's most intimate friends who represented the best that there was of both traditions, such, for example, as the English-Canadian who was a great grandson of Philippe Aubert de Gaspé. It was thus traumatic to stand on the steps of Colonel Wood's house and to watch cavalry, armed with axe handles, followed by infantry with fixed bayonets in open order, charge down Grande Allée, with the object of dispersing the anti-conscription rioters on those Easter-week nights in 1918. Rumours of threats to burn down the house of our next-door neighbour, a French-Canadian Conservative Senator, gave rise to comfortless thoughts. These things and many more were not forgotten. Within a few years I would find myself a student in Fredericton, and in the summer of 1927, a graduate, which brings me to the point at which I began this statement.

I have now to mention the kind and courteous attention given to my work by Miss Nan Gregg and her staff of the Reference Department of the Harriet Irving Library; and of how much I have appreciated collaborating with Professor David Farr, Professor Carman Bickerton, and Mr. James Marsh in the production of this volume of essays. I have been encouraged over the years in the writing of them, and much else besides, by my friend Malcolm Mackenzie Ross, an old Frederictonian, now of Dalhousie University. It only remains for me to say that to my wife, and, in their day, to my parents, I am indebted for their concern and encouragement.

A. G. Bailey,
Fredericton, N.B.,
July 17, 1971

Confederation Debate

In eighteen sixty-six on the floor of the House
Billy Needham said "Mr. Speaker . . ."
and the Union men knew what was coming.
Wary of words, drumming fingers on desks,
their faces went bleaker.
White-haired David Wark called them to action
for the Province's and the Empire's good;
admonished the visionless and the factional,
sounding the changes on obstructionism and rejection;
stultification and penury written in ledgers
with statistical precision; the timber shipments
that might last the century out – with prayers:
prayers and a question of hard cash,
a typical New Brunswick contingency.

Or anyone's contingency, for that matter.
They could not repeat forever identical processes
in a world that would not stand still.
Some said the timber rafts would soon be a
        thing of the past:
and the great fleets of sail, the ships,
dolphin-strikers plunging, making way down
                        the Bay,
in a span of numbered years
would no longer be seen clearing the ports.
Grass and silence, the derelict warehouses,
empty and derelict.
They could listen to the voice of the wind.

But there was more than trade reports that
                        made men dream.
There were those like old David Wark
                        who would
live to be a hundred, and even Mitchell and Tilley,
men who many supposed were shy of the
far-fetched, the grandiose, the insubstantial,
who seemed to see something else, something beyond them

that even gave pause to the prophets
of the economically, financially,
and politically disastrous.
Even Billy Needham with his statistics was
ultimately unable to cope with it.
It grew somewhere deep down in the

magmal regions of men's souls.
It went beyond promises, inchoately glimpsed,
of prosperity, prestige, and the enticements
                of power.
Perhaps it was partly a sense of the largeness
                of things, of the land;
although they could not actually see
a gull flying over the Strait of Georgia,
another ocean, the roll of the Pacific,
the beaten smoke-stacks and the freight of China;
dimly beyond the Lakes, the summer prairie,
and Palliser's Triangle, someday to be
                celebrated
by those trained to read
the meaning of landscapes.

Perhaps it was something that could not be
                put into words
like a railway advertisement
of a sequence of magnificent vistas;
but a way for men to live in peace and
                freedom,
with mutual forbearance,
speaking in half the languages of Europe
                and Asia,
with rights grounded in law.
Whatever else it was it could have been all of
                these things,
but there were not very many who could see this
in the session of eighteen sixty-six,
and not many the year after.

Alfred G. Bailey

I | EXPANSION AND CONFLICT

1. Vanished Iroquoians

When the first Europeans of whom we have a distinct record ascended the St. Lawrence in the sixteenth century they found tribes of Iroquoian[1] stock in occupation of the river from the site of Quebec to where Montreal now stands. In the early part of the following century the Hurons, of a like culture, dominated economically the more westerly reaches of the waterway, including the region of the lower Lakes. It has been suggested that if these populous communities had survived to recent times, in occupation of the territories where first encountered, the course of Canadian history might in all probability have been quite different from what it actually became. In marked contrast to the sparsely distributed Algonkian-speaking hunters of the eastern seaboard and the northern forest terrain towards Hudson Bay, the Hurons, who were the most numerous of all the Iroquoians, may well have numbered over twenty-five thousand souls. The Tobacco nation, and the Neutrals to the south-west, as well as the peoples encountered in 1535 by Cartier at Stadacona and Hochelaga, and other points on the lower reaches of the St. Lawrence, probably greatly exceeded the Hurons in the aggregate but together with them they may be said to have been paramount, in both a cultural and a political sense, in the great river system that in due course was to give access to the central and western region of the continent.

No facts of Canadian history are more imperfectly known than those relating to the identity and disappearance of the Iroquoians who inhabited the St. Lawrence valley in the sixteenth century. While our ill-defined and fragmentary knowledge with respect to them contrasts sharply with what we know concerning the destruction of Huronia and the dispersal of the Hurons, there are in the latter case as well uncertain elements which it is the task of historical and anthropological scholarship

[1]The lingustic stock of which the Iroquois proper were members, that is, the Mohawk, Oneida, Onondaga, Cayuga, and Seneca. Among other members mentioned in this paper were the sixteenth-century Laurentian Iroquoians of Stadacona, Hochelaga, and other towns in the St. Lawrence Valley, the Huron, Neutrals, Tobacco Nation, and the Cherokee, the last-mentioned, far to the southward.

to dispell. At least from one point of view, no facts might seem to be more portentous. Indeed, I have suggested elsewhere that if these peoples had remained and multiplied, Canada might today be in large part an Indian state as is Mexico, with a cultural heritage deriving in many respects from the remote American past, rather than almost exclusively from the incoming Europeans since the beginning of modern times. To many this may seem an idle speculation and an unlikely eventuality, but men's minds are haunted by the might-have-beens of history, and in any case such thoughts may serve to deepen our understanding of the meaning of the historical process, and to bring into greater clarity the nature of the problems that may be conceived to be the historian's legitimate concern. How can we then say that there might have been a different outcome since the influences that could have brought it about did not in fact occur? The doctrine of inevitability may appear to be an almost inescapable tenet, since we can alter the past only in the sense that by learning from it, can we transcend what might otherwise be its consequences, in ways that would be impossible without the knowledge and will required to do so. We may will, but if we have not willed, from one point of view the moment is forever lost. There is a limit too to the degree to which we can allow for the free exercise of the will, for we are hedged about with necessities and near-necessities which will permit only certain things to be done, and these imperfectly. Even Vico's dictum that man can understand his own history because he is the maker of it, does not give us leave to suppose that he could have made it differently, since the whole burden of Vico's Scienza Nuova rests upon the notion of recurrence as an outward manifestation of an inescapable unity of mind. We must for the moment therefore take into account the purposes and no others, with which Europeans in the sixteenth and seventeenth centuries came to these shores, and note what befell the Iroquoians as a consequence of the European presence.[2]

No one can doubt the purity of the missionary impulse, but just as truly no one can safely underestimate the demonic drive of European commercial capitalism in its haste to exploit the newly discovered territories overseas and to bring their inhabitants into unequal partnership in an emerging system of metropolitanism and expanding world trade. The implementation of

[2]A. G. Bailey, "The significance of the identity and disappearance of the Laurentian Iroquois," Royal Society of Canada, *Transactions*, 3rd series, sec. 2, Vol. XXVII (1923), pp. 97-108.

such a motive entailed a deadly competition between the Indian
tribes, and at the same time exposed them to all those catastro-
phic influences emenating from the eastern hemisphere that
they were ill-equipped by prior psychological conditioning, and
the quality of their technology, to withstand. We know that as
the fur trade grew from an unimportant industry dependent on
the cod fishery to an enterprise pursued on its own terms, and
with an organization suited to its purpose, it swept relentlessly
westward, engulfing the native peoples who happened to find
themselves in its path, and whose involvement was essential to
its progress. The late Harold Adams Innis has left us, in the
pages of his classic of the fur trade, an account of the monoga-
mous and sedentary habits of the beaver, the reasons why his
fur was suited as was no other to the demands of the European
felting industry, the imperative need to maintain the optimum
volume of export, and ancillary reasons for expanding into ever
new and undepleted fields of exploitation.

The first impact of the new economy was felt by the
Micmac, and to a smaller extent by the Malecite, of the Maritime Provinces, and by the Nascopi and Montagnais of what
are now southern Labrador and northeastern Quebec. As these
tribes became equipped with iron weapons, such as axes and
arrowheads, as well as other products of the European metal-
lurgical industry, they were able to drive the more remote
Iroquoians, still handicapped by their Stone Age culture, from
the sites of their towns in the St. Lawrence valley, which may
have extended, as far as present intimations allow us to believe,
from the neighborhood of Natashquan in the northeast to the
island of Montreal in the west, and perhaps somewhat beyond.[3]
Of these Iroquoian peoples we know almost nothing beyond
what we may read in the Cartier-Roberval narratives, although
an increasing body of evidence is being unearthed as a result of
the work of certain archeologists. Thanks to their patient industry the identity of these peoples is less in doubt than it once was.

Cartier's exploration of the St. Lawrence in 1534, 1535-36,
and 1541-42, lifted the veil at one moment of time upon these,
to Europeans, exotic and populous towns and villages, but we
still cannot conclude with certainty as to which branch or

---

[3] *Ibid.*; see also H. A. Innis, *The Fur Trade in Canada; an introduction to Canadian economic history*, (1930); See Bruce G.
Trigger, "Archeological and Other Evidence: A Fresh Look at the
Laurentian Iroquois," *American Antiquity*, Vol. 33, No. 4 (Oct.
1968), p. 437 for reference to Wintemberg's find at Kegaska.

branches of the Iroquoian stock they may be said to have belonged. Some students of Cartier's vocabulary have suggested that they were a distinct people, members of an outer ring of Iroquoian peoples, including the Cherokee, rather than affiliates of those more centrally located tribes such as the league of five Iroquoian nations who in the seventeenth century were encountered by Europeans in what is now northern New York State.[4] We are reminded also of Sir William Dawson's pioneer study, "Fossil Men and their Modern Representatives," in which he gives it as his opinion that the Laurentians were not closely affiliated with any later-encountered Iroquoian group, and were on the point of extinction at the time of the Cartier voyages. Other scholars find an affinity, or perhaps an identity, between the languages of Stadacona and Huronia, and some believe that the people of Stadacona later withdrew to Huronia to confederate with other Hurons towards the close of the sixteenth century.[5] Alleged cephalic resemblances with the Eskimo could be accounted for through intermarriage with the latter during long residence in the northeast, predating European contact and the supposed withdrawal to the Huron homeland. In contrast with Stadacona and its immediate neighbors, there appears to be some degree of certainty with regard to the identity of the Iroquoians situated above Quebec from Achelacy, where Portneuf now stands, to Hochelaga and other town-sites on and in the environs of the Island of Montreal. With regard to this up-river group of settlements, we possess an increasing body of archaeological evidence, a source of information which is almost totally lacking with regard to Stadacona and the towns

⁴Floyd G. Lounsbury, "Iroquois-Cherokee linguistic relations," in W. N. Fenton and John Gulick, eds., *Symposium on Cherokee and Iroquois Culture*, Smithsonian Institution, Bureau of American Ethnology, Bulletin 180 (Washington, 1961), p. 17.

⁵See for instance Percy J. Robinson, "The Huron Equivalents of Cartier's Second Vocabulary," *Transactions of the Royal Society of Canada*, 3rd series, sec. 2, Vol. XLII, (1948), pp. 127-146. On the other hand, in a most scholarly study of the question, Professor Bruce G. Trigger concludes that Laurentian is not identical with other northern Iroquoian languages. See his "Who Were the Laurention Iroquois?," *Canadian Review of Sociology and Anthropology*, Vol. III, (November, 1966), p. 211. In his paper, "Trade and Tribal Warfare on the St. Lawrence in the Sixteenth Century," *Ethnohistory*, Vol. IX, No. 3, (Summer, 1962), p. 240, Professor Trigger had previously expressed this view, as follows, ". . . today research favours granting Laurentian Iroquois status as a separate language within the Iroquoian family."

near the site of Quebec. Is it not strange that not even the location of Stadacona is known? Wintemberg believed it to have
been situated not far from where Quebec's City Hall now
stands, a place accessible to supplies of fresh water from the
little rivulet that once flowed near Ste-Ursule Street, actually
slightly to the west of the line of that thoroughfare.[6] Whereas
Stadacona was probably an open village of lodges not dissimilar
to those of the nomadic hunters who roamed the nearby forests,
Hochelaga was a palisaded town of several thousand people
who lived in the typical Iroquoian longhouse, and who had
extensive fields of Indian corn, beans, pumpkin, and squash.
That Hochelaga and Stadacona were politically separate as well
as culturally and linguistically divergent seems a likely inference
from the attempt of the Stadaconas to prevent Cartier from
going to Hochelaga. They could not think of a more effective
way than to attempt to terrorize Cartier's people by means of
three Indians who, disguised as devils, purported to bring warn-
ings from their god, Cudouagny, of the perils that awaited those
who might be foolhardy enough to venture up the river. As
though to give emphasis to the warning one of the Indians, who
had been in France, shouted "Jesus, Jesus, Jesus", and another
"Jesus, Maria, Jacques Cartier", but they failed to dissuade the
Captain from making the journey. It may be that the beginning
of political alignments among the St. Lawrence villages occurred
as a response to Cartier's kidnapping of Donnacona, the Chief
of Stadacona, and other Indians, and that Iroquoian hostility to
the French, aroused by such behaviour, was effective in preventing the French from ascending the river for several decades
following the Cartier and Roberval voyages. Although the chief
of Achelacy, near modern Portneuf, was friendly to the French
at the time of the second voyage, that of 1535-36, this same
chief was said in 1541 to have gone to Canada[7] to conclude
with the successor of the kidnapped chief "what they should do
against us." The grim and fragmentary narrative of the third

[6]Personal statement to the author by the late W. J. Wintemburg.
Information as to the existence of the rivulet was obtained from the
late Ernest Goldsworthy Gale, M.D., whose family lived in Ste.
Ursule Street (no. 37) from the late eighteenth century to the mid-
twentieth. With regard to Hochelaga, or the "Dawson site" which
has been presumed to be Hochelaga, Professor Trigger has warned
us of a too confident acceptance of archeological evidence as final.
See his "Archeological and other Evidence," *op. cit.,* pp. 432-33.
[7]H. P. Biggar, ed., *The Voyages of Jacques Cartier,* Publications
of the Public Archives of Canada, No. 11, (Ottawa, 1924), p. 259.

voyage leaves no doubt that native hostility made Cartier's fort at Cap Rouge[8] no longer tenable. In encountering Roberval on his way to Canada, he "enformed the Generall that hee could not withstand the Savages, which went about daily to annoy him; and that was the cause of his return to France." Captain Carleill stated in 1583 that the French were still trying to overcome the distrust of the Indians which Cartier's kidnapping actions had created.[9] As there appeared to be no hindrance to Cartier's nephews ascending the river in 1587 as far as Lachine, it seems safe to conclude that the Laurentian Iroquoians had by that time been driven away by Algonkian-speakers armed with ironware. They had clearly vanished by 1600, the year in which Pierre Chauvin, the French Protestant merchant, built at Tadoussac "the first house in Canada;" and in 1603 Champlain confirmed both the fact of their absence and the existence of the war between the departed Iroquoians and the Algonkian hunters.

These facts are confirmed, perhaps too neatly, by the old trader and bureaucrat, Aubert de la Chesnaye, when he wrote in 1697 that ". . . the true Algonquins possessed the land from Tadoussac as far as Québec, and I have always thought that they came from the Saguenay; it was a tradition that they had driven the Iroquois from the site of Quebec and the neighbourhood which was their former home; they used to show us their towns and villages covered with wood newly sprung up."[10]

<hr />

[8]*Ibid.*, p. 259. See also p. 264.

[9]A. G. Bailey, "Laurentian Iroquois," *op. cit.*, p. 103.

[10]*Ibid.*, p. 106. While historical evidence points strongly to this explanation of the disappearance of the Laurentian Iroquois there is still doubt as to their identity and the reason for their removal. For a comprehensive study of the possibilities, the reader is referred to Professor Trigger's paper, "Archeological and Other Evidence," *op. cit.*, especially pp. 436-437. See also his "Cartier's Hochelaga." He here would appear to suggest a variant pattern of events, namely that the Laurentian Iroquoians, or at least some of them, were driven out by Five Nations Iroquois in their endeavour to break through to the east and make contact with European traders. Cartier's Hochelaga and the Dawson Site by Bruce G. Trigger. In this paper Professor Trigger has written as follows: "It seems quite clear from Champlain's accounts that the St. Lawrence Valley was deserted in 1603 not because the Indians who lived in this area had moved inland in search of furs but through fear of the Iroquois. The most likely reason for the Iroquois to have attacked this region was a desire to eliminate tribes that were collecting tolls or acting as middlemen in the fur trade and thus to gain direct access to the

Yet we cannot lightly dismiss the words of a man whose memories of the colony extended back for nearly half a century. In the belief that the vanished people were represented in the seventeenth century by one or more members of the Iroquois League, the bitter enemies of the Hurons, who were their fellow Iroquoians, as well as of the Algonkian hunters and the French, La Chesnaye is supported in some measure by Nicholas Perrot who observed that "the county of the Iroquois was formerly the district of Montreal and Three Rivers. . . ." The view was shared by Bacqueville de la Potherie, Lafitau, Cadwallader Colden, Lewis H. Morgan, W. M. Beauchamp, all students of Iroquois history and culture, or having special knowledge of the subject.[11] If the Stadaconans spoke an Iroquoian dialect that ressembled Huron, and not one of those spoken by the members of the Iroquois League, who were enemies of the French as well as of the Algonkian, throughout the greater part of the seventeenth century, La Chesnaye's statement would be difficult to accept at its face value.

It was not incompatible with an old theory once put forward by A. C. Parker, and others, but now largely discarded, which had appeared to provide a framework for the supposition that the Stadaconans were Mohawks.[12] According to this theory the Iroquoian peoples were recent migrants into the northeast from some southern point of origin. It was supposed that as they moved northeasterly they had bifurcated at Detroit and perhaps again at Niagara, one branch moving north of the Lower Lakes, and others such as the Seneca and Cayuga, taking the more southerly route to their historic territories in northern New York. The extremity of the northern prong of the fork was supposed to be represented by those Laurentian Iroquois

European ships that came to Tadoussac." (Bruce G. Trigger, "Iroquois Culture, History, and Prehistory," Proceedings of the 1965 Conference on Iroquois Research, edited by Elisabeth Tooker, The University of the State of New York, The State Education Department, New York State Museum and Science Service, Albany, 1967, pp. 63-63.)

[11]A. G. Bailey, The Conflict of European and Eastern Algonkian Cultures, 1504-1700, a study in Canadian civilization, 2nd ed. Vol. XIII, (Toronto, 1969). Emma Helen Blair, ed., The Indian Tribes of the Upper Mississippi Valley and Region of the Great Lakes, Vol. I, (Cleveland, 1911), p. 42.

[12]Arthur C. Parker, "The Origin of the Iroquois as suggested by their Archeology," American Anthropologist, N.S., Vol. XVIII (1916).

who were encountered by Cartier. Then, as has already been suggested, these peoples centering principally at Stadacona and Hochelaga, were said to have been driven away to become the forebears of the seventeenth century Mohawks and perhaps the Onondaga and Oneida as well.

It must be said at once that many of the assumptions upon which this theory was based are no longer tenable. The blow-gun and perhaps the eagle dance which were once thought to be evidence of a southern origin, may have been diffused to the Iroquois as late as the seventeenth or eighteenth centuries.[13] Rather than having been recent migrants there is now much reason to believe that they had been in the northeast for a very long time, as the research of Dr. R. S. MacNeish into pottery sequences would seem to suggest.[14] But for how long no man yet knows, although it is now established that humans — those known as paleo-Indians — were in northeastern North America in terminal Pleistocene times, some ten thousand years ago. Much later were the Archaic cultures, and later still, after a hiatus of some thousands of years, other cultures such as the Point Penninsula which, at least in west-central New York, may have passed into one identifiably Iroquoian. To be accept-able a solution to the mystery of the vanished Iroquoians cannot ignore these facts and suppositions; and we are driven to conclusions markedly at variance with what was once believed.

Perhaps, however, too much stress has been placed on the consequences of incipient fur trade as the means whereby the Algonkians became better armed and were able to wage suc-cssful war against the Iroquoians of the St. Lawrence valley. Other inferences must be grasped if we are to account for the

[13]W. N. Fenton, "Problems Arising from the Historic North-eastern Position of the Iroquois," in *Essays in Historical Anthro-pology of North America,* Smithsonian Miscellaneous Collections, Vol. c, (Washington: Smithsonian Institution, 1940), pp. 164-5.
[14]Richard S. MacNeish, *Iroquois Pottery Types,* National Museum of Canada, Bulletin 124, Anthropological Series 31, (Ottawa, 1952), pp. 57, 71, 74, 86. See also William A. Ritchie, *Traces of Early Man in the Northeast,* New York State Museum and Science Service, Bulletin 358 (University of the State of New York, June, 1957), and in addition, two other papers by Dr. Ritchie, namely, *The Pre-Iroquoian Occupations of New York State,* Rochester Museum of Arts and Sciences, Rochester Museum Memoir 1, (Rochester, 1944); and "Iroquois Archeology and Settle-ment Patterns," in Fenton and Gulick, eds., *Symposium on Chero-kee and Iroquois Culture,* p. 35.

disappearance of these peoples. The difficulty of persisting in an economy based on the cultivation of maize in such a rigorous climate must not be excluded as a cause, though perhaps a minor one. More cogent is the argument that devastating diseases, previously unknown in the New World, worked havoc among the sedentary and more densely peopled Iroquoian communities. Cartier reported of the Stadaconans that they had "another very bad custom connected with their daughters who as soon as they reach the age of puberty are all placed in a brothel open to every one, until the girls have made a match. We saw this with our own eyes;" the author of the narrative continues, "for we discovered wigwams as full of these girls as is a boys' school with boys in France."[15] The occurrence of the "French pox" at this time, is documented and we cannot be in any doubt as to the effect of the introduction of venereal disease among a population never before exposed to its ravages.[16] We can acknowledge that it would have been a crucial factor without abandoning the contention of which we have made so much in this essay, and elsewhere,[17] concerning the consequences of a war with the Algonkian-speaking Montagnais and their allies. Recent archeological research, suggesting Onondaga-Oneida affiliations for Hochelaga and its neighborhood, accords closely enough with Perrot's assertion of Iroquois occupancy of the country from Montreal to Trois Rivières. If Dr. F. G. Lounsbury's "Laurentian" language had reference to Cartier's Stadacona vocabulary, we might be tempted to disregard LaChesnaye's identification of the Stadaconans with the seventeenth century nations of the Iroquois league, and conclude that they, unlike their affiliates further up the river, found refuge in Huronia.[18]

[15]H. P. Biggar, *The Voyages of Jacques Cartier,* Publications of the Public Archives of Canada, No. 11, (Ottawa, 1924), p. 214.

[16]J. J. Heagerty, *Four Centuries of Medical History in Canada,* (Toronto, 1928), Vol. 1, p. 270. See also Alfred G. Bailey, *The Conflict of European and Eastern Algonkian Cultures, op. cit.,* Chapter 7, *passim.*

[17]Alfred G. Bailey, *The Conflict of European and Eastern Algon-Cultures, op. cit.,* pp. XII-XIII.

[18]Floyd G. Lounsbury, *Iroquois-Cherokee Linguistic Relations, etc.,* p. 17. In a thorough canvass of the subject in the light of recent research, Professor Trigger has drawn attention to a number of crucial points. Particularly, in this connection, he cites James V. Wright's opinion that the Pickering culture, related to that of people

If the Stadaconans did in truth flee the environs of Quebec
to seek asylum in the land between the Georgian Bay and Lake
Simcoe, they were merely putting off the day of their own
destruction, for the new country, to which they would have
gone, became in the sixteen-forties, a dark and bloody ground
as the Five Nations of the Iroquois League swept over it with
fire, massacre, and torture in their drive to destroy the Franco-
Huron fur-trading empire, and capture the trade for themselves
and their Dutch allies on the Hudson-Mohawk river system.
The problem of historical knowledge presented by these events
is, as we have already noted, of a quite different nature from
that of the disappearance of the Laurentian Iroquoians from
the middle reaches of the St. Lawrence in the sixty-year interval
between the voyages of Cartier and Champlain. Although the
tragedy of the destruction of Huronia was enacted in the full
light of history, there is still an element of uncertainty as to
why the powerful and populous Huron confederacy went down
like a house of cards before the admittedly fierce onslaught of
the Five Iroquois Nations as they issued from their fastnesses
below Lake Ontario and the upper waters of the St. Lawrence.
The notion that it was a simple case of "failure of nerve" may
appear less convincing than it once did, but something akin to
this notion must not be dismissed out of hand; and we are
reminded of Toynbee's emphasis on self-imolation as the key
to the downfall of nations, and even at times of the larger
societies of which they form constituent parts. It might indeed
expose one to the risk of error if the question of imponderable
divergences between Iroquois and Huron cultural complexes
of the mid-seventeenth century were overlooked. The explanation of Iroquois superiority has been sought in the circumstances in which the members of the League found themselves
in the period with which we are concerned. Native arts and
crafts were being rapidly lost, and virtual dependence on
European materials, which could be purchased only with furs,
forced them, so it has been said, to "export or die." If they
could not lure the Huron traders away from the French, they
must destroy them. So much is true and such an argument,
according with the views of Innis and his school, is reinforced
by George T. Hunt, who prefers it to an explanation in terms

who were probably ancestral to the Huron, "flourished north of Lake
Ontario between A.D. 1100 and 1300, and may have extended down
the St. Lawrence." See Bruce G. Trigger, "Archeological and Other
Evidence," *op cit.*, p. 436.

of the possession of superior armament.[19] Certainly we need not take time to consider seriously the allegation that they possessed the "natural ferocity" attributed to them by Parkman, nor the "political genius" which Morgan found as the source of Iroquois achievement; and we are entitled to ask whether the "materialist" thesis propounded by Hunt would not apply equally well to the situation in which the Huron victims of the Iroquois League found themselves on the eve of the terrible ordeal of 1648-50.[20] While conceding that the Iroquois may have had to strive harder because they were a deprived people, one can probably find the full explanation only in a congeries of interrelated causes. Epidemics introduced from Europe appear to have reduced the Hurons from between twenty-five and thirty thousand to approximately ten thousand during the quarter-century that culminated in the destruction of their country.[21] All the while conversion to the new faith was inducing a profound spiritual and political cleavage which prevented the Hurons from presenting a united front to their enemies at the moment of greatest need.[22] Charles Seeley has stressed the unsettling effects on children growing up in a society composed partly of Christians who believe their pagan brethren to be lost souls destined for Hellfire. A profound psychological change marked by mounting fear and anxiety must be sought as a factor in the situation during the years of the great Iroquois

[19]George T. Hunt, *The Wars of the Iroquois: A Study in Intertribal Relations,* (Madison, 1940), *passim.* See also the review of this work by A. G. Bailey in the *Canadian Historical Review,* Vol. XXI, No. 2 (June, 1940), p. 212.

[20]This question was raised in the review of Professor Hunt's book mentioned in Note 19 above.

[21]The disease that killed off so many of the Hurons between 1635 and 1640 has generally been assumed to have been smallpox, but in the most authoritative paper yet published on the events leading up to the dispersal of the Hurons, Professor Bruce G. Trigger, of McGill University, refers to it as either measles or smallpox. The reader is referred to his "The French Presence in Huronia: The Structure of Franco-Huron Relations in the First Half of the Seventeenth Century," the *Canadian Historical Review,* Vol. XLIX, No. 2 (June, 1968), p. 127. For the effects of imported diseases on the neighbouring Algonkians in the seventeenth century, see A. G. Bailey, *The Conflict of European and Eastern Algonkian Cultures, op. cit.,* Chapter 7.

[22]Bruce G. Trigger, "The French Presence in Huronia", *op. cit.,* pp. 133-135.

War.[23] By contrast, Iroquois possession of superior arms, we may be sure, imbrued that people with an arrogant self-confidence in the fact of all discernible challenges. The Jesuits' success in some cases in inducing the Hurons to substitute square forts, admitting of crossfire, for the traditional rounded structures, was no adequate substitute for the firearms that the French failed to supply in effective quantity. Terrified survivors fled their burning villages only to succumb too often to starvation in the place where they found temporary refuge.

The student of Canadian history, contemplating as he must the full range of his subject, cannot fail to perceive, as a recurrent motif, the forceful removal of populations at intervals of varying duration, resulting from mixed motives and intentions, but often, although not always, having an ethnic component. War and disease may account in large part for the Laurentian Iroquoians, and the Hurons and their neighbors in the following century, in both cases accompanied by a measure of cultural disintegration as a consequence of the European impact. The deportation of the Acadians, and the persecution and flight of

[23]Charles Leonard Seeley, "The Disintegration of Huron Culture in the Seventeenth Century," (Master's thesis, University of New Brunswick, 1951), pp. 157-9. Mr. Seeley stresses the factor of cultural disintegration, as a consequence of European contacts, as a prime cause of the collapse of the Hurons in the face of Iroquois aggression in the sixteen-forties. The problem has been dealt with by both Dr. Elisabeth Tooker in her paper, "The Iroquois Defeat of the Huron: A Review of Causes," *Pennsylvania Archeologist*, Bulletin of the Society for Pennsylvania Archeology, Vol. XXIII (1963), and by Professor Trigger whose data Dr. Tooker interprets in a neat and thoughtful manner. "The suggestion," she writes, "that social disorganization of the Hurons contributed to the Huron defeat can be applied only to the Huron-Iroquois conflict and not to the Iroquois wars with other Northern Iroquoians. The Petuns, Neutrals, and Eries had even less contact with the Europeans than did the Iroquois and their culture must have been less affected by it. They could not have suffered the social disorganization that the Hurons might have as a result of French contact. Trigger's hypothesis then must be interpreted as suggesting that the Hurons suffered from too much contact with the Europeans while the Petuns, Neutrals and Erie suffered from too little contact with the Europeans, and that the Iroquois had just the right amount — contact that enabled them to get the European goods they wanted and at the same time allowed them to develop their native institutions to meet this situation without great social disorganization and so defeat the other Iroquoian leagues about the same time."

the United Empire Loyalists, stand however in marked contrast to the treatment of the French Canadians at the Conquest, whose lives and property were protected by the terms of the Treaty of Paris, with the result that relatively few sought refuge in France.[24] Some displacement of Métis and Indians was a consequence of the settlement of the issues that had been raised in the Northwest rebellions. Also the removal of the English Protestant population from areas of the province of Quebec was, according to the author of *The Tragedy of Quebec*, a matter of slow but steady attrition resulting from a policy of calculated extirpation.[25] The removal during the Second World War of the Japanese Canadians from the coastal areas of British Columbia on grounds not unlike those which motivated the expulsion of the Acadians, might appear to afford some doubt as to the certainty of progress over the course of the last two centuries.

Crucial, however, as some of these events may appear to have been, none can compare with the destruction of Huronia either as to the magnitude of the tragedy experienced or with respect to the far-reaching nature of the consequences. Dominating as they once did the industrial heartland of the future Dominion of Canada, they might have constituted, had they remained, a dense and forward-moving population during that long era when their country was in fact bereft of all inhabitants. It may be asserted with some degree of cogency that the negative effects of the loss of the Hurons and their neighbors warrant consideration equally with the positive consequences of the increments of French and Loyalist, Scot and Ukrainian, to name only a few, who in their own time and condition shaped the course of Canadian history.

Only with the arrival of the Loyalists and their camp-followers at the end of the American Revolutionary War could the slow processes of social growth be resumed in the area dominated by the once populous Huronia. Disease, disintegration, and war, had set Canada immeasurably back. The destruction of the Hurons had marked a turning point comparable in its effects only to the Conquest of 1759-60 or the consequences

---

[24]The British treatment of the French Canadians after the Conquest stands in marked contrast, *pace* Garneau, to the monotonous record of persecution and population removals that mar the record of Canada's development.

[25]Robert Sellar, *The Tragedy of Quebec: the Expulsion of its Protestant Farmers*, (Toronto, 1916).

of the Treaty of 1783. For the Laurentian Iroquois, the Hurons, the Neutral and Tobacco Nations, the advent of Europeans had spelled unrelieved catastrophe, of a kind and on a scale from which they could never recover. There was nothing in their pre-European experience to prepare them for what they were called upon to face in the era of European expansion. Pre-Columbian wars were comparatively mild in their effects, though the choice of village sites near the headwaters of small streams, instead of on large navigable waterways, indicates some concern for the necessity of defencible positions.[26] The transformation of warfare, resulting from the European presence, occurred in two phases; the first involving iron weapons that were responsible in great part, so we have claimed, for the sweeping away of the Laurentian Iroquoians in the second half of the sixteenth century; the second, characterized by the direct involvement of the French, and before long by the increasing use of firearms, that may be said to have begun with Champlain's first meeting with the Montagnais at the moment in 1603 when they were celebrating a recently won victory over the Iroquois. Champlain has described, with his usual clarity of expression, the barbaric rites that marked the occasion.[27] The place was Pointe des Allouettes, a long flat-topped point of partially wooded sand and gravel near the mouth of the Saguenay. It was the beginning of an entirely new and more deadly phase of the struggle that had been going on since the time of Cartier. But standing there, as one often did in childhood, with the great blue capes beyond Echafaud aux Basques on the one hand, and to the eastward the dunes of Moulin Baude, looking out over miles of sea towards the

[26]J. V. Wright, *The Ontario Iroquois Tradition,* National Museum of Canada, Bulletin 210, Anthropological Series No. 15 (Ottawa, 1966), p. 95. Investigation of Glen Meyer and Pickering sites indicates village locations some distance from navigable water on some tributaries and frequently palisaded. Mr. James F. Pendergast, in his monograph, *Three Prehistoric Iroquois Components in Eastern Ontario,* National Museum of Canada, Bulletin 208, Anthropological Series, No. 73, pp. 86-87, notes that defence considerations varied from site to site, although defence remained a factor throughout the whole of the period considered. However, he infers that was not a continuous characteristic of Iroquois history; and concludes ". . . that the enemy threat to the Iroquois was not so significant in early times as it became in late prehistoric and early contact times."

[27]H. P. Biggar, ed., *The Works of Samuel de Champlain,* Toronto, 1922, The Champlain Society, Vol. I, pp. 107-109.

highlands of Bic, on the very edge of space, it was hard to think of savage war, overcome as one always was by the peacefulness of the place.

2. The Ordeal
Of the Eastern Algonkians

The close relations which are developing between the natural and human sciences[1] have increased the importance of the work of the anthropologist, since he seeks to apply the method of natural science to the study of human affairs. That branch of anthropology which treats of the evolution of culture is concerned with the processes of diffusion and invention, and with environmental influences. Diffusion and invention cannot be entirely separated since an individual may manufacture traits in his endeavour to adapt himself to an ever-changing environment, and invention is therefore involved in the diffusion which may cause cultural changes. We need not concern ourselves here with the several ways in which diffusion may occur; we need only recall that the culture of any given group has been blended from diverse sources into a vivid entity which resists the diffusion of traits from other cultures. Thus, when a people migrates into an already inhabited area, a conflict almost inevitably arises between the culture of the immigrants and that of the indigenous population. The result of such a conflict may amount both in intensity and magnitude to nothing less than an economic and social revolution.

The history of Canada might well be treated from this point of view since Canada is an area into which diverse peoples have from time to time migrated. In the course of the conflict between rival cultures some of the constituent groups in the Dominion of Canada have forged ahead, others have merely maintained their place, and still others have fallen behind, several having suffered extinction. The Indians, for example, often failed to survive the shock of the conflict. Sometimes, however, a fusion of Indian and European elements occurred and resulted in new cultural traits which were neither European nor Indian. To the fusion from Indian and French sources have been added throughout succeeding years elements from other

[1]See, for example, the article by Principal R. C. Wallace of Queen's University, "Co-operation in the natural and human sciences," *Canadian Historical Review,* Vol. xiv (Dec., 1933), p. 371.

immigrant groups. The permutations which have resulted from the process of fusion are distinctively Canadian, and are unique since they have not occurred in precisely the same way elsewhere. The process merits a close study, and its first chapter must necessarily begin with the contact of the eastern Algonkians[2] with the French fishermen, traders, and missionaries in the sixteenth and seventeenth centuries. The following pages which deal with this theme offer some general observations sinc a detailed examination is obviously impossible within the scope of a short article.

II

During the thirty years that intervened between the first authentic French voyage and Cartier's voyage of 1534, there were intermittent contacts of the French with Montagnais and Micmac bands. These years were in some respects the mythical period of the relation between French and Indians; not only because there is little or no documentary evidence concerning it, but because it is the period in which the visitations of Europeans were regarded as supernatural by the Indians. Moreover, it was characterized by the early disturbance of eastern Algonkian material culture. The first objects bartered were valued by the Indians as novelties which had a religious, aesthetic, and utilitarian significance. The first attempts at barter began that infiltration of European materials which forced the disruption of previously stabilized communities. By Cartier's time the Micmacs were already familiar with the custom and procedure of barter, and iron had already attained a material significance in their lives. Indeed, it was perhaps due to their use of iron that the eastern Algonkians were able to drive the

[2]Although the distinction between the central and the eastern Algonkian is arbitrary, the latter may be taken as the Algonkian of the Ottawa valley, the Misstassini Cree of the south-eastern coast of Hudson bay, the Montagnais-Nascopi of Labrador and Quebec, the Micmac, Malecite, and Passammaquoddy of the Maritime Provinces, and the Abenaki of Maine. It is important to distinguish between the term "Algonkin" which designates a tribe that inhabited the Ottawa valley in the seventeenth century, and "Algonkian" which designates a linguistic stock to which the Algonkins and other tribes considered in this article belonged. The Five Nations Iroquois and the Hurons belonged to a totally different linguistic stock, namely the Iroquoian.

Laurentian Iroquois from the St. Lawrence valley during the second half of the sixteenth century. Before this took place, the Iroquois towns blocked the advance of the French into the upper waters of the St. Lawrence. Their hostility to the French appears to have resulted from Cartier's kidnapping exploits, and if it had not existed the French might have been able to establish themselves in the interior of the continent half a century before the first Dutch and English colonies were founded. That the Iroquois were able to maintain their position on the St. Lawrence for several decades after Cartier's time was, therefore, of vast import to subsequent European colonizing efforts in North America.[3] Acadia rather than the St. Lawrence was to be the first arena of concerted French effort to combine fur trading and colonization.

The developments which led to the founding of Port Royal were manifold. The change from green to dry fishing which occurred during the third quarter of the sixteenth century led to a search for harbours at remote parts of the coast, and thereby fresh tribes were brought within the sphere of European influence. Competition between the various nationalities engaged in the fishery led the French to Isle Percé, Gaspé, Canso, and elsewhere. Moreover, during the last years of the sixteenth century the fur trade emerged as independent of the fishing industry, partly on account of a change in the style of clothing in western Europe which created a demand and supplied a market for the fur resources of the new world. Whereas hitherto Cape Breton had been the area of maximum contact, the founding of Port Royal indicates that by the beginning of the seventeenth century the fur trade was leading to the penetration of areas beyond those affected by the fisheries. Although monopolies retarded its growth, the heavy cost of the prosecution of the fur trade, which limited it to valuable and abundant commodities, such as beaver pelts, contributed to its rapid expansion.[4] Moreover, on account of the rapid depreciation of European goods which resulted from wear, trade to remote peoples, and disposal at burial feasts, the demand for imported articles was persistent and cumulative.

The economic revolution on the gulf coast by which stone, bone, wood, bark, and antler implements and utensils were

[3]A. G. Bailey, "The significance of the identity and disappearance of the Laurentian Iroquois," *Transactions of the Royal Society of Canada,* ser. 3, xxvii, sect. 2, (1933).

[4]H. A. Innis, *The fur trade in Canada* (New Haven, 1930), pp. 9-12.

displaced by those of copper and iron, affected every aspect of the life of the Indians. The ancient crafts were rendered useless so that skilled workers in stone and other indigenous materials found themselves without employment. They were faced with the necessity of hunting more extensively or lingering idly about the posts and cod stages,[5] drinking themselves to death, ruining their digestive systems with decayed European foods, and remaining indifferent to, or resentful of, the debauching of their women by the intruders. But whether they hunted or idled the division of labour between the sexes, which had attained a stable equilibrium through long adaptation to a particular environment, was thrown out of kilter. Although it is probable that the crafts of the women were less disturbed than those of the men, yet as makers of clothes and pots they, too, were superannuated to a life of comparative leisure by the use of copper kettles, European cottons and woollens, and implements of foreign importation. As far as the men were concerned, some of the leisure time which resulted from the increasing use of iron arrow points, the axe, the musket, and other weapons, was taken up by more widespread hunting of all types of fur-bearing animals, in particular the beaver. It was on this account that the game animals in the area contiguous to the gulf coast suffered a rapid depletion which threw the population more and more upon resources other than its own, in particular on European meat and vegetable products. Moreover, the problem of leisure was partly solved by the more deadly warfare which resulted from competition in the trade. Warfare, liquor, and an unbalanced diet contributed to the decline of the eastern bands of Micmac and Montagnais. Liquor and the new foods together facilitated the spread of disease which increased mortality to a marked degree. The Indian medicine men were unable to cope with such imported diseases as tuberculosis and syphilis, and realizing that they had no adequate weapons against these insidious enemies, the Indians were seized with despair which reacted on the birth-rate, cutting it to a fraction of its former proportion.

Social intercourse in general and sexual relations in particular promoted the dissemination of the new diseases effectively and with speed. Moreover, the competition between the Indian men and the European fishermen and traders, who brought no

[5]Marc Lescarbot, *History of New France* ed. W. L. Grant (Toronto, Champlain Society), Vol. III, p. 168; R. G. Thwaites, ed., *Jesuit relations and allied documents* (Cleveland, 1896-1901), III, pp. 105-9.

women of their own kind with them, deprived the Indians of potential wives, with the result that jealousy and violence tended from time to time to disrupt the friendly relations which were entertained by each group towards the other.[6] The disproportion of the sexes resulted also in a highly unsettled state of existence for the excess male Indians. On the other hand, the high mortality rate resulting from the use of fire-arms tended to restore the balance, and apart from the fact that the French and the Indians were economically indispensable to each other, the Indians at times appeared to display a real affection for the French. Whenever offspring resulted from mixed marriages the ties of friendship were strengthened and the bonds of the marriage themselves were made more secure. Thus, the rise of a group possessing mixed blood and a culture which was fused from diverse sources exerted a modifying influence upon the pristine cultures involved. Although there is evidence that the language of each group was enriched by some knowledge of that of the other, Lescarbot exaggerated greatly when he declared that the language of the coast bands was half Basque.[7]

The failure to grasp the basic principles of the native tongues did, in fact, retard the missionaries in their endeavour to promote Christianity. It was difficult to translate terms of Christian theology into a language which was rich in concrete terms denoting sensible and material things but which was not strongly developed in abstract terms, although abstract ideas were entertained. Thus, although there appeared to be no word for justice, the Indians loved and respected a just man or a just deed. On the other hand, Christianity was disseminated by the fact that Christian ritual appealed to the Indians; by the fact that the native shamans failed to cure the imported diseases as the French were able to do, and suffered ridicule and a loss of power in consequence; by the fact that the Europeans were economically indispensable to the Indians; and by the great zeal of the missionaries. Nevertheless baptism was at first understood only as a pact of friendship and an admission to the political fellowship of the French;[8] the deeply-seated religious beliefs and social customs resisted modification by external forces, and the jealousy of the shamans conjured up a personal enmity in more than one instance. Although some Indians

---

[6]*Jesuit relations,* Vol. III, p. 69; Vol. II, p. 101; Lescarbot, *History of New France,* Vol. III, p. 167.

[7]Lescarbot, *History of New France,* Vol. II, p. 24; Vol. III, p. 207.

[8]*Jesuit relations,* Vol. I, p. 163.

became genuinely converted, their numbers were small prior to the destruction of Port Royal in 1613.

III

Before the beginning of the seventeenth century the Iroquois frontier had been thrust south and west to the waters of the Hudson and its tributaries, so that the French were able to establish a headquarters at Quebec for the prosecution of war and trade. Thus Champlain's battle with the Iroquois in 1609 was perhaps only an incident in the struggle for raw materials which had been in progress ever since the days of Cartier. At certain times throughout the seventeenth century the Iroquois almost succeeded in regaining their lost territory from the French and Algonkians. But the settling of New England at the beginning of the seventeenth century more immediately influenced the destinies of those eastern Algonkian tribes who dwelt south of the St. Lawrence. The territory of the Abenaki became a buffer state between New France and New England, and its people were willing to trade with the highest bidder until the decline of the fur trade in the English colonies, together with a mutual dislike between Puritan and Indian, brought the Abenaki definitely to the French side. Before this occurred, the French could never be sure that the Abenaki were not diverting the Saguenay trade to the English.[9] Whatever diversion of trade there may have been was due to the fact that the depleted resources of Acadia could no longer supply the continental demand for beaver pelts. Indeed, the Saguenay and the St. Maurice were superseded early in the century by the more direct route of the Ottawa. It was only when the Iroquois made the Ottawa unsafe for transportation that the Montagnais bands, who had formerly supported themselves in their own depleted territories by acting as middlemen between the French and the interior bands, could regain something of their heyday status. But even at that their tenure was made precarious by the Iroquois who after 1649 followed up the destruction of the Hurons and the Algonkins by an invasion of the northern interior which proved disastrous to the bands inhabiting that area. Thus, whether the Iroquois lost or won, the eastern Algonkians were always the losers. Moreover, the French never intended the complete destruction of the Iroquois

[9] *Ibid.*, Vol. XII, pp. 187-9.

lest there own allies should turn against them, and the invasion of the Iroquois territory in 1665 by Tracy and Courcelles was just decisive enough to allow for the establishment of the fur trade with the Ottawas in 1681. Of all the eastern Algonkian peoples the Misstassini Cree, of the east coast of Hudson Bay, alone came for a time to occupy the enviable position once held by the Abenaki, that of fur producers between two competing sets of traders. It was even more enviable than that of the Abenaki because the economic interest of the English on Hudson Bay was more closely aligned with that of the Indians than was that of the Puritans in New England. Both English and Indians were, therefore, spared the bloody wars that harried the latter region.

The use of European weapons, the growing need of the Indians for imported implements and utensils, and the persistent demand of the European market for furs, depleted the game upon which the Indians had formerly relied as a means of sustenance and made them increasingly dependent upon their French allies. Micmac and Montagnais bands tended to cluster around the settlements and exist upon doles of peas, prunes, bread, flour, and other vegetable products which promoted disease, and increased the mortality rate. Although the stimulation of the maple-sugar industry was a minor compensation of the contact, the Indians seldom succeeded in adapting themselves to an agricultural existence, even in the face of starvation. Whereas the demand for food was incessant, European clothing was unsuited to forest life and was seldom worn in the interior except for ceremonial purposes, although it influenced the styles of native clothes to a large extent. Like the poorly ventilated European dwellings, stuffy clothing appears to have been detrimental to the health of the Indians.[10] The melancholy that resulted hindered diffusion by rendering the Indians apathetic to the imported culture, and prevented them from raising their standards of living by means of the implements and utensils available through trade, donation, salvage, theft, and pillage. The Abenaki sometimes secured materials by pillaging New England towns, the Micmac by salvaging refuse and vessels stranded upon their coasts, and all the Indians by means of trade and donation. Theft was extremely rare at all times, violations against property not being characteristic of the eastern Algonkians until after they were

[10]*Cf.* G. H. L.-F. Pitt-Rivers, *The clash of culture and contact of races* (1927), p. 58.

influenced by competitive methods which destroyed their self-sufficiency and left them at the mercy of the dispensers of iron axes, copper kettles, and fire-arms. The widespread use of these articles by the bands whose territories lay along the trade routes destroyed the old crafts, disturbed the division of labour, and created the problem of forced leisure which contributed to drunkeness, disease, and depopulation. This problêm was not solved by the recession of the fur frontier beyond the territories of the eastern Algonkians. Some peoples, such as the Malecite of the St. John river and the Betsiamites of the lower north shore of the St. Lawrence, had formed pockets of relatively unadulterated culture even while the fur trade remained important in contiguous areas, and their reception of foreign traits in the second half of the century was due to factors which were once or twice removed from commercial expansion.

Other peoples, such as the Micmac of the gulf coast and the Sillery and Tadoussac Montagnais, who for some years enjoyed the position of middlemen in the fur trade, were left high and dry in territories depleted of game when the frontier was thrust beyond their reach. Those who clung about the settlements on the St. Lawrence came to be a shabby hoard of beggars without purpose and without hope. Even if they could have maintained their economic status, it is doubtful whether they could have resisted the corrupting influences of the liquor traffic, which must in any case have reduced them to a condition of nakedness and starvation. Even if there had been no rift between church and state, it is doubtful whether French officialdom could have checked the avowed interest of the fur trade any more easily than it could have bottled the smallpox, syphilis, and tuberculosis germs that stalked through the eastern woodland with horrid strides in the van of European pene-tration. Imported materials were often germ-carriers, and brandy undermined the resistance to disease. Both bade fair to extinguish whole communities before the slow process of im-munization could ensure a precarious survival.

IV

The ownership of hunting territories which had in pre-European times been vested in the kinship group tended, with the progress of the fur trade, to become increasingly individualistic.[11] Not only did contact with the French at the posts place a new emphasis upon land ownership, but the fur trade brought formerly isolated bands into closer and more frequent contact with each other, which tended to obliterate their distinctive traits. Moreover, the ruthless exploitation of fur-bearing animals forced the bands to split into smaller and smaller units as time went on, since a group of Indians, travelling as a horde, could not subsist in any one area. In addition, the need for more systematic farming of the beaver, the desire of the French to deal with individuals rather than with groups, and the marriages of white trappers with native women, all tended to break the solidarity of the primitive kinship group which had before the era of commerce existed in collective ownership.[12] Added to this, the individual ownership of pelts was by easy transference extended to hunting territories.[13] The solidarity of the bands was broken down by these forces, and by war, disease, drunkenness, and the dependence upon an outside source for technical equipment. The disintegration was further promoted by the missionaries who endeavoured to divide the bands in order that their members might be reduced to a sedentary and agricultural status in which proselytizing could proceed under their own sharp and constant eyes, unhampered by an obstinate public opinion. The new alignment of Christian against pagan

[11]For an account of the ownership of hunting territories as it exists to-day, see F. G. Speck, "Boundaries and hunting groups of the River Desert Algonquin," *Indian notes,* Vol. VI (April, 1929) p. 97; "Family hunting territories and social life of various Algonkian bands of the Ottawa valley," Memoir 70, Geological survey of Canada, anthrop. series 8 (1915); Family hunting bands as the basis of Algonkian social organization," *American anthropologist,* n.s. XVII, p. 280. In aboriginal times ownership appears to have been vested in the band, and territories seem to have been allotted semi-annually to individual families for the duration of the hunting season. See Baron de Lahontan, *New voyages to North America,* R. G. Thwaites ed., (Chicago, 1905), Vol. II, p. 481; *LeClercq, New Relation of Gaspesia,* W. F. Ganong ed., (Toronto, Champlain Society, 1910), p. 237.

[12]A. G. Bailey, *Conflict of European and Eastern Algonkian cultures, 1504-1700: A study in Canadian civilization,* Monographic series no. 2, Publications of the New Brunswick Museum (1937) pp. 84-8.

[13]*Ibid.,* p. 88; see also D. Jenness, *The Indians of Canada,* Bull. 65, National Museum of Canada (Ottawa, 1932), p. 249, *passim.*

cut across the old kinship organization so that sometimes a
father was disowned by his son, a husband by his wife, brother
by brother. But although the Iroquois often drove the eastern
Algonkian bands to seek the shelter of a French fort, the
agricultural experiment was unlikely to succeed among a people
who were unsuited by experience to a sedentary economy and
who were beset by a concurrence of adverse social forces which
excluded hope of material or spiritual prosperity.

From its basis in the band in which behaviour was controlled by public opinion – a powerful force in primitive communities – in which justice was executed by the blood feud,
and in which the individual's behaviour was directed by definite
social observances to kinsmen, eastern Algonkian society became an aggregation of individuals who were no longer responsible for each others' actions, but some of whom were invested
with that responsibility by the French. By a natural evolution
some came to be commercial representatives for the band in
its dealings with French traders, and these assumed the style
and dignity of French officers and something of the rapacity
of the traders.[14] As qualifications for chieftainship, skill in war
and the hunt was displaced by piety and friendliness towards
the French. With the disintegration of the bands the new chiefs
sometimes became petty officials in the feudal system of New
France. It became their duty to see that justice was executed
in accordance with French law under which the group was not
responsible for the actions of its members as it was among the
Algonkians, whose judicial procedure consisted of vengeance
or compensation by gifts. The open conflict that sprang from
divergent legal systems was averted at the outset only by a
temporary compromise on the part of the French who feared
the numerous Montagnais and who argued that by rigidly
maintaining the French code "trade might be injured."[15].
Although French law sometimes protected the Indians from
pillage and trespass, it was foreign to their understanding, and
its enforcement contributed to the collapse of their morale
which was already undermined by liquor, disease, and economic disruption.

The civil and criminal law was interwoven with, and sup-
plemented by, the Roman Catholic ecclesiastical law as pro-

[14]N. Denys, *The Description and natural history of the coast of
North America (Acadia)* W. F. Ganong ed. (Toronto, Champlain
Society, 1908), pp. 195-6.

[15]Champlain, *Works,* H. P. Biggar, ed. (Toronto, Champlain
Society, 1922-36), Vol. III, pp. 188-200.

mulgated by the missionaries who did not recognize the validity of Indian marriages, which for obvious reasons continued to be current among isolated bands. Moreover, a conflict arose between the priests and the Indians; the former maintaining that marriage as an act of God could not be dissolved, and the latter resisting on the ground that marriage was a contract between free parties which could be broken at will. Although the exchange of gifts and the force of public opinion exerted a stabilizing influence upon Algonkian marriages, compulsion was unknown until the French instituted dowries and imprisoned recalcitrant mates. Of all eastern Algonkian institutions the practice of polygamy was the most difficult to eradicate. If a Christian Indian's wife left him and he refrained from taking another, in accordance with church law, he could not continue to live, subject to the conditions imposed by a hunting economy. If he possessed several wives he could conform only by killing the extra wives and thereby breaking a commandment of God.[16] Moreover, often one wife was not sufficient to shoulder the burden of work that fell to her lot. Polygymy survived among outlying peoples throughout the century, but the institution of cross-cousin marriage[17] was broken down; first, because the marriage of cousins was not tolerated by the church, and second, because miscegenation, which was encouraged by the preponderance of males over females of French stock, deprived the Indians of their appointed mates, incidentally awakening their jealousy and resentment. With economic decline, political rupture, war, drunkenness, and disease, these social factors hastened the decay of the native cultures in the seventeenth century.

The new sense of sin, achieved by conversion, was rooted in the doctrine of individual responsibility, and of the dreadful expiation of the misdeeds of this life in the next. It was foreign to Indian ideas which precluded the salvation or the damnation of an individual on his own account; and its inculcation by the

[16]*Jesuit relations,* Vol. XI, p. 177.

[17]The marriage of children of brothers and sisters, as distinct from parallel marriage, that is, between children of brothers, or children of sisters. For accounts of the vestiges of this institution see A. I. Hallowell, "Was cross-cousin marriage practised by the north-central Algonkian?," *Proceedings of the twenty-third International Congress of Americanists* (New York, 1930), pp. 519-44; and W. D. Strong, "Cross-cousin marriage and the culture of the northeastern Algonquin," *American anthropologist,* n.s. Vol. XXXI, (April-June, 1929), p. 277).

Jesuits contributed to the dualism of later Indian cosmogonies which were characterized by the opposition of the flesh and the spirit, hell and heaven, and of the good and evil spirits. The horror of contemplating the images of beloved relatives writhing in the flames of the pit struck many into a blind coma in which the will to live was submerged in a ubiquitous despair.

On the other hand, their own intensely vivid religious beliefs provided a basis for the acceptance of Christianity. Thus, the belief in mysterious beings, or manitos, such as the culture-hero, provided terms with which they could apprehend God. The departmental deities or guardian spirits of the animals made easier the acceptance of the Catholic hierarchy of saints, but there was a number of circumstances which made the conversion of the Indians difficult. The idea of individual salvation, which was so unlike their own belief that the other world was an automatic sequence of this life, together with the linguistic barrier, the isolation and nomadic existence of many of the bands, the abandonment by the missionaries of bands that were broken and decimated in the wake of the fur frontier, the omnipresence of disease and drunkenness, the political rivalries of church and state, the professional jealousy of the native shamans, and, finally, the superfluity of further deities when their own were real and usually adequate, all contributed to render the record of baptisms an unsafe guide to the real success of Christianity among the eastern Algonkians. Many unreservedly sincere converts there undoubtedly were, but the patterns of native culture, involving the incongruity to a hunting economy of such observances as Lent,[18] provided obstacles to conversion which could not have been eradicated within the duration of a third or a fourth generation. Many failed to achieve the adjustment and died, life having lost its meaning. The effort of the Jesuits was noble and generous, by contrast with that of other groups, but from the humanist point of view it must be judged to have failed.

V

It may be taken as evident that every frontier has two sides, and that the advance of the one is invariably conditioned by

---

[18]Lahontan, *New voyages to North America,* Vol. I, p. 326; *Jesuit relations,* Vol. XVIII, pp. 229-31; LeClercq, *New relation of Gaspesia,* p. 110.

the recession of the other.[19] The factors of Indian retreat before European invasion partly determined the nature, extent, and direction of that invasion. Not only were the Indian cultures modified by the thrust of European civilization into the new world, but the latter was modified as a result of the resistance of those cultures. Moreover, European culture became scattered and spare in its passage of the Atlantic, and many of the traits that achieved importation were unsuited to the American environment. Although many household articles were brought by the immigrants, many were of necessity left behind, and often the settlers were almost entirely lacking in the technical equipment which was essential to survival in the new country. The Puritan settlers and the French traders alike were incapable of exploiting the flora and fauna of the eastern woodland without the aid of the Indians' knowledge which was the result of centuries of careful adaptation to the specific environment.[20] The Puritan had to be shown how to cultivate corn and how to make the implements and utensils which were necessary to grow and prepare it. The French were schooled by the Indians in the methods of hunting, fishing, and gathering edible roots and berries.

Of great significance was the influence of the Indian cultures upon the social and political development of the Canadian dominion. The present boundaries of the Dominion of Canada testify to the pervasive influence of the fur trade with the Indians in the colonial period. It was also the wilderness economy that bred an individualism and impatience of restraint in the Canadians, which renders the revision of the old story of paternalism long overdue. On the other hand, it is not so certain that the Indian contributed much of his blood to the European peoples of eastern Canada. In the English colonies where miscegenation is supposed to have been rare, a number of cases have been recorded involving white women and Indian men. That no such phenomena appear in the records of New

[19]W. C. MacLeod, *The American Indian frontier* (London, 1928), preface.

[20]For accounts of the English Puritans' relations with the Indians, see H. U. Faulkner, *American economic history* (New York, 1924), p. 60; H. W. Schneider, *The Puritan mind* (New York, 1930), p. 38; T. J. Wertenbaker, *The first Americans, 1607-1690,* Vol. II of *A history of American life,* Schlesinger and Fox, eds., (New York, 1927), p. 83; J. T. Adams, *The founding of New England* (Boston, 1921), pp. 15-6.

France was doubtless due to the immense preponderance of males over females of European blood, a circumstance which was, however, conducive to the intercourse of Frenchmen with native women. Although the linguistic barrier, physical and cultural differences, the new sense of sin achieved by many of the converted Indians, and the monastic segregation of Indian girls, all hindered miscegenation, it nevertheless occurred widely. But as the mothers were Indian, and as the children no doubt followed the mothers into the Indian tradition, the movement was centrifugal as far as the French were concerned. Church marriages in the settled area were apparently almost unknown, although in the hinterland marriages were undoubtedly frequent both with and without benefit of clergy.

In the area under consideration the influence of the Indian has been cultural more than biological. Although the Indian culture was essential to Canadian development, it was weaker in many respects than that of the European. It suffered disintegration in consequence, with the result that eastern Algonkian society had ceased to be of much continental importance by the end of the seventeenth century. As the fur frontier moved westward new tribes rose to an ephemeral affluence, but collapsed through their failure to integrate with the changed social conditions. In south-eastern Canada little of the Algonkian way of life has survived further immigration and settlement, the growth of agriculture, mining, and the forest industries, and the diffusion of the products of the industrial revolution.

II | PROVINCIAL EFFLORESCENCES

3. Creative Moments
In the Culture
Of the Maritime Provinces *

I

Twice in the history of the Maritime Provinces literary works have appeared that in retrospect can be seen to have marked the beginning of developments of high significance to Canada's cultural growth. The first of these was *The Clockmaker* by Thomas Chandler Haliburton, which was published in Halifax in 1836. Forty-four years later, in the neighboring province of New Brunswick Charles G. D. Roberts published *Orion and Other Poems,* which he had written while he was a student at the University of New Brunswick and which appeared in the year following his graduation with honours from that institution. Haliburton's tales of Sam Slick enjoyed an immediate and wide popularity on both sides of the Atlantic, running ultimately to over one hundred editions, and being translated, before the century was out, into several European languages. Although Roberts' first volume of poems enjoyed no such vogue, it has long been recognized by students of Canadian literature as the earliest expression of a note that was then new to this country but which came to dominate Canadian poetry for almost half a century afterwards. It inspired Archibald Lampman, then an undergraduate in Toronto, with high hopes for the future of Canadian letters. No one can read Lampman's account of the excitement with which he was seized on reading *Orion* without realizing what it meant to the young men of that time and without becoming aware of the seminal influence that Roberts' work exerted upon the subsequent cultural development of this Dominion.

*Address presented to the Canadian Humanities Research Council, Maritime Regional Conference, Halifax, 10 June, 1949, by Alfred G. Bailey, Dean of Arts and Professor of History in the University of New Brunswick.

Although a French critic of the middle of the nineteenth century expressed astonishment that Haliburton did not indulge in the current mode by composing Romantic descriptions of the Nova Scotian landscape, modern students of Canadian history appear to accept without question the phenomena of a Howe and a Haliburton. In the light of recent researches into the social and intellectual life of Nova Scotia the achievements of these two men in the fields of politics and literature occasion no surprise. V. L. O. Chittick has given us the definitive study of Haliburton, and the writings of Ray Palmer Baker have thrown much light on the early literary movements of the Martime Provinces. Above all we are indebted to Dr. D. C. Harvey, whose articles in the *Dalhousie Review* and elsewhere, have shown the spacious days of Haliburton and Howe to have been the logical culmination of a prior intellectual awakening experienced by Nova Scotia during and immediately following the Wars of the French Revolution and of the era of Napoleon.

No such light has yet been shed upon the social and intellectual milieu out of which Roberts and Bliss Carman emerged. The numerous eulogies and the few serious biographical studies of these authors both fail to sketch more than the haziest of backgrounds, in which the observer can see nothing but the looming figures of Canon Roberts and George R. Parkin moving mysteriously out of the shadows. If one did not guess that the hand of Thomas Carlyle lay heavy upon these belated exemplars of romantic individualism, one might be tempted to suspect the deliberate fabrication of a myth. No historian or sociologist has yet undertaken the task of research into the origins of the Fredericton School of Poets, and it is therefore not surprising that a profound misconception has existed in the minds of eminent scholars, as well as the general reading public, concerning the nature of these origins. In his otherwise admirable study of the poetry of Carman, James Cappon noted in passing that Fredericton was the seat of a small university. He neglected to mention that Carman had been a student at this university during the most formative years of his life, and that he found it congenial and stimulating enough to return to it later for post-graduate study. In 1943 Pelham Edgar, in reviewing a recently published biography of Sir Charles Roberts, was misled into remarking of Roberts' formal education "that at the Collegiate School, and during his three years (1876-1879) at the University of New Brunswick, there is not a great deal to be said. The staffs were not noteworthy in the scholarly sense,

and we may assume that the standards were not, on a comparative estimate, high." The Canadian historian who casts about
for adequate studies that would render intelligible the creative
moment of 1880 in the cultural development of New Brunswick
and of Canada finds none and is naturally baffled in his attempt
to explain the phenomenon. Professor A. R. M. Lower may
therefore be forgiven for writing in his book *Colony to Nation*
that "curiously enough it was the sterile soil of New Brunswick
which bred the Roberts family and their relative Bliss Carman."

II

In view of these quotations and of the widespread point of view
which they epitomize, it becomes a matter of some moment to
search for an explanation of the occurrence of the Fredericton
school of poets that does not do violence to the major sociological findings of the last fifty years. It will be useful also, and
necessary to our purpose, to compare the movement in New
Brunswick in the eighties with that of Nova Scotia in the thirties
and forties of the last century, and to attempt to account for
the differences in character that mark them off from each other.
It is to be hoped that such an exercise as this will yield the
answer to the question as to why New Brunswick came only in
1880 to the point analogous to 1836 in Nova Scotia's development. It seems safe to assume at the outset that such a difference in timing is a factor of significance to our enquiry, since
we are avowedly eschewing the romantic notion that sociocultural phenomena are the result of spontaneous generation.
On the contrary, some acquaintance with the culture of primitive peoples, as well as with the rise and decline of ancient and
modern nations, has convinced me that it is necessary for
societal elements to coalesce into differentiated and fluid patterns, that communities that emerge by virtue of the formation
of these patterns must experience mounting tensions through
the polarity of their parts, if there is to be a discharge of creative
energy in any field of endeavour. At the creative moment the
interacting elements out of which the society is composed are
suddenly transcended, and a proliferation of forms ensues that
are new and different from any that could have appeared at an
earlier period in the community's course. Like metropolitan
societies, which tend to be worlds-in-themselves, small communities must become as mature as their narrow limits allow
before they can fulfil the purpose that is within them.

No such communities emerged, or (given the conditions of the time) could have emerged in the Maritime Provinces before the opening of the nineteenth century. Forces of discontinuity and dispersion have tended to inhibit the growth of these provinces throughout their entire history. There was no significant and lasting continuity between the aboriginal society and that of the incoming Europeans. Although visited early, Acadia was long neglected in favour of neighbouring areas, partly for fortuitous reasons and partly because the French and the English, in their drive to possess the continent and to exploit its resources, found promise of more ample rewards elsewhere. Through the establishment of their strong outposts in New England, Virginia, and the West Indies, the English began in the seventeenth century to lay the foundations for a commercial empire in the North Atlantic, and when they wrested the valley of the Hudson from the Dutch they accelerated the thrust into the western fur-bearing areas that left Acadia outflanked and far behind. The French, too, were not long in discovering that the successful pursuit of the fur trade demanded the establishment of bases on the St. Lawrence, and it was there that their main colonial and commercial efforts were made. Their remote fishing stations on the Acadian coast survived the official colonizing ventures of Monts and Champlain, but they could not become important strongholds of French enterprise in the New World as the fishing technique later developed by the French did not demand the establishment of agricultural settlements in Acadia to serve as sources of supply for their fleets. For the sake of neither fish nor furs did the French form large permanent communities in Acadia. In other circumstances it might have been expected that the River St. John, which ran for hundreds of miles through northwestern Acadia and, among the rivers on the Atlantic seaboard, was exceeded in size only by the St. Lawrence and possibly the Susquehanna, would have served the French as a highway of commerce and a focus of settlement. But this extensive river basin was outflanked by the St. Lawrence as a means of access to the northern fur-bearing country, and its headwaters could actually be reached more easily by a short journey south from the St. Lawrence than by the long ascent of the St. John itself. So tenuous was the hold of the French upon it that, a hundred years after Champlain had discovered its mouth, it was virtually abandoned, and remained so for a quarter of a century. Frequently throughout the seventeenth century the French lost Acadia to the English, and even on occasion to the Scots or Dutch. They failed to

integrate it into their Atlantic economy, and it remained neglected, underpopulated, and remote from the main theatres of
imperialist enterprise.

As the century drew to a close, however, two circumstances
combined to enhance the importance of Acadia. One was the
expansion of New England into the northeast, which was
prompted by the need for settlements closer to the fishing
grounds that lay off the Acadian coast. The other was the
strategic value of Acadia as a potential naval base from which
to dominate the northwest Atlantic, including the approaches
to the gulf of St. Lawrence and to the Atlantic seaboard.
Because the French and English empires in America were by
1689 converging upon each other and because of the intensification of Anglo-French rivalry in Europe and on the high seas the
sovereignty of the Acadian peninsula became a matter of concern to the English. Its conquest by the British in 1710 made
possible by French neglect of sea power and their squandering
of blood and treasure in a vain attempt to satisfy Louis XIV's
insatiable dynastic ambitions, placed the Acadian settlements
under alien rule. These people, who had survived the vicissitudes
of colonial life, found themselves during the long period from
1713 to 1740 neglected by the English, as they had been by the
French. Although in the course of their history they had become
a community marked by distinctive traits, their situation on the
flank of two rival empires was in reality one of great insecurity,
and with the renewal of warfare in the mid-century, which
stemmed in some part from the heightening pressure of New
England against Acadia, they suffered the blow from which they
have never entirely recovered, at least in a psychological sense.
The Expulsion of 1755, and after, not only shattered the pattern
of Acadian community life: it removed the majority of the
people themselves bodily from the scene. Those who managed
to evade expulsion, together with those who returned to fight on
a later day in "the battle of the cradle" have, for all their fine
qualities, made no contribution to French Canadian culture
comparable to those with which we are here concerned. As a
peasant people they were quite different from the enterprising
Yankee with his enquiring mind, his political acumen, and his
cultivation of the intellectual virtues, and it is therefore doubtful
whether the Acadians would have developed the kind of social
dynamic that was necessary to high accomplishment in the field
of literature, had they been allowed to remain in possession of
their homes. Nevertheless their removal meant that the social
processes had to be commenced anew. The rejection of the

aboriginal way of life and the obliteration of the Indian culture
had been a foregone conclusion. With the expulsion of the
Acadians in the middle of the eighteenth century a hundred and
fifty years of persistent social growth was destroyed, and the
province was left less like a palimpsest than like a slate that had
been wiped clean.

III

The effective beginning of the modern organized communities
of the Maritime Provinces was thus delayed until the founding
of Halifax in 1749, the immigration of the Yankees at the end
of the Seven Years War, and the sudden inundation of the
Loyalist refugees at the close of the American revolution. In
these events for the first time lay the possibility of a diversified
economy based upon a variety of skills and techniques capable
of utilizing such resources as lay at hand and of capitalizing
upon the Province's position in the commercial empire of the
Atlantic. Here too was the promise of political growth and of
an evolution of self-consciousness that would seek and ultimately find a measure of self-expression. All this, however,
would take time, and during the War of Independence there
was clear evidence of the immaturity of Nova Scotia. It had not
yet achieved a singleness of purpose, and the neutrality to which
the majority of the Yankees tried to adhere showed the measure
of its weakness. Even after the Loyalist migration the fundamental weakness of Maritime life became strikingly evident.
Students of the subject are accustomed to contrast the institutions of the geographically scattered Maritime area with the
centralized style of those of the St. Lawrence and Great Lakes
system. The Maritime world of islands, peninsulas, and river
valleys, lacking a single entrance or unifying principle, has
always been unusually divided against itself, and from the
earliest times to the twentieth century it has bred small-scale
competition and cross purposes. The organization of the fishing
industry, operated from many different bases in Old and New
England, and in Nova Scotia itself, reinforced the particularism
of the area and stimulated many rivalries, of which that between
Halifax and the outports was only the most conspicuous, and
which continued even after the diversionary pull of New England was relaxed at the end of the War of Independence.

Up to this point we have been stressing the forces that
retarded the development of an integrated and purposeful com-

munity in Nova Scotia, but these very conditions were to contribute to the challenge to which the province would respond successfully during the first half of the nineteenth century. When the British government, for reasons that are well known, dismembered Nova Scotia in 1784, the peninsular remnant was sufficiently homogeneous and aggressive to follow the star of its own peculiar destiny. It contained the oldest and most populous part of the province, and while the Scots were filling up Cape Breton and the eastern shore, Yankee and Loyalist elements were gradually conquering their distrust of each other. The central districts comprised a narrow area – too narrow, it might be thought, to father great achievement – but the memory of the Dutch Republic warns us of the danger of accepting without reserve the generalization that "small countries make small people." It was this area more than any of the others, even the Scottish districts, that furnished the enterprise and intelligence that were to carry the Province forward to the climax of the 'thirties and 'forties.

The fivefold increase in population from 1784 to 1837 was accompanied by an accumulation of capital derived from a widening range of sources that included the increasingly effective utilization of natural products, skilled craftsmanship in the minor arts and in shipbuilding, and privateering and commerce on the high seas. The navigators returned enriched in experience from abroad, and the merchants, as Dr. Harvey has written, "were forced by the nature of their vocations to examine provincial and international conditions," and were thus "the first to break through traditional modes of thought, to arrive at intelligent conclusions" as to policy, and to raise demands for economic and political reform. Correlated with this was the impulse to enlarge the means of intelligence through the establishment of schools, colleges, libraries, museums, newspapers, and magazines, and through public debate in the assembly. While King's College at Windsor was cultivating an interest in letters and refining literary tastes, the illiteracy of many of the Gaelic-speaking Scots in eastern Nova Scotia was awakening in Thomas McCulloch a zeal for the spread of education that was to result in the founding of Pictou Academy and the inception of a distinguished tradition of scholarship. By 1828, when Howe acquired the *Novascotian* and began his career as a journalist the province was responding in full stature to the importunities and possibilities of the age.

By 1828, also, settlement had been rounded out and the period of social adjustment in a new environment was over.

Nova Scotia was at a turning point, but there was only one direction in which the province could turn if it was to avoid the stultifying consequences of irresponsible government and of subordination to a distant metropolis. The great challenge that came to it at this moment was political in nature. The destruction of the entrenched position of the Halifax oligarchy in the provincial executive would mean not only the achievement of a larger measure of political democracy, but also a position of imperial partnership within the limits of which Nova Scota would emerge as a new British nation in the western hemisphere. It was to the accomplishment of this twofold task that Joseph Howe and his associates addressed themselves with all the confidence that they could imbibe from the vibrant life around them. Howe's poems tend to derive in form, and to some extent in feeling, from an application to provincial subjects of an 18th century style, but his political statements, in editorials, letters, and addresses, strike a new, terse, and trenchant note that was born of his courageous temper, his forthright intelligence, and pungent wit. In the heat of political battle his spirit soared. In a six-hour speech in his own defence against a charge of libel, he vindicated the principle of the freedom of the press in 1835. In the following year Haliburton published *The Clockmaker*. Three years later still, Howe addressed his famous letters to Lord John Russell. Truly it may be said that in these years the creative forces at work for some time past in the provincial body politic were caught up and transfigured by Howe and his brothers in arms. He, and Haliburton in his own manner, had become masters of the political and literary media with which they worked. That they were contemporaries was no accident, and they were not eminent exceptions to a prevailing mediocrity. They were merely the brightest stars in a numerous constellation.

Their works were essentially political in nature because they were forms of response to a political challenge. Haliburton was no less a Nova Scotian for being a Tory than was Howe, but his Windsor and Kings College background, and his temperament, which was so fully conditioned by it, bred in him a degree of urbanity and detachment that were quite foreign to Howe. He was able to stand aside and castigate his fellow countrymen in the satires and caricatures through which he hoped to spur them on to greater achievement. In doing this he was turning upon himself, for the satirist must experience an identity with what he satirizes. In this way, paradoxically, and in more than a figurative sense, the satirized society is the author of the satire. He was schooled to a sharp perception of the weaknesses and foibles of character and the detachment of the provincial Tory made possible the kind of literary creation for which he is memorable. His style was wrought from the characteristic political journalism that the issues of the time and place called forth, together with certain obscure American influences that modern scholarship has been able to identify. The result was quite unlike anything else and was strikingly at variance with prevailing metropolitan styles. It was the highest literary creation that Nova Scotia was to produce.

In his later writings, Haliburton maintained his distinctive qualities, and perhaps perfected some of them, but he contributed nothing fundamentally new or different. To some extent he imitated himself, and other such satirists, if they had appeared, could have done likewise. But it may be supposed that the style would have become repetitive and therefore progressively sterile. It began with the selection of one of several possible styles, and once the commitment had been made, the range of variation irrevocably narrowed. A new style could come only from new and very different circumstances and these were not to appear when the promise that had brought forth Howe and Haliburton had been fulfilled. With the achievement of responsible government in 1848, Howe too had done what he had been given to do. Only thus can one account for the falterings and confusions of his later career. Confederation has been made a scapegoat for far-flung and complex changes in industrial techniques and their political consequences which left the Maritime Provinces isolated on the periphery of a continental economy to which they were in due course made tributary. It is doubtful if much else could have happened to them, and in any case the pattern of political and cultural life was beginning to re-form on a wider basis than could be contained within the bounds of a single province. In the moment of their greatest intensity the conditions that had subsumed these characteristic expressions of Nova Scotian life inevitably passed away.

IV

The development in New Brunswick that culminated in the Fredericton school of poets was entirely different. The passing of both provinces through analogous political stages in the nineteenth century should not obscure how entirely different it really was. It will be instructive to pause for a moment to compare the time-frame of Nova Scotia with that of the neighbouring province. *The Clockmaker* was published 87 years after the founding of Halifax in 1749. Charles G. D. Roberts' *Orion* appeared 97 years after the founding of Fredericton in 1783. The span of time between the two periods of creativity can thus be explained in part by the later formation of an effective community in New Brunswick, but the longer period of incubation in the latter was due to peculiarities of the local scene that have a bearing on the problem. For one thing the geographical and social particularism of the Maritimes as a whole was accentuated in New Brunswick, where the inhabitants of each river valley tended to develop a separate life of their own. More than half a century after the founding of the Province, the Madawaska district was still almost totally isolated from the others, and the settlements on the North Shore until a comparatively late date had few intimate contacts with those of the Bay of Fundy and the rivers that flowed into it. Moreover, the growth of the Loyalist community of the St. John valley was retarded by the reversion to primitive conditions imposed by the exigencies of settlement in the wilderness, and the community was out of touch with the rest of the Province. In addition, the city of Saint John, rather than Fredericton, grew to be the commercial metropolis, and thus the capital could never dominate New Brunswick as Halifax did Nova Scotia. Fredericton remained a small community, but the one in which the Loyalist pattern was longest preserved, and it was here that the cultural tradition that had had its inception in Loyalist times was to flower belatedly in the writings of Carman, C. G. D. Roberts, Theodore Goodridge Roberts, Sherman, and others. The creative impulse of the Nova Scotian writers had sprung from the life of an entire province. The Frederictonians were impelled to create by the impact of English Romantic nature poetry and Darwinian science upon the slowly formed but increasingly receptive intellectual heritage of a sharply restricted community. It was here, during the greater part of the nineteenth century that intellectual excellence was sought, and class distinctions were maintained. Elsewhere agriculture was disrupted and an ordered social existence rendered impossible by the lawless and speculative spirit of the timber trade. This spirit both animated and debased almost every other part of a Province that was to have been "the most gentlemanlike on earth." The rise of the timber trade after 1816 tended in most areas to engulf gentility in a sudden wave of unaccustomed prosperity, but the Fredericton bureaucracy, before it lost control of the casual and territorial revenue in 1837, could enjoy the fruits of that prosperity without having its good manners corrupted. The expansion of the trade brought hordes of poverty-stricken Irish to New Brunswick, decimated the forests, and bled the province of its wealth, but provided a modicum of revenue for the support of the little body of civil servants, lawyers, judges, clergymen and professors who made up the governing class of the capital. These Anglicans and Tories survived the loss of their political dominance because the establishment of responsible government was delayed in New Brunswick, and did not, in any case, mean as sharp a break when it did come as was the case elsewhere. Moreover, it was a closely knit company of experts and adepts in administration, education, and religion, and the Province continued to depend upon it for some of these services until long after Confederation just as it had in the early days of "Family Compact" rule. To this circle of professional people the Carman and Roberts families belonged.

In the education of its members and in the formation of their literary standards and tastes the University in Fredericton played a part that can hardly be exaggerated. This institution had had a long history, as long as any in what is now Canada. It had been projected back in 1783 by a group of New York Loyalists before the migration. The one college that was to have been founded in Nova Scotia necessarily became two when New Brunswick was made into a separate province. Kings College at Windsor, N.S., and the College of New Brunswick were thus coeval and stemmed from the same source. The institution at Fredericton was open at least two years before the Nova Scotian college received its first charter in 1789, but it was not incorporated until 1800. Among its founders were Ward Chipman, Edward Winslow, Chief Justice Ludlow, late of the Supreme Court of New York, and others of high distinction in the old colonies. They included Jonathan Odell, the leading Tory satirist of the American Revolution, whose literary propensities helped indirectly to form the tradition in which Carman and Roberts were nurtured. The slow growth of the college that they inaugurated, thus early was symptomatic of the fact that there was not then a sufficiently mature economic and social foundation for the province's institutional super-structure, but by 1826, when it acquired a new charter and the new name of "King's College. New Brunswick," it could look forward to an expanded programme of studies on a firmer basis. The bitter sectarian and self-styled reformist attacks upon it in the 'forties and 'fifties have diverted attention from its high standard of scholarship and the intelligent direction and leadership given by the members of the faculty in many spheres of provincial life. James Robb, Professor of Chemistry and Natural History, who was already well-known in European scientific circles when he came to Fredericton from Scotland in 1837, was a geologist of note, and New Brunswick's first systematic botanist. Through his encouragement of agriculture and home manufactures he hoped to wean the province away from too exclusive a dependence upon an industry that in the 'forties seemed shattered by the repeal of the Imperial timber duties. This was but one aspect of a concerted effort to conquer the pessimism of the moment by inaugurating a more diversified and self-sufficient economy, and to achieve that sense of community that had always been weaker in New Brunswick than in Nova Scotia. The old Loyalist attitude of dependence on the Mother Country had been accentuated by the almost exclusive reliance of the province on the British timber market during the early decades of the nineteenth century. Now for the first time, during the government of Sir Edmund Head, with the prospect of railway communications and reciprocity with the United States, with the initiation of new industries and the inauguration of responsible government, the whole society of the province gathered momentum, constructive energies were released, and a vigorous and self-reliant outlook took possession of its people.

Out of the new mood of confidence and the surer grasp of the times came the great educational reforms that involved the recreation of King's College in 1859 as the University of New Brunswick, on a non-sectarian basis, and with an expanded curriculum of studies in letters and the sciences. Already in 1848 Baron d'Avray had founded the first provincial normal school, and as newspaper editor, chief superintendent of education, and professor of modern languages at the university he gave an impetus to scholarship that bore fruit in the creative achievements of the poets. Sir George Parkin and the father of Sir Charles G. D. Roberts, to whom the poets acknowledged their greatest debt, were among his students in English and French literature. His romantic background, his fresh and vigorous English, his fine sense of what was best in the literature of Europe, and his "charming dry wit" were sources of inspiration that these men handed on to their successors. He was one of a distinguished company that included some of the greatest

teachers in the history of a province where teaching was prac-
ticed as an art. Edwin Jacob, James Robb, George Roberts,
William Brydone-Jack, Montgomery Campbell, George E.
Foster, Henry Seabury Bridges, and their colleagues, were not
the mediocrities that reviewers and writers of superficial biog-
raphies would have us believe. Parkin testified otherwise when
he wrote to Loring Bailey years later that in all his wanderings
he had "seldom found social surroundings and intellectual
influences more helpful and inspiring." "There was," he said,
"an old-fashioned courtesy and dignity – a real interest in
things of the mind and spirit" in the University circle of
Fredericton in the days of his youth. Far from being a curious
and inexplicable growth from a sterile soil, the poetry of
Fredericton represented the flowering of a tradition that had
been four generations in the making on the banks of the St.
John; and behind that, across the divide of the Revolution, lay
the colonial centuries.

The scholars provided the intellectual preparation without
which the poetry could not have been written. Parkin's return
from Oxford in 1875, with a novel and exciting message,
provided the moment of inspiration. One can only guess at this
late day as to the "spiritual circumstance" that caused the
hearts of Roberts and Carman to beat faster at the sensuous
images of Keats and the pre-Raphaelite poets. An ill-defined
deism inherited from the Enlightenment, reinforced by the
Darwinian thesis, may have instilled in them a sense of loss
that the poetry helped to assuage. It could have given them
another kind of hope that led them later to Emerson. But their
first elegiac poems of nature were conceived in the long twilight
of a governing class whose political ideals had never been
fulfilled. Howe and Haliburton had met a political challenge
emanating from the body of their provincial society. Carman
and Roberts experienced a crisis of the spirit after the political
battle had been lost, and something of the world along with it.
In the realistic prose of the Nova Scotian Man had been the
argument, but in the poetry of the pagan landscape and the
New Brunswick woodland Nature had taken his place. There
was a mood in which Roberts could sing the praises of the new
nation whose birth Howe had opposed. Reared in a province
that had always been more continental in outlook than Nova
Scotia, it is extraordinary that no students of his work have
remarked upon the fact that Roberts graduated from college
in the year of triumph of Sir John Macdonald's National Policy.
But the most distinctive thing about the new poetry was the

intimation of spiritual renewal that its authors caught from the wooded valleys and seascapes of the land where they were born. The origin of the school of poetry that began Canada's first national literary movement is worthy of examination by all those who are concerned to read with serious intent the pages of their country's history.

4. Literature and Nationalism In the Aftermath of Confederation

If a choice had to be made of the year, more than any other, that marked a climax in the development of English-Canadian literature in the nineteenth century it would almost certainly be 1893, for it was then that five of Canada's most accomplished poets completed volumes of verse that reflected the maturing of their powers as creative artists. As we look back from the vantage-point of more than half a century upon the works of Roberts, Lampman, Carman, Scott, and Campbell, we can see that, although earlier writers had enjoyed some successes, the general level of the new work was higher than anything that had gone before. Throughout the 'eighties and early 'nineties the poets of the school of Roberts had been engaged in perfecting their craft, and with the possible exception of Scott, it is doubtful whether their work of later date ever much excelled the achievements of that climactic moment. Its significance did not entirely escape the notice of interested Canadians, although they were inclined to magnify it by making brash comparisons with what was being done across the border, where, it is true, a relative dearth had followed hard upon the brilliant expression of the New England genius. "It may not be known to Canadians generally," stated the Rev. George Bryce to the Literary Society of Manitoba College in 1894, "that we have in Canada at present a constellation of poets, with more true power, a loftier note of inspiration, and greater elegance of diction than is to be found in the United States." Three years earlier a Canadian journalist then living in Duluth, Minn., had written to the editor of a Toronto weekly: "It is a matter of pride for every true Canadian that at present much of the healthiest and most virile verse appearing in the leading magazines of this country is the product of Canadian thought and inspiration. There is truly more than promise in Roberts, Lampman, and Campbell, there is present achievement." While Mr. Laurier, when the subject came up in the House, was not prepared to concur in Nicholas Davin's assertion that literature was the life-blood of a people, it was acknowledged that Lampman was a genuine poet, deserving of public support. It is not recorded that anything was done, and interest in the nation's culture apparently went no further than this. Poetry and politics were seldom contingent, although the writers themselves were conscious of the relevance of their work to the processes of the society that had given them birth. "This pouring out of song," wrote one of them, "is a sign and hopeful token of our national life in Canada." The poets were acknowledged to be "the outcome of a hope and belief that Canada has a destiny worthy of the confidence of her sons."

The fact of the influence on literature of the national spirit that had been born with Confederation and in its aftermath was thus clearly apprehended. The nature of that influence seems to have been imperfectly understood, even by those who were actively engaged in the attempt to produce a literature that would be worthy of the Canada to which they aspired and distinctive of its life and thought. Conceptions of social evolution that were increasingly in vogue, involving an emphasis on material causes that was characteristic of an age of realism, and mounting international economic conflict, sometimes misled them into believing that when the country reached a certain stage in its growth, a literature of merit would inevitably follow. "In point of time," wrote Graeme Mercer Adam, onetime editor of the now defunct *Canadian Monthly and National Review*, "the material progress of every country necessarily precedes the intellectual; indeed, they stand to one another somewhat in the relation of cause and effect."

While the causal relationship may be conceded, it is doubtful whether any such optimistic assumption of inevitability is warranted by the facts. Economic progress, the formation of a unified state, and a phase of rapid social differentiation were essential precedents to the growth of a national literature, but they could not ensure its occurrence. Theoretically it would have been possible for Canada to expand its territories to the Atlantic and the Pacific, and at the same time to extend its economic commitments, while remaining intellectually arrested through the exhaustion of its energies, or by diverting them to unworthy and spiritually sterile ends. It may be inferred from the evidence that both these factors operated in different degrees to check the creative impulse of the Canadian people in the period with which we are concerned. But they must be considered in relation to the opposite tendencies, simultaneously at work, the existence of which is necessary to account for the school of romantic poetry to which reference has been made.

The student in fact is confronted with what appears to be a paradox. He finds the editors and publicists who were loudest in their praise of the work of the poets, as it developed towards its peak, expressing increasingly a sense of frustration and despair as they looked about them at what was going on and counted the prospects of the future.

The truth was that a rich and varied literature of high quality had been hoped for and expected, but only the poets appeared to be fulfilling something of the promise of an earlier day. The meagre and disappointing yield seemed disproportionate to the years of social and intellectual growth that lay behind. American and British publishers testified in 1884 to the serious falling away of their exports to Canada, and local wholesale houses confirmed the fact of the decay of the better-class book trade. Mercer Adam who, as editor, publisher, journalist, and historian, gave a quarter of a century to the service of Canadian letters, found "in the ebbing out of national spirit, a growing intellectual callousness, and a deadening of interest in the things that make for the nation's higher life." The national literature, with nothing to encourage it, was fast losing the power to command attention and was perceptibly dying of inanition. "We talk with horror of political annexation," he wrote on the eve of his own departure for the United States in 1889, "yet we pay no heed to the annexation of another kind, which is drafting off across the line not only the brains and pens of the country, but the hopes and hearts of those who move and inspire them." Whistler had said that art happens, but why, asked Sara Jeannette Duncan, did it happen so seldom in Canada? The newspapers, she believed, both reflected and abetted the tastes of the people. There was no dispassionate consideration of public questions, abuse being the common substitute for reasoned argument. There were "no social topics of other than a merely local interest, no scientific, artistic, or literary discussions, no broad consideration of matters of national interest – nothing but perpetual jeering, misconstruction, and misrepresentation for party ends of matters within an almost inconceivably narrow range."[1]

Sometimes the causes of cultural backwardness seemed to be cosmic in their scope and unalterable in their incidence. They were sometimes explained as the result of an economic dispensation of an overruling Providence. The conclusion, wrote Miss Duncan, was usually that "owing to the obscure

[1]*The Week,* Toronto, Sept. 30, 1886, p. 707.

operation of some natural law" literature was not indigenous to Canada. But she herself was not prepared to accept this conclusion. As clearly as any of her contemporaries she posed the problem that has continued to this day to baffle, perhaps more than any other, the student of literature equally with his fellow-worker in the social sciences. She was not unfamiliar with the language of Coleridge and his school. She knew that genius had been regarded as a strange and beautiful flower of the ego, put forth under all climates and conditions, irreducible to a scientific nomenclature, and defying all the wisdom of the botanists of civilization. While she did not make a clear decision, she touched on the contrary view – the view that the modern student of cultural phenomena has been most concerned to explore – in accordance with which genius was regarded as a function of the social and cultural milieu, and as a supreme expression of the processes and impulses latent within it.

II

There was little that was propitious in the British North American settlements as they took shape at the end of the War of Independence. Counter-revolutionary in sentiment as the dominant elements were, they shrank from the uncertainties of social and political experiment, and fostered attitudes that were inimical to the inquisitive and free-ranging mind. Even the Yankees, already settled in Nova Scotia before the Revolution, were unable to make much impression on the conservatism of the Loyalists; and here, as well as in Upper Canada, their diffusive influence was still in part accountable, a century later, for the strongly traditional character of the Canadian mentality. Divided from each other by the barriers of distance and terrain, it was impossible, before the building of the railways, for the scattered communities of British North America to coalesce into a large and vigorous society. The future Dominion could never have been projected by the Maritime Provinces alone, or even in alliance with the mixed population of Lower Canada. While Nova Scotia matured early, and the New Brunswick Loyalists carried over from the old colonies an intellectual tradition that flowered in the Fredericton school of poets,[2] a ,

[2]Alfred G. Bailey, "Creative Moments in the Culture of the Maritime Provinces," *Dalhousie Review*, (Oct. 1949), pp. 231-244.

nationality capable of significant literary expression, founded in autonomy, and transcontinental in extent, required a numerous population of English speech and institutions, centrally located on the Upper St. Lawrence and in the southern Ontario lowland.

Events conspired to make available a territory that was essential to the purposes of the nation-builders of a later generation. Depopulated in the seventeenth century by Iroquois wars, and largely by-passed by the French in their drive for furs, its population was drawn, at the conclusion of the Revolution, almost entirely from the illiterate communities of farmers bordering the lakes to the south. Denied intellectual pursuits and aesthetic outlets by the circumstances of their existence, they nevertheless maintained their ties with the Republic from whence they had come, posing the danger, constant and increasing, of the peaceful absorption of Upper Canada into the American Union. It was the Americans themselves with their armed invasion of the province in 1812 who started the current of social forces flowing in a different direction. Successful resistance to the Americans meant support of the Family Compact, whose members took advantage of the circumstance to consolidate their arbitrary and sometimes irresponsible power over provincial affairs, with consequences that were far-reaching. Energies that might have found expression in a progressive educational programme and a general increase in public intelligence were frustrated by the bitter political conflict that mounted in intensity as thousands of British immigrants, after 1815, entered upon the empty lands of the province, augmenting the strength of the agrarian resistance to the rigid and unyielding policies of the privileged oligarchy. Hostile to the newspaper press, which would have provided a field for the exercise of literary talents, and absorbed in the lucrative business of government, the Tories, up to the time of the Rebellions, made no contribution whatever to the beginning of an indigenous literature.[3] From their opponents might have been expected a clear and zestful prose literature of political content; but little of the kind was forthcoming, and after 1837 they were cowed and beaten or dispersed in other lands. The vast number of immigrants from overseas, who kept up the invasion of the wild lands of Canada West during the

[3]John Richardson was hardly typical of the provincial Tory, although he belonged with the Tories if he belonged anywhere. For a just estimate of his place in Canadian letters, see Desmond Pacey, *Creative Writing in Canada*, (Toronto, 1952), pp. 25-28.

forties, possessed two disqualifications for cultural advancement on arrival in the new world and for many years to come. They did not represent an exact cross-section of the British population. Deriving preponderantly from the geographical and social fringes of the society of the British Isles, there were fewer men of learning and cultivation among them than were to be found in the metropolitan community as a whole. This disadvantage was accentuated by the terrific ordeal of coming to terms with a repellent bushland. The cultural consequences were an enforced relinquishment of many of the essentials of civilization, mental as well as physical, and a growing incomprehension of the meaning of civilization itself. This is suggested by Professor Delbert Clark to whom we are indebted for his study of the effects of the frontier on Canadian society.[4] Deprivation of educational institutions bred eventual indifference to education. Emphasis on exploitation of material resources drew the best men away from the despised profession of schoolteaching and left the schools in the hands of the poorer element, with consequent impairment of the intellectual faculties of large numbers of the native-born, upon whose capacities and outlook the cultural life of the future Dominion would in large measure depend.

These factors were partly offset by a relatively small number of immigrants with an Old Country background of culture and gentility. Galt came too late in life and stayed too short a time to be claimed by Canada; but a number of persons, mostly Anglicans, who settled on the Upper St. Lawrence and in the Trent Valley exerted an influence on later Canadian writers. Scottish newspaper editors, steeped in the poetry of Burns, while they sometimes fed the nostalgia of the lonely exiles in the clearings, disseminated useful information, made salty comments on local affairs, and started the first imaginative currents moving in the mind of many a bereft colonial.[5] People like the Langtons and Stewarts, and particularly their neighbours, Susanna Moodie and Catherine Parr Traill, became the exemplars of how the life of the mind, even when tempered by hardship, could bring spiritual enrichment to themselves and to the life of the colony. More than any others it was the Strickland sisters, Mrs. Moodie and Mrs. Traill, who promoted

[4]S. D. Clark, *The Social Development of Canada*, (Toronto, 1942), pp. 212-213.

[5]James J. Talman, "Three Scottish Canadian Newspaper Editor Poets," *Canadian Historical Review*, Vol. XXVIII, (1947), pp. 166-177.

the literary life, both by their own writings and by their sponsorship and encouragement of others. Apart from the Maritime Provinces, where Haliburton was, at that time, developing his humorous satires, there was little of interest until the Stricklands, with their intellectual tastes already formed, entered into and leavened with their presence the new society that was then taking shape in the Canadian back country.

Mrs. Moodie helped to stir Charles Mair's interest in literature when, as a boy, he read her poems and sketches in a magazine to which his parents subscribed. How much a mentor of Lampman Mrs. Traill became may be suggested by the effect of her personality on him during his childhood at Rice Lake. Isabella Valancy Crawford spent her girlhood in the haunts of the Stricklands and it would be surprising indeed if they had not helped to impress that gifted young woman with the possibilities of a literary life. The examples are few, but they are nonetheless indicative of some reaching of minds across the emerging vista of colonial time. The age of settlement and rebellion was not entirely without promise for the future nation and its literature.

III

With the mid-century the formative period was reaching its end. The scattered settlements were becoming a community with a degree of social consistency and a sense of identity unknown at an earlier day. The process was accelerated by a limitation placed by nature upon the capacity for physical expansion. In spite of transportation difficulties, political frustrations and deadlocks, and the ever present competition of the United States, all the good arable land of Canada West had become occupied by the early 'fifties, and the agrarian element, which was by far the largest in the population, was hemmed in and checked in its westward movement by the great wedge of the Canadian Shield. Here was a profound difference between this country and the United States. In Canada there was no Middle West, no "valley of Democracy" in which ineluctable changes of custom, temper, and ideal, could work their way on men, imperceptibly, shaping anew. Lacking an area in any way comparable with the Mississippi basin, the Canadian tendency, noteworthy from the beginning of its history, towards consolidation, centralization, and a type of social and intellectual conservatism, was accentuated in a way that has sometimes puzzled the student of Canadian institutions. Such a tendency was further accelerated by the beginnings of the railways, the increased domination of investment capital, the consequent impetus to manufacturing, and the first tentative move towards a system of protective tariffs.

A refinement of technological skills, specialization in the professions, and other symptoms of social differentiation accompanied these changes. An expansion and an improvement in the agencies of communication were demanded by a suddenly hustling community. The newspaper press and the printing trades sprang into new life with the application of steam power to the iron presses, and other technical improvements. Publishing became a vocation and men and women, stimulated by new university foundations and an increasing demand for information, edification, and entertainment, took to the making of books. Editors and publishers, such as Mercer Adam, John Lesperance, and George Stewart, fostered authorship by providing the media for publication, by giving a lead to public taste through their literary appraisals, and on occasion by joining the ranks of the authors themselves.[6] It was such men who, during the first years of Canadian nationhood, wrote the poems, essays, short stories, novels, and reviews that raised the standards of such magazines as the *Nation,* the *Canadian Monthly, Belford's* and the *Week* to levels of which the Canadian of that time could well be proud.

While newspapers continued to improve in tone, with some evident exceptions, and to multiply everywhere, especially in Ontario, the magazines played a crucial role in giving focus and direction to the literary life of the country. The editor of the *Nation,* in 1875, modestly put forward Toronto's claim to be the literary capital of the Dominion; and James Douglas, of Quebec, conceded that the *Canadian Monthly* was "the best literary periodical which has yet been published in Canada. . . ." The editor of that periodical, too, felt that the changed conditions justified his venture. "The range of study," he wrote in 1872, "has grown wider and taste is becoming critical, if not fastidious. There is an evident desire to keep up with the knowledge of the time, and . . . for the latest and noblest fruits of contemporary intellect." An acquaintance with the Greek

---

[6]The influence of Goldwin Smith on the growth of a national literature is so well known that I have preferred to draw attention to the names of men who played an important part in the affairs of the time, but who are less likely to be remembered today.

and Latin classics on the part of the new university-bred generation wrought transformations in taste, and raised the quality of prose and verse to a new level. Lampman, Campbell, Roberts, and Carman, owed a debt to their classical training. Original researches in classical archaeology won acclaim at home and overseas. Through the work of Dr. McCaul, wrote the *Nation* in 1874, "Toronto may justly claim the merit of having anticipated the Mother Country in the production of a work exclusively devoted to Britanno-Roman epigraphy. . . ." The universities in the Maritime Provinces, as well as in Quebec and Ontario, tempered their devotion to the classics with a lively concern for the sciences. Important monographs in anthropology were published, and a distinguished group of geologists, through their teaching and researches, helped also to form an intellectual climate that was favourable to the growth of a national literature. William Dawson LeSueur, a native of Quebec, and a graduate of the University of Toronto in the class of 1863, was typical of the best minds of that period. Well acquainted with the ancient literatures, he wrote extensively on the major scientific, philosophical, and literary questions of the time, and always in an interesting and persuasive manner. So wide and varied were his interests that they almost epitomize the influences, British, European, and American, then current in Canada.

These varied influences, it was felt in the seventies, entered the country in such a way as to form a Canadian point of view, divergent from those of the lands from which the influences were derived. It is true that Canadian editors tended to print only those articles which they regarded as being of interest to their readers, and also that they sometimes rewrote them, giving them what they supposed to be a Canadian slant. Nevertheless it is impossible at this day to determine either the extent of the process or its results. We know that Canadians not only adopted, selectively, ideas and emotional attitudes from abroad, but also that they were inclined to be sensitive to opinions of Canada and Canadians published in the newspapers and journals of Great Britain and the United States. It was gratifying when a London editor complimented the Toronto *Nation* on its well-written pages, the expression of ideas in clear English, and on the preservation of good manners in describing issues of public and controversial interest. It was also gratifying, when an issue of the English *Publishers' Circular* of 1873 noted the "important native literature springing up in the country. . . ." "Canada is the most vigorous of our colonies, and we are inclined to think," it stated in reference to the *Canadian Monthly*, "that this is the most vigorous of colonial literary productions and quite able to stand side by side with our home produce."

It is evident that Canada was subjected to a *mélange* of literary influences that did not come in the chronological order in which they had first appeared in the metropolitan societies from which Canadians drew the greater part of their spiritual and intellectual sustenance. Sometimes the style of the Canadian writer reflected that of a British or American contemporary, later to be replaced by another of a previous age. Sometimes the movement was the other way, or in no easily discernible order at all. Earlier in the century Byron had been an influence on Canadian poetry. Later we find an interest in Swinburne and Rossetti; and for a time it was Tennyson who, according to a journalist of the day, exercised a virtual tyranny over the style of colonial writers. Keats was the paramount influence in the eighties, on such writers as Roberts and Lampman, and there were, of course, other influences, both then and later, the determination of which would require a separate study.

Not as spectacular as the British, but nevertheless persistent, were certain American influences. Commenting on Canadian attendance at the American celebration in 1876 of the centenary of the Declaration of Independence, *Belford's Monthly* expressed the view that it would "have been the highest education of all, if our people, having seen the degree of art and other culture in the States, become dissatisfied with our present attainments . . . and seek to raise and improve them. Taking hints from our more artistic neighbours," it reassured its readers, "does not imply annexation or any diminution in attachment to home and country." Canadians, as a matter of fact, were caution personified. The *Nation*, on May 14, 1875, felt it necessary to tender advice to the youthful Toronto student-at-law, Thomas Stinson Jarvis. "Against one thing we would venture to warn him. He seems in danger of being infected by the humour of Mark Twain – the lowest, the most forced, and the most vulgar that ever usurped the name." Unfortunately it was too often the case that such poets of the literary interregnum as Aldrich, Stedman, and Faucett, rather than the great Americans, were taken as models. Bryant was a better and a discernible influence, but Canadians were challenged most, if not influenced in equal measure, by Longfellow and Parkman, to seek in their own historic past, or more particularly in that of their French-Canadian compatriots, for themes that would lend themselves to treatment in a congenially romantic vein. The spate of histories, in which the example of Parkman's style and accuracy was not sufficiently emulated, was nevertheless a sign that Canadians were seeking to establish the lines of development of their emerging society, and to discover their own place among the nations. At that date the interest in history was still largely romantic and genealogical, a fact which goes some way to explain the relative popularity of Kirby's poem on the Loyalists, and especially his novel, *The Golden Dog*, the most impressive performance in the historic and romantic genre in the entire range of the nineteenth century. The aristocratic world of the eighteenth century was still very much in the minds of men of a certain class, and was not confined to a single nationality.

A more common influence of French Canada came in the form of the spirit of emulation with which English-Canadian writers were seized as they contemplated the achievements of Garneau, Crémazie, and other members of the Quebec School. Not often did they go so far as to become French-Canadian in sentiment, as Frances Harrison was described as doing in her work, *Crowded Out*, when she expressed what was said to be an "un-English" attitude towards pain. This rather odd example of the assimilative process would probably have accorded with the hopes of some of the nationalists that the French and the English would, in time, grow into one people.

IV

Literary influences disseminated from abroad provided some of the content and affected the emotional tone and attitude of most Canadian writing. British and American patterns of style, and ways of achieving effects desired for aesthetic ends, served as models for colonial authors. Canadian national feeling[7] augmented both the desire and the capacity to turn these traits into the elements of a native tradition. Never quite succeeding in this role of catalytic agent, it arose in the first instance as a sense of attachment to the emerging provincial community of Canada West in the eighteen-fifties. Responsible govern-

[7]On the beginnings of a national spirit, see A. J. M. Smith, "Colonialism and Nationalism in Canadian Poetry before Confederation," *Annual Report of the Canadian Historical Association*, (1944), pp. 74-85.

ment, vindicated in 1849, was extended into the field of religious organization by the movements of colonial autonomy in the Protestant churches in the era of Confederation. Institutional consolidation recurred in the absorption of sects into churches,[8] the later movement for university federation, and above all in Confederation itself. A growing self-consciousness stemming especially from Ontario was enlarged and intensified by the step towards transcontinental dominion taken in 1867; but the rank and file were not greatly moved by it, especially in the Maritime Provinces. It was a small group, the founders of the Canada First movement, who caught a vision of national destiny from D'Arcy McGee, and gave form to the inchoate and diffuse intimations of nationality current in some parts of the country. William Alexander Foster and the other members of the little band in Ottawa, who in the year after Confederation pledged themselves to place the good of Canada above every consideration, were not unaware partly through the example of McGee, of the role which literature had played, and was continuing to play, in the Irish nationalist insurgence. They were all men of letters themselves in their various ways. Henry Morgan had already begun to celebrate the achievements of eminent Canadians in the first of his biographical compilations. Haliburton, the son of the author of *Sam Slick*, whose studies of African ethnology were later to win him renown, anticipated in conception and outline Macdonald's National Policy. Colonel Denison, who became a widely recognized authority on cavalry warfare, added a somewhat militant note to the movement; and Charles Mair who later alternated hair-raising adventures in the West with the authorship of the verse-drama, *Tecumseh,* had just sounded the nationalist note in his first book of poems.

Affronted by the renewal of party warfare after Confederation, the Canada First movement, given aim and direction by Goldwin Smith, ran foul of George Brown, all but became a political party under the aegis of Edward Blake, and by 1877 had dissolved into a mere aggregation of men who shared a common ideal of nationhood, rather than an organized body with coherent and practical objectives. Nevertheless it both helped to form, and facilitated the acceptance of, Sir John Macdonald's conception of a national domain of Maritime and Western lands, linked with the manufacturing centres in

[8]S. D. Clark, "Religious Organization and the Rise of the Canadian Nation," *Annual Report of the Canadian Historical Association,* (1944), pp. 87-97.

Ontario and Quebec by an inter-oceanic line of railway communications, and made viable by a moderate system of protective tariffs.[9]

There were many related circumstances out of which Canada First had arisen. Its policy, and that of the Liberal-Conservative party after it, involved attitudes to the Imperial tie and to the United States which had been in process of formation throughout the century that had elapsed since the conclusion of the American Revolution. While the nationalists were pretty well agreed on repudiating any suggestion of annexation to the United States, they differed among themselves as to whether Canada should enter a system of Imperial federation, or seek an independent status in friendly association with the Mother Country. The sentimental attachment to Great Britain, and to the Queen, was constantly protested, but there was no love lost for the Queen's ministers who, it was felt, had sacrificed Canadian interests in the Treaty of Washington in 1871. Many factors, both public and personal, determined the attitude of Canadians to the question of independence. Frequent and sometimes derogatory references to Canada by English politicians and in the English press, then much influenced by Little Englandism, gave Canadians the notion that independence would be looked upon without regret by many in Great Britain. Relations with the metropolis had bred a sensitivity in Canadians which was one of the roots of their nationalism. No Canadian book, whatever its merits might be, could find sale for a single copy in England, wrote an English publisher to the author of The Golden Dog. Real or supposed attitudes of superiority accounted for some of it. Canadian civilians attending social functions sometimes felt put in the shade by the officers of the Imperial garrison stationed in Canada. In a novel called Bluebell, the wife of an officer of the 13th Hussars cast slurs on the morals as well as on the manners of Canadian women. If Bluebell, said the Saturday Review, "is to be accepted as a faithful picture of Canadian manners, the amount of romping, flirting, vulgarity, and kissing accepted as the natural order of things in the Dominion is simply surprising, and to English women must be not a little revolting."

Fortunately, it was not a representative opinion, and matters of this kind were, in any case, hardly of major importance in themselves. There were many reasons why, before very long,

[9]D. G. Creighton, Dominion of the North, Boston, (1949), pp. 322, 336-353; W. Stewart Wallace, The Growth of Canadian National Feeling, (Toronto, 1927), p. 59.

relations between Canada and the United Kingdom began to improve. Policies of economic nationalism and the resurgence of imperialist rivalries were responsible for the Imperial Federation movement, involving proposals for the economic integration of the Empire, and colonial contributions to Imperial defence. This movement did not of itself abate the tide of Canadian national sentiment, but it grew in popularity and influence at a time when factors of another nature were conspiring to weaken the faith of Canadians in the future of their country. Before this happened, in the seventies, and then in the early 'eighties, under the stimulus of the National Policy, and because of the social and political conditions which we have been engaged in describing, a self-reliant spirit, and a confidence in their ability to succeed in great tasks, took possession of Canadians.

The hopes for something distinctive in Canadian culture, and of high quality, which had been entertained by scholars and publicists ten years before, seemed on the point of being fulfilled. The literary editor of the *Nation* had written in 1874, "One of the most gratifying features in the history of the country is the rapid growth of culture and the increasing interest in intellectual life among the people. Knowledge is descending like the first and second rain and spreading with an uninterrupted flow over the land . . . in all directions bountifully irrigating the mental soil . . . to bear fruit, we trust, ere many days." When a few years later Charles G. D. Roberts published the poems he had written while he was an undergraduate at the University of New Brunswick, he was recognized by Lampman as "the first Canadian writer in verse who united strong original genius with a high degree of culture and an acute literary judgment." These poems with their strongly pagan, earth-loving instinct, delight in the presence of life and nature for its own sake, half intellectual, half physical, touched with a passionate glow, convinced him, as he said, that Canadians were not helplessly situated on the outskirts of civilization where no art and no literature could be. The romantic stream now moved in fuller flood into a social and intellectual milieu better than ever prepared to receive it. The poets of the school of Roberts had in general a surer grasp of the technical requisites of the craft, and a larger sense of aesthetic possibilities than earlier writers had. Predisposed by his father to the influence of Canada First, Roberts quickly became the acknowledged leader of the nationalist movement in literature which, by the late 'eighties, in the form of the lyric of native and classical landscape, was clearly approaching its apogee. "A Canadian literature," wrote Wilfred Chateauclair in 1888, "promising to be fine, conscious, and powerful, is budding and blossoming book after book. . . . The nature of it shows that it is a result of Confederation. Its generation is that which has grown up under the influence of the united country." To Mercer Adam, writing in 1889, Lighthall's anthology, *Songs of the Great Dominion,* was evidence "of a mental growth and a degree of literary culture far beyond what has been thought to be the intellectual possibility of a mere colony."

V

The momentum given by the national fervour to the school of romantic poetry continued through the last decade of the nineteenth century while adverse forces were setting in, weakening the foundations of the national life, and casting the future in a doubtful light. Flaws and biases that had existed from the beginning, but which had been obscured by the phenomenal growth of the country between 1850 and 1885, became more clearly visible, especially with the execution of Riel and the renewal of conflict with the French, the resurgence of provincialism, and the prolonged and deepening depression. The early distrust of mental activity of a literary and speculative nature, contributing in no immediate way to the material advancement of provincial life, bred indifference to authorship, and restricted the market for literary productions so sharply that to live by the pen was impossible. No protection was afforded Canadian authors by the copyright laws, which allowed British and American firms to publish garbled and pirated editions of their works, for which they might never be paid. Fierce factional strife, habitual since the days before the Rebellions, continued to absorb some of the keenest minds of the country, to the ruin of their creative possibilities. Guardians of morals, sometimes self-appointed, fostered the conventional responses to time-honoured institutions. "The foreign element in the fiction of the average country-town public library," wrote an amused observer, "used to consist almost exclusively of 'Les Misérables' and 'Selections' from Balzac, with possibly a translation of 'Manon Lescaut' which had slipped in by the inadvertence of the Board of Directors," or because of their somewhat limited acquaintance with the French classics. Such boards were still "apt to be of the opinion that all foreign literary matter emanates from the devil." The treatment of breaches of the moral code in fiction was to be kept in strict conformity with colonial proprieties. "Immorality," wrote a pundit in the *Week* on October 8, 1885, "should never be allowed to prosper for more than a short time, and then its downfall should be greatly emphasized. . . . It should never be described in luxurious surroundings . . . the immoral in fiction should never be taken as a matter of course and acquiesced in as a mere foible that all at some time must give way to." Foreign realists, on the other hand, presented unrecognizable situations and complexities to the native readers, few of whom possessed the requisite sophistication and sensitivity to enable them to write in that vein.[10] Men like Robert Barr and Gilbert Parker were touched by it for a brief period, while resident abroad; and Sara Jeannette Duncan's novel, *The Imperialist,* written years later and in another country, laid bare the lives of individuals warped by the crassness and venality of small-town Ontario politics. There was not much more than that.

Indifference and depression, a narrow and inhibiting morality, a political disunity that was a consequence, in part, of the fading of the vision of nationhood, these and other factors, drove journalists, novelists, and poets, to seek elsewhere what was denied them in their own country. It is hardly realized today how large was the exodus of the leading literary figures, especially to the United States, in the last decade of the century.[11] Even the names of many of those who left are hardly remembered today. So complete was the break in continuity that in the years following the First World War new Canadian writers could find no significant roots in the earlier literature of their own country. The patterns of romantic poetry, which had reached their fullest expression in the nineties, and which had continued in attenuated forms for decades afterwards, were stale and meaningless to a generation emerging from a war that seemed to have destroyed all the traditional values. It became fashionable, and it was salutary, to deride the accomplishments of the past. They had often suffered from overpraise, and, in any case, intellectual and aesthetic realties

[10]Professor Claude Bissell suggests that realism was most palatable to the Canadian reader in the form of the local colour novel. See his "Literary Taste in Central Canada during the Late Nineteenth Century," *Canadian Historical Review,* Vol. xxx, (1950), pp. 237-251.

[11]Alexander Brady, *Democracy in the Dominions,* (Toronto, 1947), pp. 35-38.

demanded a new start. The student of the history of culture in Canada must recognize the necessity for the revolt of the twenties. He cannot appreciate its significance if he does not know the tradition that was then overthrown, its objectives and its limitations, as shaped in the historic context of the time. Such knowledge is essential to the deeper understanding of the possibilities of a national culture.

III | THE CASE HISTORY OF A MARGINAL PROVINCE

5. Railways
And the Confederation Issue
In New Brunswick, 1863-1865

New Brunswick occupies a unique position in relation to the two geographic provinces of the St. Lawrence River and the Atlantic seaboard. It stands at the apex of the angle where these two regions meet and possesses both an Atlantic and a St. Lawrence frontage. The latter is, however, not properly a frontage at all. It is rather the left flank of a province facing south and standing with its back to the Appalachian highland which runs out into the great spur of the Gaspé Peninsula. The flank is partly isolated by that spur from the St. Lawrence region.[1] No port on the "north shore" or left flank of the province has ever rivalled Saint John, which is situated on the more important Atlantic front. Hence in many respects New Brunswick has belonged more naturally to the Atlantic region than to that of the St. Lawrence.

I

Within the two geographic provinces there evolved early in colonial times two competing societies,[2] that of the St. Lawrence having been occupied first by the French and then by the British, and that of the Atlantic first by the British and then by the United States. In response to needs peculiar to themselves both societies competed for the control of the territory now occupied by New Brunswick. Which would triumph was a question long hanging in the balance. In the seventeenth century, while the British were colonizing the Atlantic seaboard, the French were attempting to link their fur-trading empire of

[1] W. M. Whitelaw, *The Maritimes and Canada before Confederation* (Toronto, 1934), pp. 9-37.

[2] D. G. Creighton, *The Commercial Empire of the St. Lawrence, 1760-1850* (Toronto, 1937), pp. 1-21.

the St. Lawrence with the fishing grounds controlled by them in their colony of Acadia. The Intendant Talon projected a line of communication between Quebec and Acadia by way of the St. John River Valley. Thus, what was one day to be the Province of New Brunswick was a key-stone in the arch of French empire in America. It was, however, a weak stone. Talon's vigorous policy was not followed up by his successors, and, partly as a result, the St. John Valley was virtually deserted during the first half of the eighteenth century. The French empire collapsed in part because of the failure to integrate the closed season of the St. Lawrence with the fishing season in Acadia, and to link both these with the hurricane and sugar seasons of the West Indies.[3]

With the arch of empire finally broken at the surrender of Montreal in 1760, New Englanders pushed their frontier northeastward into Nova Scotia. During the American Revolution, the neutral Yankees of Nova Scotia, to use Professor Brebner's apt phrase, preferred to remain aloof from the conflict. Their attempt to storm Fort Cumberland and the expression of "rebel" sympathies on the part of the settlers of Maugerville, a small settlement on the River St. John, were exceptions to an otherwise prevailing tendency. The weakness of American seapower, among other factors,[4] rendered abortive the attempts to link the destiny of Nova Scotia with that of the other thirteen seaboard colonies; and by a sublime piece of imperial strategy, whether altogether intended or partly fortuitous, ten thousand loyal refugees erected a province in the valley of the Saint John as a bulwark against further encroachments of New Englanders into the north-east.

For better or for worse the Yankees of New England and the Loyalists of New Brunswick were destined to live side by side in the same geographic region, and it was inevitable that some intercourse should surmount the mutual antipathy that is generally supposed to have existed between them. As the nineteenth century advanced and the economy of the Second Empire gave way to reciprocity, the commercial bond between New Brunswick and New England was drawn closer than it had ever been before, and it was the keen desire of certain interests in both Maine and New Brunswick to draw it closer still. With the advent of the railway era these interests became focussed on the

[3]H. A. Innis, "Cape Breton during the French Regime," *Transactions of the Royal Society of Canada*, sec. II, XXIX, (1935).

[4]J. B. Brebner, *The Neutral Yankees of Nova Scotia, a Marginal Colony during the Revolutionary Years* (New York, 1937).

project of extending New Brunswick's European and North American Railroad westward from Saint John to the American border, thus connecting it with the railway systems of the United States. Thus when Canada embarked upon the path of economic and political imperialism which was to harness the commerce of the great West to the St. Lawrence system and sweep the Maritime Provinces within its orbit by means of federation and the Intercolonial Railway, the rival project of *western extension* appeared in New Brunswick as an obstacle to the attainment of that end. The relation between the *western extension* interest and the anti-Confederation faction in New Brunswick has long been recognized, but it is doubtful if the connection has ever been given the prominence it deserves in the story of Confederation. Obviously, with the Intercolonial Railway unbuilt and the rival road completed, New Brunswick's only railway connection would have been with the United States, and *western extension* might well have acted as the spearhead for the expansion of New England's interests into that region. Situated as it was between Canada and Nova Scotia, New Brunswick was essential to any union of the provinces of British North America. It is proposed in the following pages to examine the relation of the proposed *western extension* to the Confederation movement.

II

Lord Durham clearly indicated the political significance of railways when he advocated the building of an Intercolonial Railway to link Canada with the Maritime Provinces. It was an essential step towards British North American union, and although the proposal was not practicable when Lord Durham made it, railways continued to play an increasingly important part in the economic and political life of the provinces. Advocates of an Intercolonial Railway became numerous, and two abortive interprovincial conferences were held, in 1862 and 1863, the object of which was to draft practical plans for its promotion. Since the failure of these two conferences was directly connected with the defeat of Confederation in New Brunswick in 1865, it is necessary to examine in some detail the circumstances arising from them.

The Intercolonial Railway conference held at Quebec in 1862 was followed by another conference in London in the following year. The British insistence upon a sinking fund as a necessary condition, if the imperial guarantee of £3,000,000 was to be made, was not acceptable to the Canadian Reform government in 1863, and Canada had therefore failed to pass the legislation necessary to the promotion of the project. Both New Brunswick and Nova Scotia, however, fulfilled what they conceived to be their part of the bargain by passing bills providing for the raising of funds to construct their respective sections of the road, and they were naturally dismayed and chagrined at what they regarded as Canada's repudiation of a solemn agreement. "The engagement of 1862," wrote Governor Gordon of New Brunswick, "was of a solemn character, approaching as nearly in its nature to a Treaty as the political condition of these Provinces permits."[5] In the opinion of the Governor-General, Gordon virtually charged the Canadian government with want of good faith.[6] Monk replied to Gordon on October 17, 1863, with some asperity, setting forth the Canadian view that, when the agreement had been reached in September, 1862, the provision of a sinking fund, for the extinction of the debt to be guaranteed by Great Britain, was unknown; and that, when it was laid down as indispensable by the imperial government in 1863, its unacceptability to Canada rendered the original agreement void.

In the opinion of the two Maritime Provinces, concurrent legislation on the part of Canada was a necessary preliminary to the survey of the road, but Canada took the view that legislation would be fruitless until the survey had been made and the approximate cost of the railway estimated. On October 26, 1863, Gordon laid the views of New Brunswick before the Colonial Secretary. It was useless, he wrote, to expect the Maritime Provinces to contribute a large sum for the expense of a survey, without some definite expectation that construction would be undertaken. This expectation could not be entertained if the 1862 agreement had been rendered void as was asserted by a number of Canadian legislators. Moreover, if it were void, the three provinces would, he thought, be released from their obligations, and Gordon was "not sanguine as to their being easily re-assumed."[7] It was, however, by no means certain that the British government considered New Brunswick free from her obligation under the convention of 1862 as a result of the

[5]*Journal of the House of Assembly of New Brunswick, 1864,* Intercolonial Railway Correspondence, pp. 16-17, Gordon to Newcastle, Feb. 15, 1864.

[6]*Ibid.,* p. 31.

[7]*Ibid.,* p. 28.

alleged Canadian repudiation. In view of the fact that an important group in New Brunswick was agitating for the abandonment of the proposed rail connection with Canada, and was
instead actively promoting the idea of extending the European
and North American Railway westward from Saint John to the
American border, thus linking New Brunswick with the railway
systems of the United States, it was imperative that the British
government should state its position with respect to the Intercolonial Railway agreement. So popular had the idea of *western
extension* become that during the first weeks of 1864 the local
government was solicited to make a definite declaration of
railway policy. The views of Cabinet members were canvassed
freely. The Liberal party was almost to a man favourable to
western extension. The Conservatives also strongly favoured
the road, and, there being very little party spirit, they were quite
willing that the government should undertake the work. But the
government hesitated to declare its policy, since, while there
might still be a chance for the I.C.R. agreement being accepted
by Canada and sanctioned by Great Britain, "a high sense of
honour may have led them to believe that, notwithstanding the
objections of Canada, they were justified in considering the
legislation" of 1863 as binding.[8] There was a growing opinion,
however, that the withholding of the royal assent from the New
Brunswick Facility Bill had relieved the local government of
responsibility, and that the province was now free to promote
western extension as though no I.C.R. legislation had been
passed. A section of the press which was both friendly to the
government and favourable to *western extension* had not pushed
the matter, for fear of embarrassing the government's friends.
"When, however," declared the *Saint John Globe,* "the Petitions
now being rapidly signed, containing the names of a majority of
the citizens, of persons in every calling and profession in life,
begin to pour in, showing the extent of public feeling, the
Government will prepare either to yield to the voice of the
people, or to take the consequences."[9] It was possible, continued
the editor, "that the Government as a whole might cling to the
Inter-Colonial Road. There might be imaginary promises from
visionary Grand Trunk adherents; or splendid schemes propounded by English capitalists of fabulous wealth; or there
might be some *ignis fatuus"* which the rulers of the Province
would chase, either to gain time or because they honestly

[8]*Ibid.,* p. 173.
[9]*Ibid.,* p. 173 ff.

believed that they would succeed in getting the I.C.R. As the Cabinet had been committed to this "ignis fatuus," some members might be compelled on principle to oppose *western extension,* in which case a remodelling of the Cabinet might be expected. "The country will soon recognize but two parties, a Railway and Anti-Railway party. . . ." People must prepare their minds for the encounter, counselled the editor, and irrespective of party, lend their energies and talents to maturing the measures that would develop the resources of the country and lead it to wealth and power.[10]

As the *western extension* party continued to make capital of the impression that the British government had refused assent to the provincial I.C.R. bill, and that in consequence, the Act was disallowed and was of no effect, Gordon sought a declaration from the Colonial Office. Newcastle replied on March 5, 1864. He was surprised that an impression prevailed in New Brunswick that the I.C.R. Act had been disallowed.[11] It was useless for Great Britain to sanction it before Canada should pass a similar law. It was still in force in New Brunswick. The dilemma of the New Brunswick government, in the face of this declaration was obvious. It could not proceed with the project to which it was committed, and it could not declare for the popularly desired *western extension* as an alternative. Nor could it wait idly for Canada to take action. The government, therefore, endeavoured to secure the British guarantee for the portion of the line which was to be constructed from Truro in Nova Scotia to Moncton in New Brunswick. But the Lords of the Treasury wished it to be "distinctly understood that the construction of the Line now proposed between Truro and the Bend [Moncton] is undertaken by the two provinces at their own risk; that no claim of any kind is to be made upon the Imperial government if the whole project of 1862-3 should not be carried out; . . ."[12] The views of the Colonial Secretary were transmitted to the New Brunswick government on March 18, 1864, and it was made clear that, if New Brunswick and Nova Scotia should build the Truro-Bend line and if the whole Intercolonial Railway should subsequently be built, the British guarantee would be retroactively applied to that part of the line. If, however, the larger project should fall through, the imperial

[10]*Ibid.,* p. 174.
[11]*Ibid.,* Newcastle to Gordon, March 5, 1864.
[12]*Ibid.,* p. 193, Peel to Rogers, March 18, 1864.

government would not hold itself responsible for any part of the loan of £3,000,000.[13]

Although the Canadian Reform government had shirked the commitment of 1863, there were powerful Canadian and English backers of the Grand Trunk who were anxious to bring the I.C.R. negotiation to a successful conclusion. As the Grand Trunk then terminated at Rivière du Loup, and as it had no all-year access to the sea except through American territory to Portland, Maine, there was a pressing necessity that a route through British territory should be secured in the face of the menacing hostility of the northern states as they emerged victorious from the holocaust of the Civil War. This was why Edward Watkin, the President of the Grand Trunk, viewed with alarm the failure of the negotiation of 1862 and the desire of interests in New Brunswick and Nova Scotia to abandon the attempt to secure rail communication with Canada. On February 15, 1864, he noted that the Legislatures of New Brunswick and Nova Scotia would, in the approaching session, be "urged to devote, in other directions, the capital to be set apart for the construction of the Inter-Colonial." Both provinces were "at this moment appealed to to join with parties in the State of Maine in connecting their respective Railway systems, and the Railway systems of the United States."[14] Indeed, this *western extension* project involved a much smaller financial outlay on the part of New Brunswick than did the Intercolonial, "and as it will give for New Brunswick a short route into districts with which they have a very considerable trade, such a proposal finds many ardent supporters." In the circumstances, therefore, Watkin suggested to Newcastle that the Treasury should protect the two provinces in the event of their "taking action in the right direction," without waiting for Canada. At length the Grand Trunk "sales-talks" had some small effect upon the British government, which agreed to modify its stand on the imperial guarantee so that it would be available to New Brunswick and Nova Scotia for the building of the Truro-Bend line, if within five years Canada should fulfil her part of the agreement of 1862. In these negotiations, C. J. Brydges, the General Manager of the Grand Trunk, was an active participant. The approaching end of the Civil War made rail connection with the

---

[13]*Ibid.*, p. 191, Rogers to Watkin, March 19, 1864; *The Gleaner,* Chatham, April 9, 1864.

[14]*Journal of the House of Assembly of New Brunswick, 1864,* 193-4, Watkin to Hamilton, Feb. 15, 1864.

ports of the Maritime Provinces seem imperative to Canadian railway interests, but their desire for an all-British route was not new. Indeed, down to 1864 the *Toronto Globe* treated the whole intercolonial idea as a Grand Trunk "job," and nothing more.[15] "The Grand Trunk and Mr. Watkin have fanned the flame which is always kept burning on the railway altars in Halifax and St. John. . . ." It was noted, however, as early as December 7, 1860, that the Maritime people were "afraid to trust themselves to politicians who had the reputation of the railway speculators of Canada."[16] This statement, of course, required qualification. If the lower provinces as a whole were hesitant, certain business interests of the north shore of New Brunswick looked favourably upon closer connection with Canada. A considerable quantity of flour and provisions was imported from Canada into this area. On the other hand, the dependence of the north shore upon trade with the United States was negligible. No part of British America was less dependent upon benefits accruing from the Reciprocity Treaty than the north-eastern part of New Brunswick.[17] It was, therefore, natural that the I.C.R. project should have found great support from Peter Mitchell, the chief protagonist of the north-shore business interests; and to the alacrity with which New Brunswick passed the I.C.R. bill of 1863, these interests must have contributed in no small measure.

Nevertheless, in spite of Peter Mitchell and the Grand Trunk, and their advocacy of closer commercial relations, it is evident that neither in New Brunswick nor in Canada was there any general enthusiasm for a union of interests. The mutual interests of the two provinces were, in fact, slight. New Brunswick was attached to the economy of the Atlantic seaboard rather than to Canada's commercial empire. The proof was found in terms of irrefutable statistics. Canada's trade with the Maritime Provinces was but a small part of her total trade. Of the total imports of Canada in 1861, amounting to $43,054,846 only $478,130 were derived from the Maritime Provinces.[18] Exports to the Maritime Provinces amounted to

[15] F. H. Underhill, "Some Aspects of Upper Canadian Radical Opinion in the Decade before Confederation," *Annual Report of the Canadian Historical Association,* (May, 1927).

[16] *Ibid.,* 57. For a general account of the railway politics of the day, see R. G. Trotter, *Canadian Federation* (London, 1924), especially part II.

[17] *The Headquarters,* Fredericton, Jan. 24, 1866.

[18] *Ibid.,* Sept. 28, 1864.

only 2.84 per cent of the Canadian total. There was no trade between Canada and New Brunswick's Atlantic ports. The great volume of New Brunswick's external trade was with the United States. When the overwhelming impetus to the union of the British North American provinces did come, it was not the lower provinces which cast longing eyes upon Canada; it was the Canadian commercial giant, grown suddenly straitened by her hostile southern neighbour, which reached out towards the Maritime Provinces. In this development the year 1864 was crucial. By February 24, The Quebec Mercury noted that public opinion in Canada had begun to veer in favour of the I.C.R.; and it was not merely because of the threatened withdrawal of bonding privileges by the United States, nor because of the refusal of the United States to renew the Reciprocity Treaty. It was rather the fear of losing the all-British route to the ice-free ports of the Maritimes beyond much hope of recovery. Such might be the result of the extension of New Brunswick's railway westward to the international boundary, a step which would link the Maritime Provinces with the railway systems of the United States. It appeared also "that some English capitalists have been making some propositions regarding the Railway."[19]

III

If English capitalists showed signs of enterprise in the direction of New Brunswick's railway development, they were, perhaps, matched by American overtures, and by the influence of the United States upon the economy of the province. The author of the report on trade and navigation for 1863 noted the strong disposition on the part of neighbouring American citizens to invest capital in "these colonies," perhaps in part owing to the unsettled state of the Union during the Civil War and to the light taxation in New Brunswick. Already American mining companies were actively interested in New Brunswick, and the Albert Mining Company sold its product principally in the United States where it was used for making oil and gas.[20]. Moreover, since the repeal of the Navigation Laws in 1849, American and Norwegian vessels had secured a large share of New Brunswick's carrying business.

[19]Ibid., Feb. 24, 1864.
[20]Journal of the House of Assembly of New Brunswick, 1864, Report on trade and navigation for 1863, p. 20.

Something of the close commercial relations between New Brunswick and the United States, during the years preceding Confederation, can be gleaned from the correspondence relating to the restrictions on the American export trade to British North America, imposed for the purpose of preventing trans-shipment of supplies from British American ports to the southern states during the war. So onerous were these restrictions to the mercantile interests of Saint John that grave and repeated complaints were addressed to the Lieutenant-Governor by various wealthy and respected merchants, a prominent representative among whom was John W. Cudlip who was soon to reveal his uncompromising hostility to the Quebec Resolutions. The Saint John Chamber of Commerce addressed a memorial to the Governor praying that the matter be taken up with the British Ambassador at Washington with a view to having the restrictions removed. The memorialists drew attention to the fact that the trade of the province was a growing one, and that imports from the United States consisted mainly of breadstuffs and salt meats, of which there was a rapidly increasing consumption, that these were imported for consumption only, none being shipped to destinations adverse to the interests of the United States. The British government regarded the difficulty as sufficiently serious to represent to the American government that the restrictions were imposed in violation of the treaty obligations between the two countries. The restrictions seriously affected the business of such American shippers as A. Smithers and Company of New York, who had been engaged in business with New Brunswick and Nova Scotia for fifteen years. Although the population of these provinces had largely increased in this time, they apparently raised little grain except oats and barley but imported their breadstuffs from the United States. Before 1854 Canadian flour had been shipped through the United States in bond, but after that time Smithers and Company had exported American grain exclusively. In 1863 alone their business was said to have amounted to $800,000. To the Secretary of the Treasury Smithers expressed the view that restrictions would drive the entire import trade of New Brunswick and Nova Scotia into the hands of Canada.[21]

The signs of the times were not as easy to read, however, as might have been supposed. It was true, of course, that if reciprocity and the bonding privilege were abolished, and that

[21]*Journal of the House of Assembly of New Brunswick, 1865*, pp. 118-30.

if New Brunswick were to become connected with Montreal and Quebec by a route passing through British territory, importation from the United States might be expected to decrease immediately, and Saint John might "become the Atlantic shipping port of Canada for the winter months."[22] But beneath the political animosities that clouded relations with the United States at that time, the enterprising railway promoters of New Brunswick and Maine pursued their somewhat obstructed way. It was the promoters in the State of Maine who appeared the more aggressive, and apparently took the initiative late in 1863. Plans were offered for a railroad from Portland to Halifax, to be constructed in sections in a spirit of harmony, even if not owned and managed by a single company. Every opportunity was to be offered to the Maine interests to take up such shares of stock as they might desire. All stock not taken locally would be offered in the large markets of the United States. The European and North American Railroad Company, of Maine, had secured all necessary charters and awaited only the consent of New Brunswick and Nova Scotia. As soon as this might be secured "the needful amount of stock to carry out the work" would be "readily taken up by the large capitalists of the United States."[23] To this invitation the government of New Brunswick could only reply that it could not agree as long as the correspondence with Canada concerning the Intercolonial Railway had not yet terminated.

Nevertheless the plan was not discarded as a result of this rebuff. Overtures were continued. Although the Tilley government was officially committed to the Intercolonial project, the scheme which had been kept intermittently in the public mind ever since the Portland convention of 1850, must have attracted a considerable following, both in New Brunswick and Nova Scotia. On January 27, 1864, the *Fredericton Headquarters* sounded the note that was to be prominent in the Confederation issue for several years. Although, declared the editor, the present did not seem to be the best time to enter into closer commercial relations with the United States, it was most desirable that friendly relations between the provinces and the states should be preserved, and that everything be done to allay bad feelings. "A closer commercial connection by means of railroads might be the best means to excite friendly relations. In

[22]*Ibid.*, 1864, Report on trade and navigation for 1863, p. 17.

[23]*Ibid.*, 1864, Correspondence on western extension laid before the House of Assembly: Poor to Tilley, Nov. 16, 1863; Tilley to Poor, Jan. 13, 1864; Poor to Tilley, Jan. 26, 1864.

these uncertain times, the duty of New Brunswick is to draw, if possible, into closer relations with the loyal Provinces of Canada, though it may be for her interest to connect herself commercially with the United States. Duty and interest lead two different ways. . . ." The call of duty notwithstanding, the question of *western extension* was one that, in the opinion of the editor, closely affected interests of Fredericton and York County, and deserved the serious consideration of all their merchants, business-men, and politicians.

Although closer commercial relations with the United States was a motive of the supporters of *western extension,* they had another which was ancillary to their main objective. They had no intention of allowing American interests to draw the region watered by the upper Saint John within the ambit of their railway economy thus detaching it from the rest of New Brunswick to the detriment of the provincial metropolis at the mouth of the river. Intimations that this objective was contemplated by the Maine interests were not lacking.[24] To keep the Americans from carrying off the trade of the upper Saint John by extending the Saint John-Shediac line west to connect with the American lines, so that the metropolis would remain the entrepôt of trade, was one of the avowed objects of *western extension.* Burpee's report on New Brunswick railways, published on January 27, 1864, stated succinctly that "the people of Maine . . . are determined to extend their roads. If we meet them and give them a connection with the trade of the Lower Provinces and European travel, they will naturally take the proposed route; if not, they will take their only course on reaching the Mattawamkeag, to follow the course of that stream, and up the Saint Andrews road a few miles below Woodstock station, thus appropriating to themselves the whole trade of the Upper Saint John."

As the weeks advanced there were signs that the whole province was becoming exercised about the railway question. Meetings to discuss it were held in Saint John, Carleton, Woodstock, and Fredericton. In Carleton it was resolved that the terminus should be there. Fredericton favoured it, provided the road passed through or near Fredericton. The *Colonial Presbyterian* was for immediate action and the nullification of the I.C.R. legislation. The *Church Witness,* on the other hand, maintained that the province was bound for two years by the I.C.R. bill within which time Canada might take action in the

[24]*The Headquarters,* Jan. 27, 1864.

matter.[25] None the less the movement gathered head. The Saint John Chamber of Commerce prepared to memorialize the government and Legislature with a view to promoting it. Leading men of Bangor and Augusta had indicated their readiness to meet New Brunswick on the boundary. There would no doubt, commented the *Fredericton Headquarters,* be some pressure put on the government to move in the matter. "The most enthusiastic and impetuous advocates of the scheme . . . would tear up the Inter-Colonial Railway Bill at once – turn their backs on Canada, and rush at once into a connection with Maine and the Northern States. . . ." Although no one would doubt the commercial advantage of the line, there were other considerations that, in the opinion of the editor, demanded attention. Duty and interest, he reiterated, drew two different ways. Would anyone doubt which New Brunswick would choose? "New Brunswickers will prefer in this case their duty to their interest."[26] The province's "remarkable position – in a kind of middle ground between her sister Provinces and the Northern States" was noted. Two choices lay before her, and she found Canada "taking a position . . . that renders all her effort of a connection with it ineffectual. She is tempted to act hastily, and rush into commercial connection with the Northern States – out of a feeling against Canada, in great part. . . ." The *western extension* movement was viewed with alarm by the *Halifax Citizen.* It was feared that New Brunswick would become a mere appendage of the United States. "The New Brunswickers in laying down the rails to the boundaries would be forging link after link of a chain which would bind them inevitably to the chariot wheels of the North, commercially and socially at first, and probably politically afterwards." Already there existed a tinge of American democratic sentiment. With the new railway this "would sweep in and overflow the ancient British land-marks." New Brunswick might expand its trade and commerce, but it would sacrifice its British character. The danger to Confederation was manifest. New Brunswick lay "in the middle of our great British brotherhood so that Canada and Nova Scotia depend constantly and entirely on co-operation from New Brunswick when undertaking to draw the bond of union closer. But to introduce a foreign element would be to erect an obstacle on the common pathway" which would directly forestall the i.c.r., preventing the latter from ever being really effected.

[25]*Ibid.,* Feb. 3, 1864.
[26]*Ibid.,* Feb. 10, 1864.

In spite of these admonitions from certain sections of the press, a resolution was moved in the Legislative Assembly on March 8, 1864, to the effect that, as the Canadian government had "unequivocally and absolutely abandoned" the agreement made at Quebec in 1862, the government of New Brunswick was no longer bound by it. As the people of Maine were "providing for an extension of their railways eastwards towards the boundary line" of New Brunswick, it was held to be desirable to act in concert with them to connect Halifax with the United States and to link the interior of New Brunswick with the main line by branches from St. Stephen and Woodstock. Charles Fisher, the veteran reformer, countered with a resolution in which he sketched the broad destiny of British North America of which the Intercolonial Railway would be the instrument. There was no clear indication, he held, that Canada was not anxious to carry the project through.[27] At the same time, as many of his constituents favoured *western extension,* he would regard it with favour if the province were not already committeed to the i.c.r. Some members maintained a favourable attitude towards both projects. But John W. Cudlip, the mover of the original resolution had, in January, 1864, stated that the merchants of Saint John would tax themselves to the amount of a balance of $6,500 necessary to complete the amount required to put through the *western extension* project. Now, on March 30, he moved for leave to bring in a bill to incorporate the European and North American Railway Company for extension from Saint John westward to the American border.[28] On April 9, the bill passed the Assembly without division.[29]

IV

With the passing of spring into summer and summer into autumn, the conflict between *western extension* and the Intercolonial merged more and more clearly with the Confederation issue. What had appeared originally to be a matter of commercial rivalry became increasingly a political issue as the conference at Charlottetown on Maritime union was succeeded

[27]*Ibid.,* March 9, 1864.
[28]*Ibid.,* Jan. 27, 1864; *Journal of the House of Assembly of New Brunswick, 1864,* p. 30.
[29]*Journal of the House of Assembly of New Brunswick, 1864,* p. 224.

by the conference at Quebec on British North American federation. In the campaign for power that followed, the railway
issue became clouded but never obscured. It continued, beneath
the surface, to dominate opinion in the Province of New
Brunswick. When the electorate, on March 6, 1865, gave its
decision against the Quebec Resolutions, it was undoubtedly
guided in some part by the immediate commercial interest
which it hoped would be promoted by *western extension*. Indeed, in his analysis of the defeat of the Tilley government,
expounded to the Canadian Legislature following the election
in New Brunswick, Macdonald stated that "there was the
influence to be contended against of those who were in favour
of the railways to the American frontier – the Coast Line or
Western Extension Railway – as opposed to the Intercolonial
Railway interest."[30] When a Canadian member attempted to
discount the American influence, McGee replied that "one of
the successful candidates is the agent of the American line of
steamers – the International line – which does all the carrying
trade to New Brunswick; . . ." He understood that there was
not a pound of that stock held in New Brunswick. Did anyone
suppose that the influence of that company was not used for
his election? Steamboat, railway, mining, and fishing interests
were brought to bear. "It was," McGee asserted, "a fair standup
fight of Yankee interests on the one side and British interests
on the other; and those who are here ungenerously and unwisely
rejoicing over the defeat of the Hon. Mr. Tilley, are in reality
rejoicing in the triumph of Yankee interests."[31]

The *western extension* interest was one that the government
of New Brunswick could not overcome. The assertions of the
Canadian Confederation leaders were confirmed by no less an
authority than Tilley himself in his post-mortem to Galt following the election of March 6:

At the last session we met the demand of the people for Western
Extension by providing a bonus of $10,000 per mile to any Com-
pany or Companies that would complete the connection with
Maine or build certain specified branch railways. Up to the present time no Railways have been undertaken under the provisions
of this Act.–
And the friends of Western Extension, who are mostly the enemies
of Confederation, asserted that with the facilities then provided, no

[30]*Parliamentary Debates on the Subject of Confederation of the
British North American Provinces,* 3rd session, 8th Parliament of
Canada (Quebec, 1865), p. 658.
[31]*Ibid.,* p. 669.

roads would be built, and were demanding that they should be undertaken as government works.—seeing that this could not be done under Federation they would not only oppose that measure, but would have embarrassed the Government by submitting a proposition, calling upon them to assume these Railways as government works, knowing that the members of the govt must oppose it, and in doing so, Watters and myself would lose the confidence of our Constituencies. You see therefore had we met the House we would have been compelled to have taken a course that at the Elections in June would have defeated the Government members and their supporters, 5 in all for the city and county of Saint John. The people of St. John have been so wild about this Western Extension question, that any member showing indifference upon it, was almost certain of defeat—The opposition took advantage of this state of things, made many of the people believe that in Confederation there would be no Railway Westward. . . .[32]

V

Of the many factors that combined to defeat Confederation in New Brunswick in 1865, there can be little doubt that the most potent was *western extension*. Around it gathered the forces which ran strongly against union with Canada. The facts of local geography, and of the material interests deriving from them, might in time give way to the larger and contrary forces, represented by Confederation, but this could not be accomplished without doing some violence to a disposition of nature herself. It was inevitable that the process of adjustment which accompanied and resulted from Confederation would be a long and hard one for the Maritime Provinces, especially as other momentous changes which had a profound effect on their economy were taking place at the same time. A discussion of these considerations lies, however, beyond the scope and purpose of this paper.[33] Nor is it possible here to follow the story of the *western extension* project through the tortuous course of events during the two years that followed the victory of the anti-Confederation faction. With the fortunes of that faction the fate of the *western extension* project was closely identified.

[32]Public Archives of Canada, Macdonald papers, Confederation correspondence, vol. 6, Tilley to Galt, March 6, 1865.

[33]For an account of the changes in the economic life of the Maritime Provinces in the era of Confederation, see S. A. Saunders, *The Economic History of the Maritime Provinces: A Study Prepared for the Royal Commission on Dominion-Provincial Relations* (Ottawa, 1939).

The decline of that faction is material for a separate and important chapter in the history of the Confederation issue in New Brunswick. A variety of influences combined to weaken it. The appeal for the support of imperial interests urgently pressed forward, the strength of the Loyalist tradition and of the sense of "duty," the use of Canadian campaign funds and the promise of future compensations, the abrogation of reciprocity with the United States, the raising of the Fenian bogey – these and other considerations, economic, political, and religious, contributed to the complexities of the situation. It is often supposed that "high-pressure" methods combined with certain changes in circumstance led to an almost complete reversal of opinion in New Brunswick within little more than a year after the defeat of the Tilley government on March 6, 1865. All that can be said here on this point is that the reversal may not have been nearly as extensive as has sometimes been assumed. Many leading organs of opinion in the province continued to the last to express apprehension as to the sequel which they expected would follow union with Canada. If "duty" to the Empire drew New Brunswick one way, "interest" in commercial relations with the other communities of the Atlantic seaboard seemed to many observers to draw her another. And if the province in true Loyalist fashion did its duty, it was also inevitable that locally a legacy of resentment should survive the accomplished fact of continental union. A fuller examination of the nature of this legacy is long overdue. There were those whose bosoms swelled at the thought of the great Dominion extending from sea to sea, from the river to the ends of the earth; but there were also others less resigned than the commentator who, with more wry humour than legal precision, perhaps with some prognostication of hard years to come, certainly with a belated eye to party interest, penned the following obituary notice shortly before Dominion Day, 1867: "Died, – at her late residence in the City of Fredericton, on the 20th day of May last, from the effects of an accident which she received in April, 1866, and which she bore with a patient resignation to the will of Providence, the Province of New Brunswick, in the 83rd year of her age."[34]

---

[34]Quoted from the *Saint John Freeman* by the *True Humorist*, Saint John, June 22, 1867.

6. The Basis and Persistence Of Opposition To Confederation In New Brunswick

Recent research has done much to clarify the circumstances surrounding New Brunswick's entrance into Confederation. The crucial impact of British official importunity upon the sentiments of the people of the province, and the influence of Canadian campaign funds in the critical election of 1866 have been assigned their due weight as factors in inducing New Brunswick to accept the proposed change in the constitution of British North America. The use of the Fenian scare to impress upon the people the inadequacy of existing means of defence has received the attention which the importance of the subject warrants, and something of the effect of the failure to renew the Reciprocity Treaty has been noted. Yet there still remain certain aspects of the story which deserve a fuller treatment than they have hitherto received. Adequate consideration, for instance, has not yet been given to the causes for the rejection of the Quebec Resolutions in the New Brunswick election of March, 1865, or to the ensuing circumstances in the face of which the anti-Confederation cause gradually deteriorated to a point at which opposition became politically ineffective. This article attempts, therefore, to examine the grounds upon which opposition to union was based, and to describe how certain of those grounds became increasingly untenable throughout the year that followed the defeat of the Tilley government.

I

It is evident that in the early stages of the union movement there was a misapprehension of its significance, together with some degree of apathy, rather than a reasoned opposition.

There was an inclination to regard Confederation "as intended to produce, by its agitation, some immediate effect on the condition of existing political parties rather than as designed to inaugurate a new constitutional system."[1] But apathy and a "willing ignorance" of the whole matter gave way to an increasing hostility throughout the autumn of 1864 on the part of influential sections of the press. Many, wrote one editor, as early as October 19, did not understand why the delegates who had gone to Charlottetown to consider Maritime Union, were now at Quebec, having given the lesser question the slip. It was insinuated that they were carried captive by the Canadians who "have a definite purpose to effect, a pressing internal difficulty to overcome . . . and it is not to be wondered at that they should strain their views to effect a union with the Lower Provinces, that will give them peace within themselves, besides some considerable material advantages."[2] But it would "not be very gratifying . . . to see . . . a portion of the revenue of this Province drawn off to widen and deepen and extend Canada's magnificent canals, as the Toronto *Globe,* with scarce concealed exultation, says will be done. It would be a source of regret to many to see their roads, byeroads, bridges, and schools going down, down, down, while they see Canada growing great partly by aid of their money."

Money was a prominent feature of a long article carried by the *Headquarters* of Fredericton, on October 19. The assimilation of tariffs, it predicted, would mean the adoption of those of Canada. "Unless Canada consents to economize and curtail its expenses to a very considerable degree, which is not likely to happen, the Lower Provinces will have to raise their tariffs to that standard, as they will require a greater revenue to meet the expenses of government under the new confederation. It appears that they will have to make sacrifices and pay something handsome for the privilege of entering it, and seeing their representatives starring it in the Magnificent Parliament House, with its quadrangle, towers, and turrets at Ottawa." More than half the yearly expenditure of Canada had already been incurred. It must be clearly understood that none of this must be charged upon the revenue of the provinces, under the

[1] *Correspondence Respecting the Proposed Union of the British North American Provinces, etc. Presented to both Houses of Parliament by Command of Her Majesty, 8th Feb. 1867* (London, 1867), p. 85.

[2] Fredericton *Headquarters,* Oct. 19, 1864.

general government, but that it must be made a matter in which Canada alone would be liable.

Canada, however, was not the only villain in the piece. With some prescience the editor wrote, "The idea can hardly be ignored that this confederation business is more than a political move on the part of Canada – that the British government are at the bottom of it, and that the reversal of their colonial policy is not far distant."[3] British sentiments regarding defence were becoming known in the provinces, since the views of Englishmen were quoted at some length in the local papers.[4] It could not, however, yet be said positively that Britain would support Confederation on this ground. "In the uncertainty it would be a great relief to know positively what the British government expect the colonies to do." It would make "all the difference in the world" if it were known that the British government had expressed not merely approval, but desire.[5] The editor's remark requires qualification. A large body of opinion continued hostile, even after a year of constant appeal to "loyal" sentiments. In the meantime it was necessary to use other means to mitigate the hostility.[6]

It is safe to say that the larger part of the New Brunswick press looked unfavourably upon Confederation throughout the autumn of 1864 and the winter of 1865. The reception accorded to Tilley and Gray while campaigning in Saint John was reported as cold and critical. However, this attitude was attributed by one editor, who had not yet become irrevocably committed to the support of either faction, to the fact that Confederation was a new subject concerning which the audience had only half-formed opinions. Although Tilley "delivered himself with his usual facility and energy," the speeches were not calculated "to convince their judgement and arouse enthusiasm" for Confederation. The sceptical editor was puzzled by the peculiar state of opinion early in the campaign. Everyone, he reported, admitted that the union must take place sooner or later; nevertheless there was a disposition evident on the part of some persons "to put the matter off," and of others, "to

[3]Compare Chester Martin, "British Policy in Canadian Confederation," *Canadian Historical Review,* Vol. xiii (March, 1932), pp. 3-19.

[4]See for example the article by A. A. Bridgmen in the *Headquarters,* October 12, 1864.

[5]Fredericton *Headquarters,* Oct. 19, 1864.

[6]Public Archives of Canada, Macdonald Papers, Confederation Correspondence, vi, 43, Tilley to Macdonald, Nov. 23, 1864.

make the road rough." Tilley had shown "what he thought the people would get by the scheme, but he did not clearly make out what they would have to pay for it." He had scouted the idea that higher taxes would be imposed, or that the Canadian tariff would be the standard of assimilation. But he failed to convince his opponents, and the lukewarm among his constituents, that the general government, with its railway obligations and its provincial subsidies, could be carried on without raising the imposts on dutiable articles coming into the provinces. "He said the Canadian tariff was not to be the standard, at one time, because the forty-seven Lower Province members . . . would resist its imposition; at another he maintained that it was not in reality higher."[7] It was asserted that Tilley pitched his hopes too high and his figures too low. In truth, none knew what the project would cost. "For all the outcry against Mr. A. J. Smith's figures, he is as likely to be correct as any of them."[8]

Soon after the adjournment of the Quebec Conference it had become known that Albert J. Smith would lead the opposition. He and his associates, drawn largely from among the opponents of the Tilley government, soon had a numerous following with the aid of which they hoped "to alarm the people and carry the elections."[9] As public opinion warmed, the fight began to take on the aspect of a personal tilt between the two champions. The province became alive with public meetings as the leaders stumped the country proclaiming their respective faiths. Early in January, 1865, Tilley invaded Smith's home county of Westmorland.

Then welcome be Samuel L's tongue to the shock,
Though his figures be strong as the Westmorland rock,
For woe to his figures and woe to his cause,
When Alfred [*Sic*] the dauntless exposes his flaws

sang one anti-Confederationist. Borrowing epithets from the prize ring, Smith, with grandstand bravado, was hailed as "the Lion of Westmorland" and the "Douglas of Dorchester."[10]

Although the provincial intellect was no doubt titillated by such superficial chaff, it never lost sight of the real issues that

---

[7]Fredericton *Headquarters*, Nov. 23, 1864.

[8]*Ibid.*, Dec. 7, and Dec. 21, 1864.

[9]Macdonald Papers, Confederation Correspondence, VI, 49, Fisher to Macdonald, Dec. 6, 1864.

[10]Fredericton *Headquarters*, Dec. 28, 1864.

beat with an ever insistent and fateful rhythm upon the public consciousness. Politicians, editors, farmers, manufacturers, and financiers, wrestled with the crucial problem of hard cash. What was Confederation to cost? Would it increase taxes? Would it stimulate business? Would it facilitate trade, ensure the safety of New Brunswick and the Empire generally? How were the signs of the times to be read and interpreted?

Early in the campaign the Smith faction gained a powerful supporter in the person of William Needham of Fredericton, who, throughout the ensuing months, raked the Quebec scheme with his broadsides. Referring to the resolution concerning the development of the West, he asked what New Brunswick could do, with only fifteen members in a House of one hundred and ninety-four, to prevent the expenditure of any amount in such undertakings.[11] And in addition to Canada's canals, the people of New Brunswick would "have to pay also for making a high-way – a railroad – between Canada and the Pacific, a project on which old George Brown has breakfasted, dined, and supped for the last twenty years."[12] In the railways to the North-West the Maritime Provinces could have no present or future interest, but they would bring upon present or future generations large burdens of taxation.[13] It seemed clear to him that New Brunswick, with its small representation in the proposed federal Assembly, could not hope to block a large expenditure on public works from which the anti-unionists conceived she would derive no benefit.

If the development of the West were the price the Maritime Provinces would have to pay for securing the Intercolonial Railway, provided this railway were held out as a bait on the hook of Confederation, what constitutional guarantee was there that the railway would be built forthwith? This was, perhaps, a difficult question for Tilley to answer, even to his own satisfaction. On February 13, he placed the issue squarely before Macdonald:

We have always regarded it as the policy of the conference that the subsidy to the Local Governments and the building of the Inter-colonial Railway would be secured to us by Imperial Act. The delegates from the Lower Provinces could never have consented to the union on any other terms, and so understanding it have repre-sented it to our people. . . . It is said that you stated that there would

[11]*Ibid.*, Dec. 14, 1864.
[12]*Ibid.*
[13]*Ibid.*, Feb. 22, 1865.

be no Imperial Legislation on the subject of the Intercolonial. Now I can assure you that no delegate from this Province will consent to union unless we have this granted. And we will certainly fail in all our elections unless I have word . . . saying that this security will be given us. All will be lost without this; as it is, great alarm and anxiety has been created.[14]

Macdonald had stated publicly that an agreement to build a railway could not be a portion of a constitution. But a week later he telegraphed his assurance to Tilley that, as the railway was one of the conditions on which the constitution was adopted at Quebec, it would be inserted in the imperial Act giving legal effect to the union.[15] But in spite of Macdonald's assurance to Tilley, and Tilley's assurance to the electorate, that the railway would be provided for in the imperial statute, it was as yet by no means certain that the provision would be agreed to by the British government. It was at least felt by Governor Gordon that the imperial government would incorporate in the Act only those provisions of a general constitutional nature, and that the details would be left to the good faith of the provinces themselves.[16] There is no doubt that the measure of uncertainty with regard to the railway contributed to the defeat of the unionists in March, 1865.

Even if the securing of the Intercolonial Railway appeared certain to some observers, the vaguest notions were entertained as to which sections of the province would benefit by the railway, since the route would be decided by the general legislature of the union. That the northern route would be chosen seemed probable, as it was favoured by half the members of the New Brunswick government, and by the whole of Nova Scotia. Moreover, it was in the interest of Canada East to have as much of the road as possible within its own territory, namely, by building it across the Gaspé highland from Rivière du Loup to the Baie des Chaleurs. It would serve the steam-mills of Buctouche, Richibucto, Miramichi, Bathurst, and Dalhousie, all of which shipped large quantities of deals and lumber to Canada, which would thus support them in pressing for the northern route.[17] No consistent statement could be secured

[14]Macdonald Papers, Confederation Correspondence, VI, 61, Tilley to Macdonald, Feb. 13, 1865.

[15]Ibid., Macdonald to Tilley, Feb. 20, 1865.

[16]Correspondence Respecting the Proposed Union of the British North American Provinces, Gordon to Cardwell, Feb. 27, 1865.

[17]Fredericton Headquarters, Feb. 1, 1865.

from the government. Charles Fisher of Fredericton asserted that the road would pass north through the Saint John and Keswick valleys. Mitchell and Johnson, both of the North Shore, stated quite as definitely that their section would have it.

> Mr. Tilley, will you stop your puffing and blowing
> And tell us which way the railway is going?[18]

wailed an exasperated rhymster. How would Saint John benefit from a railway along the North Shore? asked Smith. Even if it were run up the Saint John River valley, the effect, he asserted, would be to cause a flow of the products of the up-river counties into Canada, instead of bringing them down to the provincial metropolis at the mouth.[19]

While the different sections fought over the railway route, speculation ran rife concerning the possible effects of Confederation upon the industrial structure of the province. The cleavage of opinion seems not to have followed either occupational or class lines. The manufacturing interests were divided, some strongly favouring union. Having viewed it "in all its bearings" they felt satisfied that it would prove beneficial not only to domestic manufacturers, but to every other interest throughout the province. But dissenting voices were loud and long. In a measured oration delivered early in December, 1864, Needham asked how union would open up to the manufacturers of the province an immense market in Canada.

> I ask you tanners, I ask you foundrymen, is it possible, is it likely that you will flood that country with your wares. If so, why is our Province flooded, our shops crammed with American goods! Look at it—where we have one foundry, one tannery, one distillery, they have thousands. After the Union you will be in a worse position than you are now; for you will . . . have the Canadians flooding you with goods also.[20]

According to this school of thought Canada would have no need for the manufactures of the Maritime Provinces, but would have no objection to flooding them with her goods. With arguments such as this one anti-Confederation editor wrote that Needham had "Knocked Fisher higher than a kite."

While the fight waxed hot over local issues a measure of attention was given to the imperial implications of the proposed

[18]*Ibid.*
[19]*Ibid.*, Feb. 8, 1865.
[20]*Ibid.*, Dec. 14, 1864.

change. The argument for Confederation as a means toward improved defence did not go unchallenged. It was publicly alleged that Canada was trying to get the Maritime Provinces into Confederation, to share the burden of her defence as agreed with the British government.[21] It was easy to prove, maintained one orator, that the mother country was determined to drive these colonies into some kind of union, and the ravings of those who were determined to resist it "might as well be addressed to the planet Saturn." The *Headquarters* expressed a forthright disbelief that the British government were determined to force the colonies into union.[22] Moreover, it was ridiculous to suppose that Confederation would put British North America into a better state of defence. With or without it, if there were an invasion, it would be as impossible for New Brunswick to resist as for a shad to walk up a bean-pole.[23]

When other arguments were deemed insufficient, high constitutional principle was invoked against the delegates who had abandoned the legislative union of the Lower Provinces for the Quebec scheme without the consent of the legislature to which they owed their appointments. It was denied that the Governor-General had called the Quebec Conference with the assent and approbation of the Queen. More probably, no one on the other side of the Atlantic had heard anything about it.[24] It was on the ground of the well-understood principle of responsible government, that Needham declared that the wish of the people should first have been heard through their representatives; that the Governor-General had had no right to call the Quebec Conference "there to sign and seal and deliver over to himself a protocol making a radical change in the constitution of the country, without going to the people and asking them whether they would have it or not."[25]

As early as the first week in December, 1864, A. J. Smith announced his objections to the Quebec scheme and foreshadowed the platform upon which his party would appeal to the electorate. The adoption of the Quebec plan could mean increased taxation; the loss to the province of political influence and status; the expenditure of vast sums on Canadian canals;

[21]*Ibid*. Disapproval of Confederation as a defence measure was by no means unanimous. See *The Borderer and Westmorland and Cumberland Advertiser,* Sackville, N.B., Feb. 24, 1865.

[22]Fredericton *Headquarters,* Dec. 21, 1864.

[23]*Ibid.,* Jan. 18, 1865.

[24]*Ibid.,* Dec. 14, 1864.

[25]*Ibid.*

the unfairness of eighty cents a head as a basis for taxation, since it would not be increased, whereas the revenue of the general government would be increased; and the unconstitutional behaviour of the delegates at Charlottetown and Quebec. Moreover, he asserted, the Inter-colonial Railway would be "no great boon."[26]

In the light of the ubiquitous blasts of the anti-Confederation press, it is difficult to discover the basis for the Lieutenant-Governor's optimistic belief in the victory of the union party. According to his diagnosis, local interests and local partialities would decide the issue. Only in three constituencies, Saint John, York, and Westmorland, would Confederation affect the result. Fisher was less sanguine of immediate success. He recognized that a hard fight lay ahead. "Some of us may go down for a while in the operation but we will carry it finally," wrote Fisher to Macdonald early in the campaign.[27] If Governor Gordon remained unimpressed by the gathering clouds of opposition he might at least have received some intimation of the approaching *débâcle* from the defection of G. L. Hatheway, an influential member of the government, who became no ineffectual agent in securing the defeat of his former colleagues.[28]

The desertion of Hatheway only served to increase the popular suspicion of the government that stemmed in part from the diatribes of the opposition leaders against the Quebec Resolutions; and these leaders themselves pursued a policy of opposition because they were identified or involved with certain interested groups who believed that the realization of cherished objectives would be baulked if the proposed union were accomplished. Prominent among these groups were the banking community of Saint John, the Roman Catholic church, and the mercantile element who were eager for more effective communication with the United States. The testimony of John Hamilton Gray, a defeated candidate, justifies the emphasis placed upon the crucial role of the bankers in the overthrow of the government. A week after the election Gray informed

[26]*Ibid.*, Dec. 7, 1864.
[27]Macdonald Papers, Confederation Correspondence, VI, p. 49.
[28]*Correspondence Respecting the Proposed Union of the British North American Provinces,* Hatheway to the Lieutenant-Governor, enclosed with Gordon to Cardwell, Jan. 30, 1865. See also the *Headquarters,* March 8, 1865: "Mr. Hatheway has been mainly influential in bringing about the signal defeat that Mr. Tilley and his government have sustained on the question that they were forced to submit to the people." It was, however, an over-statement.

Macdonald that ". . . the banking interests united against us. They at present have a monopoly and their directors used their influence unsparingly. They dreaded the competition of Canadian banks coming here and the consequent destruction of that monopoly[29] – and many a businessman now in their power felt it not sage to hazard an active opposition to their influences."[30]

Equally decisive was the action of the Catholic section of the population. Fear of the Protestant influence of Canada West and especially of Grand Trunk control of the Intercolonial Railway were salient motives. Control of the projected railway, if it were secured by the Grand Trunk, would give that company a guiding hand in land settlement adjacent to the railway line. The Bishop of Saint John had for years taken a great interest in the settlement of his co-religionists on the wilderness land of New Brunswick.[31] But by far the strongest single element opposed to union with Canada was the business fraternity who had been endeavouring for a decade to integrate the commerce of the province more closely with that of the United States, and thus to make the most of New Brunswick's historic position as the north-eastern extension of the Atlantic geographic province.[32] Separated as New Brunswick was from Canada by the Appalachian barrier, trade with that province was negligible in comparison with her expanding commercial relations with the United States. It is, therefore, not to be wondered at, that the rival Intercolonial Railway, which was so closely associated with the Confederation movement, did not appeal to practical business leaders who were intent upon promoting the extension of New Brunswick's European and North American Railroad westward to the Maine border where it was to connect with the railway systems of New England. Such an alignment of forces proved too strong for the government to withstand, and it is by no

[29]Their fears were apparently justified. In the first Dominion Parliament it was necessary for Galt to explain: "The Bank of Montreal did the government business in the greater part of the Dominion, and it was natural that they should extend an agency of that institution to do the public business in the Maritime Provinces" (quoted in the Ottawa *Times,* Nov. 12, 1867).

[30]Macdonald Papers, Confederation Correspondence, VI, p. 68, J. H. Gray (N.B.) to Macdonald, March 13, 1865.

[31]*Ibid.,* VI, p. 95ff., Tilley to Galt, March, 1865.

[32]A. G. Bailey, "Railways and the Confederation Issue in New Brunswick, 1863-5," *Canadian Historical Review,* Vol. XXI, (Dec., 1940), pp. 367-83. See also E. E. Chase, *Maine Railroads* (Portland, 1926).

means surprising that it suffered defeat at the polls on March 6, 1865.

II

On March 27, 1865, the Tilley government resigned from office and an anti-Confederation government was formed by Albert J. Smith and R. D. Wilmot. Prominent among its members were Timothy Warren Anglin, Irish editor of the Saint John *Freeman,* and G. L. Hatheway who had resigned from the Tilley government before the election as a protest against the Quebec Resolutions. The new government, with a large majority in the legislature, seemed in a strong position. None of the important men of the union party possessed seats in the new Assembly, although in the Legislative Council, Mitchell and Chandler were to continue ably to uphold the unionist point of view.

In the session which opened in March, 1865, no new position was taken up by either party, and the old arguments, already familiar on the hustings and in the press, were repeated on the floor of the House. Owing to the absence of Tilley, Fisher, and Gray, and because of the small number of unionist representatives, the new government and its supporters were able to present their case more forcefully than were their opponents. It was doubtless for this reason that the broad vision of a new British-American nation, which had found such conspicuous expression in the public addresses following the Charlottetown Conference, was now totally absent. In its place was to be found, notably from the tongue of Smith himself, the expression of a fairly definite, if not intense, local feeling and of pride in the achievement of a self-government which he claimed had been violated by the delegates who had proceeded to Quebec to alter the constitution of the province and had exceeded their powers, in a way for which history provided no precedent.

These delegates who assembled on Prince Edward Island for a particular purpose, abandoned their business and arrogated to themselves powers that did not legitimately belong to them, and undertook to alter the institutions of the country and surrender the independence we have so long enjoyed. Is it not the duty of the Government to exercise their functions within the four corners of the Constitution? Is it not their duty to preserve inviolate the independence of the People?

It would, however, doubtless be an error to stress this element in the anti-Confederation point of view. More practical considerations continued to weigh heavily. Although one member waxed sentimental over the destruction of the link with England, which he envisaged if the Quebec Resolutions were adopted,[33] dollar-and-cent considerations received the greatest attention. There was no guarantee that Canada would keep faith in the matter of the Intercolonial Railway.[34] The Lower Provinces would be dragged in to bear their proportion of the expense of the great canal project of Canada West. "Canada has to borrow money to pay the interest on her own debts, and then wants to assume ours. It is like a bankrupt wanting to assume the debts of a rich man." So ran the argument, which Needham took up on the question of status. Powers of local government "would be confined to making laws to prevent cows from running on the commons, providing that sheep shall wear bells, and to issue tavern licenses."[35] "Forty-eight thousand men in this province have said we don't want Confederation, and that should be the end of it."

MacMillan, former member of the Tilley government, took up the cudgel for Confederation. "I do not believe," he said, "that to unite these British North American Colonies under one rule would be a political injury to them, neither do I believe the people of the country think so. I do not believe that the people are prepared to say that it will be commercially injurious to them to have a free intercourse in all articles and manufactures between the Provinces, setting aside the barriers of the Customs House." He asserted, moreover, that provincial opinion was veering, and that another election would show two-thirds of the people of the province in favour of Confederation. Indeed, Tilley thought he observed some indication of a change of heart on the railway question. The state of the public revenue, and the prospect of a decrease during the ensuing year, together with the discount at which provincial debentures were being sold in the English market, would prevent any government from undertaking Western Extension as a government work. This fact was becoming recognized in the financial circles of Saint John, which "began to fear that they have not acted wisely, hence the reaction in Saint John on the confedera-

[33]*New Brunswick, Debates of the Legislative Assembly*, May 31, 1865, p. 111.
[34]*Ibid.*, May 30, 1865, p. 110.
[35]*Ibid.*, p. 111.

tion question."[36] Nevertheless the reply to the Speech from the Throne expressed "regrets that existings laws preclude immediate action for the accomplishment of the extension of the European and North American Railroad westward from Saint John to the American border."[37] Realizing that to commit the province to carrying out Western Extension as a government work would prevent the raising of New Brunswick's share of the loan for the building of the Intercolonial Railway, Fisher declared his unequivocal opposition to the project, stating that it should be built by a private company.

An amendment was moved to the reply to the Speech from the Throne, embodying the view that the road should be built by private enterprise aided from public revenues, but it was defeated by a vote of twenty-nine to ten.[38] It was necessary "to act conjointly with the people of the United States, for they have to meet us at the boundary," declared Smith.[39] The road must be "a part of the great highway to the United States." J. W. Cudlip, diehard "Anti," voiced the view of the commercial interests of Saint John when he asserted that ". . . it was necessary to connect with the United States. It would then give the people who travelled and who had an eye to our resources, an inducement to come in and develop them, and would greatly further the trading influence and make American people come into the Province who never came before. The commerce between the Province and the United States had very greatly increased, and was increasing year by year." New Brunswick now received vast quantities of goods from the United States which formerly came from England. On June 6, Cudlip moved that the government should proceed with the construction of Western Extension as part of the European and North American Railroad, but that, as haste was essential, a private company should not be prevented from undertaking the work with the aid of the provincial subsidy of $10,000 a mile as provided by the Facility Bill of 1864.[40] The same provisions should apply to "Eastern Extension" from the Bend to

[36]Macdonald Papers, Confederation Correspondence, VI, p. 95, Tilley to Galt, March, 1865.

[37]*Ibid.*, p. 33.

[38]*New Brunswick, Journals of the Legislative Assembly,* 1865, pp. 26-8.

[39]*New Brunswick, Debates of the Legislative Assembly,* May 26, 1865, p. 96.

[40]*New Brunswick, Journals of the Legislative Assembly,* June 6, 1865, p. 223.

Truro so as to link Nova Scotia with the United States. The unionists endeavoured to block the move on the ground of inexpediency. The province should not commit itself to such an outlay at a time when there was such a heavy drain on public finances and a large debt due to creditors in Great Britain. Nevertheless, Cudlip's resolution was carried by a vote of twenty-five to thirteen.

In spite of the seeming assurance with which the government proceeded with the legislative programme, it was not as strong as it appeared. The completeness of the late victory at the polls could not disguise the divergent interests and views among members of the Cabinet. To some extent the attrition suffered by the government throughout the ensuing year, stemmed from Cudlip's resolution concerning Western Extension, which did not exclude the building of the road by private enterprise. Anglin, who had stated on nomination day that "it must be built as a government work," continued to sit in the government. The opportunity was not to be missed, and he did not go untaunted by the unionist press.[41] Although he had declared that he would use his efforts to turn out any government which would not build Western Extension as a government work, the administration endorsed a grant to assist a private company in its construction, "and still Mr. Anglin is its apologist and tame public servant."[42] Although he continued to support the anti-Confederation cause, Anglin had resigned from the Cabinet before the issue was again joined at the polls.

III

In the meantime, while "interest" became divided on the question of railway policy and on other matters, the people of New Brunswick were to suffer no misapprehension concerning the path of "duty" as decreed by the Colonial Office. That the Canadians contributed in no small way to the formulation of the view held at the Colonial Office is so well known as to need no stressing. On the other hand, the reaction of New Brunswick opinion and policy to the course set for it by the British government is important to delineate, because it was conceived to be the task of imperial policy to modify this opinion so that it should harmonize with imperial interest.

[41]*Morning News,* Saint John, May 8, 1865.
[42]*True Humorist,* Saint John, May 26, 1865.

The effect of the defeat on Canadian policy had been marked. In that province the Quebec Resolutions had carried in both Houses by majorities of three to one. Tilley's defeat had so frightened the legislature of Nova Scotia that Tupper forestalled a hostile vote only by side-tracking the discussion in favour of the question of Maritime Union. Drastic action to reverse the verdict in New Brunswick was the immediate concern of Macdonald and his associates. Three weeks after the defeat he wrote:

We now send four of our ministers to England to take stock . . . with the British government to see what can be done. . . . We intend also to arrange, if possible, the subject of defence. I do not despair of carrying out our great project sooner or later. I quite agree . . . that the British Government will carry their point if they only adopt measures to that end, and we shall spare no pains to impress the necessity of such a course upon them with what success remains to be seen.[43]

In 1865 A. T. Galt stressed Confederation as a means to the continuance of the British connection when he declared that a decided expression of policy on the part of the British government would have "a most marked effect on the loyal and high-spirited people of the Maritime Provinces."[44] Accordingly "the strongest delegation which had ever left Canada," Galt, Macdonald, Brown, and Cartier, set out for England within a few weeks of Tilley's defeat to impress the Colonial Office with the dire necessity of reversing the verdict in New Brunswick.[45] Fisher, Tilley, and Tupper were parties to the plan, bluntly declaring that the actions of the Governors of New Brunswick and Nova Scotia had ensured the defeat of the measure.[46] On April 5, Fisher wrote to Macdonald that he was "satisfied if the press here learn that the British government are anxious for the union it will influence their mood." It would be well "if the dispatch indicating that opinion could be got out before the middle or latter end of May. . . . It is said our governor has resigned or intends to. I hope it is true. . . . I know everyone that he might be supposed to have the least influence with, or associates with in any way, violently opposed Confederation, a state of things I cannot think could exist without his procure-

[43]Macdonald Papers, Confederation Correspondence, VI, p. 66, Macdonald to Gray (P.E.I.), March 24, 1865.

[44]Martin, "British Policy in Canadian Confederation," p. 18.

[45]Ibid., p. 11.

[46]Ibid., p. 17.

ment in some way." Macdonald was admonished to be sure, if a new incumbent were appointed, "that he is honestly and faithfully at heart in earnest to carry confederation." With such a man acting "friendly and in earnest," Fisher believed it could be carried in three months after his arrival. "That is the tendency of the public mind."[47]

The New Brunswick press was not slow to grasp the implication of the Canadian plan. The public must "keep watch on this Canadian Mission."[48] Nevertheless the anti-Confederation press affirmed their belief that the British government had their interests at heart, and might at most persuade, but would not attempt to coerce the province. "We do not think that there will be any attempt made to force any unpalatable measure upon this province, but there will be some pressure brought to bear. . . ." Doubtless, surmised the *Headquarters*, the thought was running in Macdonald's head that "it is intolerable that New Brunswick with its paltry 250,000 of a population should stand in the way of a great scheme that Canada with 2,500,000 is desirous of adopting, and no doubt if it is properly represented the Imperial government would see it in the same light, and 'reason with' this stubborn province." "It is evident," was the conclusion "that these Canadian politicians will have to be narrowly watched." In June the Montreal *Gazette* took it upon itself to lecture to the Maritime Provinces concerning their duty to the mother country and the Empire, exploiting the sentiment of loyalty so constantly protested in those provinces:

The Imperial Government . . . will not dictate to the Maritime Provinces what they shall do in matters of local legislation or concernment; but it can and we believe it will, say upon what terms the Imperial navy will protect their coasts and . . . garrison their towns. It is idle for them to conceal the fact from themselves—confederation or union of some sort is a condition of the continuance of British connection. They have to decide now at how much they esteem that connection . . . or whether . . . it is mere lip loyalty.[49]

Since the British government had already expressed its approval of Confederation on the ground of imperial defence, the reception of the Canadian delegation at the Colonial Office was extremely cordial. Cartier pointed out that the British government could exercise a very great influence through the

[47]Macdonald Papers, Confederation Correspondence, vi, Fisher to Macdonald, April 5, 1865.
[48]Fredericton *Headquarters*, March 22, 1865.
[49]Quoted in *The Borderer*, Sackville, N.B., June 16, 1865.

decided expression of its views, in order to reverse the verdict. Cardwell replied that the government would "use every proper means of influence to carry into effect without delay the proposed confederation." The attention of the Smith government was to be drawn to the intimate connection between the small population and the measures that would be necessary for the defence of the province. New Brunswick was to bear in mind that as a separate province it could make no adequate provision for its own defence and that it would therefore "rest in a very great degree upon the defence which may be provided for it by Great Britain." "It will consequently be likely to appear to your advisors," wrote Cardwell to the Governor on April 12, 1865, "reasonable and wise that, in examining the question of the proposed union, they should attach great weight to the views and wishes of this country. . . ."[50] Gordon was to impress upon his legislature the concern felt in England for imperial defence. The publication in the *Royal Gazette* on July 15, of the Monck-Cardwell correspondence could have left no doubt in the minds of New Brunswickers concerning the wishes of the British government.

The fears expressed earlier in the year by the Fredericton *Headquarters* were now realized. Its readers had been warned that the Canadian mission to England would have to be watched narrowly, for they intended to steal a march on New Brunswick. "It is evident they have done so. . . . It is evident that the Home authorities have only looked at the grand outline . . . from an Imperial point of view; they have not curiously examined the details, and how they were likely to affect most injuriously the interests of this small province . . . the negotiations were conducted as between the British Government and Canada alone. The conduct of Canada throughout has been most arrogant, irritating and insulting to this Province."[51] The scheme originated in the political necessities of Canada and "the Imperial approval was only an after-clap." And the Saint John *Evening Globe* asked:

How many English publicists have examined the features of that obnoxious scheme of confederation agreed upon at Quebec? . . . How many of them know anything about the Northwest territory, about the enlargement of Canadian canals, or the building of Canadian fortifications, in so far as these matters affect us? How many of them know that our taxation will be double the moment we enter upon

[50]Macdonald Papers, Confederation Correspondence, VI, p. 117.
[51]Fredericton *Headquarters*, July 19, 1865; Sept. 6, 1865.

Confederation? How many of them know that the Canadians are a
people with whom we have little or no trade; that they are a people
for whom we have no more affection than we have for the people
of . . . any other British Colony.[52]

The *Freeman* could not contain its indignation, "expressed
with Fenian venom" at the British Colonial Secretary for acting
as though union were a *fait accompli*.[53]

There is little doubt that when Smith and Allen set out to
lay the "true" situation and feelings of New Brunswick before
the Colonial Office, they had the support of the majority in
their own province. The *Headquarters* expressed confidence
that the British government would give their views every consideration. But in view of the strong representations of the
Canadian delegation, with whom the British government was
now publicly in accord, the hopes of the editor were far too
sanguine. Nevertheless the mission bore strong views across
the Atlantic. Cudlip had stated in the House that false statements were being circulated in England by the Canadian delegation to induce the imperial Parliament to legislate for New
Brunswick in the matter of intercolonial union. "If there is
anything of that kind in contemplation, they had better pause
before they attempt it, for we would resist coercion whether
it was brought against us directly or indirectly." He had then
moved that the delegation be sent to England to make known
the view of New Brunswick, that "the consummation of the
said Scheme would prove politically, commercially, and financially disastrous to the best interests" of the province. The right
of the people to decide all questions affecting their own local
interests for the promotion of their prosperity and welfare
issued from their right of internal self-government. Moreover
the committee of the House had "reason to fear that Her
Majesty's Government are but imperfectly aware of the true
feelings of the people of this Province on the subject." The
resolution had passed by a vote of twenty-nine to ten. The
Governor had been asked to inform the Secretary of State
"how entirely this scheme has been rejected by the people of
this province." On July 15, Gordon had forwarded to Cardwell
an enclosure from the Executive Council, giving as the reason
for having repudiated Confederation that "they were unable
to discover anything in it that gave promise of either moral or
material advantage to the empire or themselves; or that it

[52]*Evening Globe,* Saint John, Sept. 8, 1865.
[53]*Morning News,* Saint John, Nov. 13, 1865.

afforded a prospect of improved administration or increased prosperity." To confer on this Province a right of self-government would have been a mockery" if the wishes of the mother country were in all cases to be followed when they did not coincide with the views of "those on whom alone the responsibility of action in the Province falls." In spite of these representations, Cardwell informed the delegates that he "could give no countenance to any proposals which would tend to delay the confederation of all the Provinces. . . ." The failure of the anti-Confederation mission was hailed as another milestone on the road to ultimate triumph by the unionist press.

IV

Long before Cardwell's rebuff, the Smith government showed a certain lack of strength. It had difficulty in filling vacancies in a number of public offices. By April 5, it had not appointed a postmaster, solicitor-general, or any legislative councillor,[54] through fear, an opponent stated, of suffering reverses at the polls. Uncertainty over railway policy was partly the cause, and British pronouncements may have had some effect, although the anti-Confederation faction continued to believe that the British government would not use coercion. "Rather poor comfort," commented Fisher privately.[55] The hope was expressed by the supporters of union that the Canadians would use means to influence the Orangemen of the province to vote for Confederation by playing up "loyalty" and the British connection through the lodges. Roman Catholics appeared to be as strongly opposed as ever. There were about six hundred Catholic voters in York County, and Fisher despaired of getting more than twenty of them in his forthcoming election campaign. "I find them," he wrote, "still in a solid phalanx united against confederation, and I know that no argument but one from the church will reach them."

In spite of this opposition, the unionists continued to plan how they could capitalize upon the weakened position of Smith's government, which had refused A. R. Wetmore the attorney-generalship because this would have necessitated his risking re-election in Saint John. Smith decided to take that

[54]Macdonald Papers, Confederation Correspondence, VI, Fisher to Macdonald, April 5, 1865.
[55]Ibid. Fisher to Macdonald (confidential), Aug. 13, 1865.

office himself, and the unionists believed that he would be returned without opposition as he had strong backing in his own county of Westmorland. Tilley was confident of victory in Saint John when that riding should be opened.[56]

It was in York County, however, that the most conspicuous battle was to be fought. Attorney-General Allen having been raised to the Bench, the constituency was opened. Both sides prepared to engage in a major offensive. Fisher, who was the most likely unionist candidate, feared that the government might bring forth a strong lumber merchant and spend an enormous amount of money. Fisher might raise the cry of Fenianism against his opponent and arouse the Orange lodges, with the connivance of the Canadians, but as to money, he stated bluntly to Macdonald, he did not have it to spend.[57] It was felt that Fisher could be returned with an expenditure of eight or ten thousand dollars, and the Canadian unionists were solicited to contribute to the common cause.

When Smith arrived in Fredericton after his unsuccessful mission to England, a party caucus was held to determine what should be done to fight the election in York County. Although it seemed evident that the Catholic bishop and his followers would continue to oppose Confederation, Anglin was distasteful to the majority of Protestants, particularly those of Loyalist descent and the immigrants from the north of Ireland. In order to meet this situation it was determined that John Pickard, a wealthy lumber merchant and an Orangeman, should run on the anti-Confederation ticket. A Catholic candidate was also presented on the same ticket with Pickard, but on nomination day he retired in favour of Pickard who thus perhaps secured the bulk of the Catholic vote although he himself was an Orangeman. Moreover, Pickard could afford to spend a considerable sum of money on the election, and was in a position to pay it if he were elected. Only an outlay on the part of the Canadians could meet competition of this kind, because although Fisher did not lack resources of his own, it was suspected that the Smith government would spend "any amount of money."[58]

Fisher did not present himself as a candidate until a short time before nomination day, and many in the county did not know that he had decided to run until after he was nominated

[56]*Ibid.*, Tilley to Macdonald, Sept. 13, 1865.

[57]*Ibid.*, p. 138 ff., Fisher to Macdonald (confidential), Aug. 13, 1865.

[58]*Ibid.*, p. 167 ff., Fisher to Macdonald, Nov. 11, 1865.

as Pickard's opponent. On nomination day Fisher branded the government with Fenianism "without much mercy," but was compelled to state that before Confederation was adopted it must again be submitted to the people at a general election. As the campaign proceeded the whole province became excited from one end to the other. Although Fisher never left his office until the polling day,[59] Pickard, Needham, and other anti-Confederation leaders scoured the country. A lot of young men, acting in Fisher's interest, followed them around to refute their statements. Orangemen and Loyalists were not unmoved by the intense British feeling created by Fisher, and, according to one account, "all sorts of intimidation forced many of the voters to change their tickets." It is uncertain as to what part Governor Gordon played in the election. Although officially committeed by his instructions from the British government to support Confederation, his personal views may have remained unchanged. His gardener, coachman, and grocer, it was stated, voted against Fisher.

Fisher wrote jubilantly to Macdonald about his victory in York County and of the moral effect on public opinion throughout the province. But he politely reminded Macdonald of the day of reckoning. His expenditure had been large: "We look to you," he wrote, "to help us out of the scrape, for if every dollar is not paid it will kill us at the general election. If it is met fairly, we have a plain course open for confederation. . . . Do not allow us to want now or we are all gone together."[60] He represented the victory as the turning point in the great Confederation struggle. It had inspired Confederationists everywhere with visions of ultimate success. The jubilation was general in official circles, although Cardwell was disheartened by the unopposed return of Smith from Westmorland. On November 22, Lord Monck wrote to congratulate Macdonald and his colleagues on the return of Fisher for York County. "I think," he declared, "that this is the most important thing that has happened since the Quebec conference, and if followed up judiciously affords a good omen of success in our spring campaign."

There are, however, reasons for believing that the official optimism was unwarranted and that Fisher's election did not in fact represent a marked swing of opinion toward Confederation. Fisher's friends did their best to keep the issue out of the campaign, and he himself only succeeded in checkmating the

[59]According to his own statement. See *ibid.*, p. 167 ff.
[60]*Ibid.*, p. 167 ff., Nov., 1865.

anti-unionists by pledging himself to oppose Confederation if it were presented to the then existing legislature. Moreover, his supporters diverted attention from the real issues involved by invoking the red herring of Fenianism. "The Fisher party have worked the Fenian cry well, and it has been successful . . . the absurd, and as it is now known, fearfully exaggerated telegrams about Fenian doings in Canada, were artfully taken advantage of to work upon the fears of the electors . . ." So ran the *Head-quarters'* post mortem. Furthermore, the belief was publicly stated that "the Canadian government have largely aided their party here by hard cash. . . ."

Similar means were employed by the "Antis," although the origin of the funds remains partly undisclosed. The Saint John *Telegraph* revealed one source of support when it denounced the Smith government "for giving a certain enterprising lumber operator [Alexander Gibson], who happens to be a very active Anti-confederate, . . . the privilege of purchasing certain tracts of land." The sale was denounced as a political act and awoke an outcry from the unionist opposition. "Antis" countered with the assertion that the land, comprising two tracts of 4,903 and 10,000 acres in York County, was, in any case, unfit for settlement. Nevertheless the opportunity for sniping was not to be lost. The *True Humorist*, tireless ridiculer of "Anti" politicians, concocted for the occasion an imaginary conversation between members of the Smith government, in the course of which they referred to themselves as having swapped away "15,000 acres of the Public Lands to one man for a few hours strutting around the polls," and as having paid out "the public money drawn from the emaciated vaults of the People's Bank!" The government of 1862 refused to go beyond a mere survey when it found Gibson wanted 15,000 acres of prime land on the central route of the Intercolonial Railway – "That's true, and Gibson turned against the Government from that hour, and got nothing until we came in; and then we rescinded the order. How he used to dog me around till we rescinded the order."

The resignation of R. D. Wilmot from the Cabinet proved to be a more serious problem for the Smith government than the jibes of the *True Humorist.* Wilmot afterwards declared that the abrogation of the Reciprocity Treaty had converted him, and denied that he had changed his opinion while on a visit to Canada in reply to the insinuation that he had been "bought." Whatever may have been the reasons for Wilmot's change of front, the Governor planned to capitalize upon it as a means of driving Smith from office, by retaining Wilmot whom Smith refused to meet at the council table. The Governor could not be blamed for the failure of the plan, although the unionists continued to suspect him for remaining "at heart opposed to union" when he appointed two inveterate "Antis" to the Bench to the neglect of Wilmot's claim. "Wilmot is a methodist," wrote Fisher on February 13, 1866, "and the methodists, baptists, and presbyterians feel especially insulted at this appointment. These denominations are four-fifths of the confederation party alone. . . . Anti newspapers publicly speak of the policy of delay as a means by which they intend to worry out Canada until the coalition fails."

There can be no doubt that the more earnestly the Governor promoted union, as the representative of the British government, the more the effort to exert influence became distasteful to numbers of persons in the province. The Canadians, it was averred, had "brought all the pressure they could to break down the opposition in New Brunswick. . . . They have induced Mr. Cardwell to write a series of irritating despatches by way of exercising upon New Brunswick what he calls the just authority of the Imperial Government, and they are now waiting anxiously to see if New Brunswick will break down under the pressure."

V

A review of evidence gleaned from the press and from the public and private pronouncements of political leaders reveals that the opposition to Confederation was based upon economic, political, and religious considerations. Moreover, certain elements of the population, such as the Roman Catholic, appear to have been opposed to union on any terms on the ground that it would be harmful to their interests. Into this category also a section of the manufacturing group would appear to fall. On the other hand, there were those who directed their attacks not against the principle of Confederation so much as against the specific terms of union which had been embodied in the Quebec Resolutions. These, they held, would mean increased taxes, higher tariffs, Canadian competition in the provincial market, and loss of local monopolies. Some did not stress the positive evils of Confederation so much as doubt the benefits that would accrue from it. The most influential representatives of the commercial interest, particularly in the southern part of the province, were intent upon pursuing a project of a different nature, that of fostering trade with the United States by linking New Brunswick's railway with the New England system, and this development they feared Confederation would impede.

It is clear, however, that throughout the year that followed the defeat of the Tilley government, new circumstances arose which rendered several of the grounds of opposition to union no longer tenable. The decline of provincial debentures in the English market and the probability of a decrease in the public revenue prevented the government from extending their railway westward from Saint John to the American border as a government work, and when the task of construction was offered to a private company, Anglin, who had been a tower of strength, resigned. When the government's inability to complete the railway was linked with the failure of the Reciprocity negotiations the prospect for increased trade with the United States dwindled, and Wilmot followed Anglin out of the councils of the government to become later a Father of Confederation.

By contrast with Wilmot, other leaders, like Cudlip, persisted in their opposition to Confederation either in the hope of a renewal of the Reciprocity negotiations and the successful completion of the railway, or in the belief that even without these advantages the interests with which they were identified would be better off under existing conditions than if the province were merged in a larger union. The latter continued to find support among the Roman Catholic element, for nothing seems to have occurred in the interval to alter the policy of the Church. Furthermore the Quebec Resolutions remained the basis for the proposed union and the objections which had been levelled against them in the previous year were still in 1866 regarded by many as valid. Such considerations help to explain in part the remarkable persistence of opposition in spite of loss of government personnel and support in the face of deteriorating conditions. In this connection it will be recalled that Smith still commanded a majority in the Legislative Assembly at the time of his forced resignation from the premiership in April, 1866. Up to that time neither he nor his "anti" majority appear to have been sufficiently impressed by the declared wishes of the British government to change their policy on the union question.

Space does not permit a full examination of the reaction of the province to British policy, nor of the complex attitude of Smith himself in the light of the altered circumstances. All that can be said here is that, although privately persuaded of the difficulty of following his original party line, and under constant pressure from the Governor to adopt a policy favourable to union, he continued to adhere publicly to his "anti" position. This divergence between private opinion and public profession prevented Smith from giving effective leadership to those forces which, in the early months of 1866, still continued to resist the union of the provinces. Smith's hesitating and uncertain course must therefore be added to those factors already considered as having weakened the anti-Confederation position during the period under consideration, and which prepared the way for the later intensification of the appeal to support union on the ground of loyalty to the British connection. This, conjoined with the exaggerated menace of Fenian invasion and the persuasive power of Canadian campaign funds, carried New Brunswick into Confederation.

7. New Brunswick: Keystone of the Arch

In the afternoon of April 7, 1866, at a few minutes to three, Premier Albert J. Smith, drove hurriedly up what was then the muddy main street of New Brunswick's diminutive capital to keep an overdue appointment with the Lieutenant-Governor, the Honourable Arthur Hamilton Gordon. He went in response to an urgent message informing him that the Governor had arranged to receive an address from the Legislative Council at 3 p.m. The Premier went in spite of the fact that it forced him to leave the House of Assembly at a critical time, since a debate on a motion of want-of-confidence in his government was approaching a critical phase. But the Governor's proposed action appeared to him as a more immediate threat, since a favourable reply to the Legislative Council by the Queen's representative would force Smith's government, because it was committed to a different policy, to resign.[1]

Smith's fears were confirmed on his arrival at Government House. The Governor stated that as the Imperial Government were anxious for the Union of the provinces at the earliest possible moment, and because of his impression that Smith had earlier given him assurance that he would not be unfavourable, he proposed to commend the Legislative Council for their address praying for an Imperial Act to bring about Confederation. Smith expostulated with the Governor and an angry

[1]This was in accordance with the principle of responsible government, which had been in effect hardly more than a decade. It should be noted also that to become law a bill had to pass both houses of the Legislature before going to the Governor for his signature. The members of the Legislative Council or "Upper House" were appointed by the Crown. The Lower House or Legislative Assembly was elected by the people. Premier Smith, who had the support of a majority in the elected house, thought that the Governor should express the majority opinion against the wishes of the majority of the merely appointed house in order to maintain a democratic form of government, that is to say, expressive of the will of the people of the province.

altercation ensued, lasting for three quarters of an hour. It was Smith's view and he expressed it in terms that left no doubt as to his meaning, that the Governor had no right at all to do what he intended. Smith pointed out that he himself was the head of the government that had been elected in the previous year to oppose Confederation, and that he still had a majority backing in the Legislative Assembly. According to existing constitutional practice it was the Premier and his government, and not the Governor, who should decide the terms of the Governor's reply to the Legislative Council. Smith denied that he had ever given the Governor any idea that he could proceed along this line. He made it clear that to do so would be a violation of the well-understood principle of colonial self-government. But the Governor remained unmoved and said that he would take the consequences, whatever they might be. The delegation from the Legislative Council were waiting in an adjoining room. There was nothing more to be said. Smith left the building, and a few days later his anti-Confederation government resigned.

This historic encounter which we have just described not only marked a turning point in the history of New Brunswick, but could also be construed as having had a significance far beyond the place where it occurred and the lives of those who took part in it. Both men were in some degree the unwilling protagonists in a struggle the import of which could not then be clearly perceived. It is only in the perspective of history that we can see the effect of Gordon's action on subsequent events. Confederation was a regional embodiment of forces that were world-wide. But history is made by men, and Confederation came about when and in the form that it did, as an outcome of the meeting between Smith and Gordon. We can see with equal clarity that the objectives which Smith and his colleagues had set themselves on their assumption of power in March, 1865, became, long before that dramatic meeting, impossible of realization.

Apart from all else there is an irony in the argument between Governor and Premier on that spring afternoon nearly a century ago. It is more than likely that Smith had come to doubt the viability of his anti-Confederation policy, and that Gordon's personal convictions also ran counter to the course that had been set for him by the British Government. It may be that a kind fairy should have allowed them to change places, but we cannot be really sure of this because of the number of ambiguities that cloud the situation. What we do know is that

Gordon in his despatches to the British government in the autumn of 1864 had opposed the Quebec Scheme for inter-provincial union, and had asked to resign rather than be forced to be a party to its adoption. This escape from a situation that was personally repugnant to the Governor was denied him, and he was instructed to remain at his post and do everything in his power to bring about Union.

Did he do so? Who would know better than the members of his cabinet, those men who by virtue of the offices which they held, were in daily association with the representative of Her Majesty's Government during the months preceding the election of March 6, 1865, in which they were so roundly de-feated, and which had brought Albert J. Smith to power in opposition to them, in the first place. Some of them certainly thought otherwise. Samuel Leonard Tilley[2] had urged A. T. Galt[3] "to send us a man who is heartily in favour of union and no one else." Charles Fisher[4] expressed the hope that the rumour of Gordon's resignation was well-founded. He was convinced that everyone the Governor had had any influence with had violently opposed Confederation. He urged John A. Macdonald to help to secure a new governor who would work faithfully in the cause of Union. His suspicions remained un-shaken nearly a year later. On February 13, 1866, he wrote

[2]S. L. Tilley, 1818-1896, a leader of the temperance movement, represented Saint John in the Legislature for many years and became, together with Peter Mitchell of Newcastle, the leading exponent in this province of the movement for the union of the provinces. Later he held several cabinet positions, notably that of Minister of Finance at Ottawa. He served as Lieutenant-Governor of New Brunswick and was knighted for his public services in 1879.

[3]Alexander Tilloch Galt, 1817-1893, son of the Scottish novelist, John Galt, came to Lower Canada at an early age. From his concern with land settlement schemes he became interested in railways. While Minister of Finance in the Canadian Government of 1858 he came out strongly in favour of Confederation, and was associated with John A. Macdonald in all the later conferences leading to the union of the provinces in 1867. He was the first High Commissioner in London, 1880-1883, and received knighthood in 1869.

[4]Charles Fisher, 1808-1880, a native of Fredericton, and one of the earliest graduates of King's College, New Brunswick, now UNB, was Premier of New Brunswick from 1854 to 1856. Through his advocacy of Confederation he lost his seat in the Legislature in 1865 but regained it in a hotly fought by-election in York County later in the year. He eventually became a judge of the supreme court of New Brunswick.

that "our Governor continued at heart opposed to the union," and that "although he is pressed by his instructions he moves about reluctantly and with a very bad grace."

There seems, however, little doubt that Fisher's views were coloured by party animosity. He was particularly irritated at the Governor's action in raising two inveterate anti-Confederationists to the bench, with one of whom the Governor was alleged to be implicated for his "anti" views. Fisher himself favoured the claims of Robert Duncan Wilmot, who had gone over to the Unionists. The Governor had flouted the Churches and the Confederation party in one stroke. "Wilmot is a Methodist, and the Methodists, Baptists, and Presbyterians feel especially insulted by this appointment. These denominations are four-fifths of the Confederation party alone," wrote Fisher. Adverse comments on the governor were not confined to confidential letters, but were boldly stated, ". . . if rumour speaks truly, His Excellency promised the Home Government, if they would but give him back his gubernatorial office, he would not be profoundly indifferent to Confederation any longer . . ." This statement appeared in *The Headquarters,* a Fredericton newspaper.

What are we then to believe, in the light of these strictures? Was the Governor merely making an outward show of supporting Union? All that can be said in reply is that, in spite of what Fisher thought, there is no evidence that Gordon dishonoured his office by playing a double game, whatever his private views may have been. On December 20, 1865, the Governor-General, Lord Monck, who was then in England, wrote to John A. Macdonald that the Colonial Secretary "showed me the private communications from Mr. Gordon, and from them I have come to the conclusion that the success of the Union next spring in New Brunswick is *certain.*" He wrote more explicitly a week later. The Smith government "will be compelled *before* the meeting of the Legislature, to adopt a Union policy, or to make way for one that will do so." At the same time he expressed his opinion to Tilley that "he may trust confidently in the action of Mr. Gordon."

These views, rather than Fisher's, seem to be borne out by what Gordon actually did. There was first of all a plan to have Smith accept a judgeship, but it fell through. Then the Governor determined to take advantage of the internal dissension in the Government. One of the strongest members, the Irish editor of the Saint John *Freeman,* Timothy Warren Anglin, had already resigned after a disagreement with his colleagues over a crucial question of railway policy. Anglin insisted that the Western Extension Railway from Saint John to the American border should be built as a government work, but the government had been unable to raise the funds and had turned to private capital, without much success. Now there was a first-class row between Smith and R. D. Wilmot. As the two refused to meet each other at the council table, the Governor thought that by holding on to Wilmot he could force Smith's resignation, but Wilmot could not be induced to go along with this. He insisted upon resigning, and went over to the side of Confederation. It was only when all his other plans had failed that Gordon determined to use the action of the Upper House, or Legislative Council, to force Smith's hand.

The extreme course finally taken by Gordon in his fateful meeting with Smith on the question of the reply to the Legislative Council, can only be explained in the light of the powerful influences that were then at work to bring about Confederation. The most weighty reasons of state impelled him to this action. It is true that it was only after the Quebec Conference had concluded its deliberations in the autumn of 1864 that the British government saw in the plan for Confederation, then adopted, a means to relieve the British taxpayers of some of the financial burden of imperial defence. The public in the northern states had emerged from the Civil War in a hostile frame of mind, and it was felt that if the provinces should unite they would be able the better to withstand any attack which might be made upon British territory in North America. The Province of Canada was particularly vulnerable because of its long land frontier with the United States, and because it was difficult to send troops there in winter in the closed season of the St. Lawrence. An intercolonial railway to the ice-free harbours of Saint John and Halifax was therefore a necessity. From a commercial view as well the position of the province of Canada was precarious. The threat of armed vessels on the Great Lakes, the institution of a passport system, the withdrawal of the bonding privilege enjoyed by Canadian trade over the railroad from Montreal to Portland, Maine, and the fear that was beginning to be felt that the United States might abrogate the Reciprocity Treaty with British North America, all combined to force on Canadian minds the need for some drastic solution to their difficulties.

They were also beset by internal problems of an acute kind. Neither the partition of the St. Lawrence Valley in 1791 into Upper and Lower Canada, nor the reunion of these provinces in 1841, had afforded a solution, and both schemes had been marked by outbursts of violence. By the 'sixties the situation was such that no Canadian government could remain in office long enough to carry out a constructive legislative programme unless it commanded a majority in both sections of the province. As the clash of French and English, farmer and merchant, Tory and Radical had clearly shown in the occurrence of the rebellions of 1837 and the disorders in Montreal attendant upon the triumph of Responsible Government, the two areas of Canada seemed unable to live either together or apart. It was hoped, therefore, that the Maritime Provinces, acting as a third component, might mitigate the impact of the two Canadas upon each other, and give some assurance of a viable political settlement.

Canada's need for Confederation was far greater than that of the Maritimes. Newfoundland and Prince Edward Island had seen little advantage in it, and had withdrawn from the Quebec Conference before it was concluded. Joseph Howe led a powerful opposition movement in Nova Scotia. Smith's triumph over Tilley in March 1865 had so frightened the Legislature of Nova Scotia that the Unionist leader, Dr. Charles Tupper, was able to forestall a hostile vote only by side-tracking the discussion on to the subject of Maritime Union.

In Canada the reaction was immediate and pronounced. The unexpected triumph of Albert J. Smith had put the whole Confederation movement in jeopardy. Since New Brunswick occupied the intervening space between Canada and Nova Scotia, no union of the provinces was possible without New Brunswick's participation. The Intercolonial Railway that was essential to Union had to cross New Brunswick soil. Lying between Canada and Nova Scotia, New Brunswick was the keystone of the arch of Confederation. When it is understood that without the inclusion of New Brunswick, the dream of a transcontinental dominion could not have been realized, the importance of Gordon's action in forcing Smith's hand on that April afternoon in 1866, becomes abundantly clear.

No one understood this better than the Canadian Union leaders. For thirteen months, ever since Smith's election, they had been trying, with the aid of the British government, to force a reversal of New Brunswick's stand. As the distinguished historian, Chester Martin, once wrote, the strongest delegation ever to leave Canada – John A. Macdonald, George E. Cartier, A. T. Galt, and George Brown – had gone at once to England to urge upon the British government the necessity of putting all possible pressure on New Brunswick to change its verdict. It was only when all other expedients had failed that Gordon had recourse to the occasion which is the principal subject of this article.

During the first week of December, 1864, Smith in his appeal to the electorate made the following argument against the plan of union embodied in the Quebec Resolutions. He asserted that the adoption of the Quebec Plan would mean increased taxation, the loss to New Brunswick of political influence and status, and the expenditure of vasts sums of money on Canada's canal system which would, in his opinion, be of no benefit to New Brunswick. Neither could he see that the Intercolonial railway would be of any great advantage to the Province.

Behind these arguments and others like them were the groups that for one reason or another feared union with Canada. The Catholic vote was almost entirely directed against it. The Catholic clergy were fearful of the strong Protestant influence of Canada West, later called Ontario, and they did not want the great business interest of the Grand Trunk Railway, with its subsidiary, the Intercolonial, to get control of the wild lands of the Province which they hoped to reserve for settlement by their co-religionists. Some of the old Anglican families surviving from Family Compact days simply wanted to leave well-enough alone. The manufacturers were divided on the potential danger of competition from Canadian goods in the provincial market. The bankers anticipated a possible breaking of their monopoly by the opening of branches of Canadian banks in Saint John and other centres. Strongest of all was the desire of the mercantile community of Saint John to develop their already important trade, not with Canada, but with the United States, by extending New Brunswick's Shediac-to-Saint John railway westward to the American border to connect with the railway systems of that country. The Reciprocity Treaty which the British Minister to Washington, Lord Elgin, had "floated through Congress on oceans of champagne" back in 1854, was still in force and would make such a railway a most profitable venture. The commercial men were afraid that if the financial resources of the Province were taxed to build the Intercolonial, there would be no money left to carry out their cherished plan of a western extension of their road to the Maine border. That this "western extension" lobby was the most powerful force at work against Confederation was attested to by no less a person than S. L. Tilley, who suffered defeat at the hands of Smith and his supporters in the election of March 6, 1865.

It is clear that Smith's party were swept into office by a coalition of some of the most powerful interests in the Province. "Forty-eight thousand men," declared Billy Needham of Fredericton, ". . . have said we don't want Confederation, and that should be the end of it." In the spirit of this observation the Legislature immediately empowered the new government to send a delegation to England to make known to the British government their views that Confederation would prove politically, commercially, and financially disastrous to the best interests of the province. The Governor was asked to inform the Secretary of State how entirely the scheme had been rejected. But when Smith and one of his colleagues went to England to present these views, the Colonial Secretary categorically informed them that he "could give no countenance to any proposal that would tend to delay the Confederation of all the provinces. . . ." He claimed a right to speak in this vein on the ground that Confederation was not merely a domestic issue, but one that impinged upon the important question of imperial defence.

We can have no doubt that the cogency of this argument was not lost upon Smith, but what could he do in the circumstances? And what would his followers and the New Brunswick electorate do? There seems to have been no outward sign that he had been persuaded to change his mind at this time, nor does it appear very likely that the by-election in York County in the autumn of 1865 was indicative of the swing of opinion towards Confederation that many of the Unionists supposed it to be. It is true that the pro-Unionist, Charles Fisher, was elected with the aid of Canadian campaign funds, but only on the solemn promise that he would not promote Confederation until the return of a new House of Assembly in a general provincial election. To say the least, it was a limited victory, indicating no profound change of public sentiment.

Although Lord Monck, the Governor-General, and the Canadian government, counted Fisher's election a victory, they could not have considered that the temper of the province was reassuring. Many Maritimers thought that they were being asked to pull Canadian chestnuts out of the fire for the welfare of the Empire and out of devotion to the Crown. Such an appeal had a problematical response. Imperial sentiment both in England and the provinces was at a low ebb. Britain's repeal in the 'forties of the timber duties and navigation acts had not been forgotten. The provinces, with their primitive economies, had withstood the shock only be recoiling upon the United States. Even grandchildren of United Empire Loyalists found it heartening to see a flourishing trade with the Yankees. J. W. Cudlip of Saint John, son of a British naval officer, boldly asserted that the Imperial government had better not try coercing New Brunswick into union with Canada as any such attempt would be resisted. There was evidently a degree of resentment against Canada and the British government. The Canadians, wrote one New Brunswick editor, had induced the Colonial Secretary "to write a series of irritating despatches by way of exercising upon New Brunswick what he calls the just authority of the Imperial government, and they are now waiting anxiously to see if New Brunswick will break down under the pressure."

Partly for this, but mostly for other reasons, the position of Smith's government was progressively undermined. The rebuff by Britain and the defection of Anglin over railway policy had been followed by the greatest of all blows, namely the failure to get the government of the United States to agree to a renewal of the Reciprocity Treaty. Smith had gone as a member of a delegation to Washington in an effort to secure this prize. He was back in Fredericton on February 14, 1866, with his mission a failure. The ground had been swept from under his feet. The Western Extension railway project, the cornerstone of anti-Confederation policy, was left hanging in mid-air. The project had been embraced in the belief that Reciprocity would augment the trade and make the line a profitable undertaking, but this hope was now shattered. R. D. Wilmot, who had already quarrelled with Smith, became convinced that the anti-Union policy he had been following was meaningless without Reciprocity, and he went over to the Confederationists amid the howls of the "anti's" and their press. Smith, still with a majority backing in the Legislature, was beset from all sides. Already, whether he knew it or not, he was on the road that was to lead him to his dramatic altercation with the Governor, and his subsequent resignation.

There is some reason to suppose that the seeds of doubt as to the wisdom of his course had begun to grow in Smith's mind even before the failure of his Washington mission. He seems to have given the Governor the impression that he might support a union proposal if better terms than those embodied in the Quebec Resolutions could be secured. The Governor doubted whether Smith could swing his party to the Confederation policy, and he tried to bring about a coalition between

Smith and the leaders of the opposition. Mutual jealousies prevented it, and the only upshot was to give Smith the impression that the Governor was in collusion with his political enemies. A consequent lack of candour in the relations between Premier and Governor became evident. Gordon began to believe that Smith was deliberately stalling and would neither combine with Tilley and Peter Mitchell nor bring in a Confederation proposal of his own. Smith may have been stalling, but it seems probable that he was all the while casting about desperately for a way out of his difficulties.

The debate on the vote of want of confidence in the Smith government continued in the House. The Governor became impatient. He had promised the Colonial Secretary that he would bring about a change long before this. It was in these trying circumstances that Gordon determined to send a congratulatory reply to the Legislative Council's petition for Imperial legislation to bring about union. There is some reason to believe that while he felt he must do this, it was personally distasteful to him. He had always had a respect for Smith, and appreciated the predicament in which such action would place him. By accident or design the message from the Governor to Smith, informing him of what was intended, did not reach Smith at the Legislative Buildings in Fredericton until an hour and a half after it had been sent.

As stated at the beginning of this article Smith hurried to Government House, but he could not dissuade the Governor from making a favourable reply to the Legislative Council. He would not accept responsibility for the Governor's reply and had no choice but to resign, which he did several days later. Gordon called on Peter Mitchell[5] to form a government, and a provincial election was fought, and the outcome was that Smith's party were defeated and a majority in favour of Confederation were elected. Delegates were appointed to go to England to unite with the representatives of Canada and Nova Scotia in drawing up terms of union. These terms became incorporated into the British North America Act which established the Dominion of Canada.

[5]Peter Mitchell, 1824-1899, was a prominent lawyer, ship-builder and lumberman, of Newcastle, N.B. He entered politics in 1856 and was premier of the Province in 1866, negotiating New Brunswick's entrance into Confederation. He was later a Senator, proprietor of the Montreal *Herald,* and first Minister of Marine and Fisheries in the Canadian government, 1867-1873.

IV | A CONSCIOUSNESS OF CENTRALITY

8. William Alexander Foster And the Genesis of English-Canadian Nationalism[1]

I

The strongest impulse to create a centralized federal state on the northern half of the North American continent in the sixties of the last century was felt in that section of the old Canadian Union which in 1867 became the province of Ontario. The eastern section that became Quebec, because of the centrifugal factors operative there, was unable to play a role equally impelling or of like character. On the other hand the countervailing forces were sufficiently strong to insure the passage of the measures necessary to bring the confederation of several of the provinces into formal being. The fact that this was not the case with the two colonies that remained aloof, namely Prince Edward Island and Newfoundland, was not unrelated to their geographical location and their insular character. Nova Scotia, which had played a distinctive role in the political and constitutional struggles through which all provinces had passed earlier in the century, and whose oceanic concerns as well as pride in political and cultural achievements rendered her unwilling to merge her identity in a continental community that appeared to many of her people to offer little of advantage, was brought in only through the exercise of extraordinary pressures that have left to this day some sense of injury which may well persist for a long time to come.

While New Brunswick was drawn to New England on account of her increase in trade with that region under the terms of the Reciprocity Treaty of 1854, she also, because of

[1]In 1955 I was allowed by Mr. Harold Foster to read the papers of his father, W. A. Foster, which apparently had never been made accessible to scholars. Some were in the form of a scrapbook, which Mr. Foster allowed me to have microfilmed for the Canadian Library Association, and which I entitled the "Canada First Scrapbook." This essay is based in part on the Foster Papers.

her location, was more continental in outlook than Nova Scotia, and was not by any means without interest in the possibilities of the union of the provinces as proposed at the Charlottetown Conference in 1864. Thus although her position was marginal to both the northeastern extremity of the United States, and to the continetal union of provinces urged by Canada, it was to the latter, under British official pressure, that she came to adhere in 1866, having at first shown a disinclination to do so in the previous year. In almost all respects New Brunswick stood in sharp contrast to Ontario, located as the latter was, in a central position, upon the St. Lawrence and Great Lakes system which always constituted the main highway of commerce and communication of the northern half of the continent, and which would, under the new dispensation, continue to do so with increased advantage to the communities fortunate enough to be located on the lands bordering the great waterway.

It was not until the close of the American War of Independence that a numerous population of Loyalists and frontier farmers moved in upon the fertile lands, situated to the north of the river and the lake, which had lain almost entirely uninhabited since the destruction of the Hurons and other populous tribes at the hands of the Iroquois in the middle decades of the seventeenth century. Once resumed under favourable circumstances, and vastly augmented by immigrants from the British Isles following the conclusion of the Napoleonic Wars, Upper Canada, as Ontario was at first called, attained to a measure of prosperity from the development of her resources in timber and wheat in spite of adverse factors attendant upon the political struggles of the Rebellion era, and the effects of sporadic but necessary recourse to free-trade legislation on the part of the parliament of the United Kingdom, culminating in the repeal of the Navigation Acts in 1849.

In contrast to these influences Responsible Government, and Reciprocity soon after, gave an impetus to productive forces that were expanding agriculture to the limits of available land, and effecting the growth of secondary industry in ways that promised new alignments and new perspectives, the implications of which were just then beginning to be grasped. The Galt tariff of 1858, and the vision of westward expansion which men like George Brown and Alexander Morris were moved to proclaim, increasingly as the decade of the fifties drew to a close, were evidence of the dawning conception of a transcontinental economy made viable by the exchange of the manufactures of central Canada with the Maritime provinces to the eastward, but particularly with the large numbers of potential consumers that shortly might be expected to people the great grasslands of the western plains. At the same time the growing density of population, the diversification of industry and the concomitant phenomena of urbanization, affluence, and specialization of occupation subsumed the growth of a professional class possessing the expertise necessary to meet the requirements of the more complex society then coming into being.

The nature and outlook of this professional class must command the attention of the student of Canadian history, for the new university foundations, the libraries and the periodical press, and the vigorous book trade, were responsible for an expansion of public intelligence which became peculiarly its hallmark.

One may surmise that few of its members could have been altogether unaware of the forces of almost worldwide provenence that were at that moment transforming loosely aligned territories and peoples into large and often highly centralized national consolidations. While the Confederation of the British North American provinces was, as Professor Arthur Lower once aptly wrote, a carpentered rather than a forged occasion, participants in the event were not completely devoid of a sense of the coming-into-being of a new nationality conceived though it undoubtedly was largely in political rather than cultural terms. While several of the Fathers of Confederation perceived their creation as something potentially more than a virtually necessary political arrangement, none possessed the vision, in anything like equal degree, of the erstwhile Irish nationalist, Thomas' d'Arcy McGee who, as is so very well known, before being struck down by an assassin's bullet, succeeded in inspiring numbers of his adopted fellow countrymen with a newly-perceived and almost poetically experienced national sentiment. Among those who responded to the appeal of McGee's words was the young Toronto barrister, William Alexander Foster who, at the age of twenty, graduated from the University of Toronto. As a professional man of intelligence and a native son for whom, lacking first-hand experience, the old land was a little remote, Foster felt involved in the problems that were beginning increasingly to beset the political and commercial institutions of the old Canadian Union that had been born in 1841 out of the turmoil of the Rebellion era, and which was soon to be incorporated in the larger entity of the new Dominion.

We know enough to assert, from the meagre evidence that has survived from this period, that Foster's early career was marked by a concern for public questions, and it is possible to perceive something of the outlook with which he approached the affairs of the day. Aware as were many of his class of the forces that were tending to bring about the formation of states conceived on the basis of nationality, he must also be regarded as representative of the stage of social development reached by the provincial society of which he was a member in the decade preceding Confederation. Ontario perhaps more than any of the other areas of British North America had then achieved a degree of maturity, reflected in the outlook of its more discerning residents, that was indicative of its readiness to embark upon the novel course of political consolidation. As a matter of fact it is certain that Foster perceived something of the nationalist implications of Confederation in the years when the idea was before the public and when it had not yet been finally consummated.

II

Foster's early excursion into the field of journalism, while still an undergraduate in the late eighteen-fifties, was continued at intervals throughout his professional life. On July 10th, 1863, we find his name listed in company with those of Charles Sangster, Mrs. Leprehon, Louisa Murray, Cornelius Kreighoff, and of McMullan, the historian, as a prospective contributor to a forthcoming publication advertised as the Canadian National Magazine, a monthly serial to be devoted to literature, science, and art, under the editorship of the Hon. Thomas D'Arcy McGee, with Henry J. Morgan of Quebec as one of the associated editors.[2] He was, however, to find his metier as a publicist rather than as a litterateur, as is evident from the articles soon to be published in the Westminster Review. The first of these appeared in April 1865, under the title of "The Canadian Confederacy." Although written as though by a resident of the Mother Country, and addressed to readers of the parent state, authorship by a "colonial" was not long in becoming known. In the meantime as an article written in a clear and persuasive style, reinforced by relevant statistics,

---

[2]The project as then conceived under this title does not seem to have materilized.

indicative of the author's thorough knowledge of his subject, and published in one of the most influential periodicals of the day, it may well have exerted some effect on the course of events.[3]

Not only because his views became known through this article and others soon to appear, they must also be of interest to the student of a later day, from the fact that Foster had evidently anticipated opinions afterwards put forward in the service of nationalist aims as entertained by himself and the group with whom at the end of the decade he was to become associated. While the tendency to explain cultural or acquired traits in biological terms was not confined to the century of Darwin, it was without question a more obtrusive one in the years immediately following the publication of the Origin of Species than at any other time. It was therefore not out of context for Foster to assert in 1865 that "That self reliance, that innate vigour, which defies misfortune and begets self-confidence, is a characteristic of our race, and, when grafted, in other lands, reproduces its inherent qualities with the characteristics of the parent stock."[4] Such an affirmation of the unity of the "race," made in the decade when anti-colonial sentiment in Great Britain was perhaps at its height, could have served more than one purpose. Foster did not share the belief or the wish that the British provinces should be absorbed into the United States as was thought inevitable in some influential quarters "at home." On the other hand the respectibility of Little-Englandism in British Official circles insured that references to the "independence" of British North America were neither heretical nor anathema in 1865, however they were to be looked upon in the changed climate of opinion on this question, increasingly, in the ensuing decade. It is necessary to bear such factors in mind when noting Foster's remark that

The colonists advance with excessive timidity to whatever has the appearance of ultimate independence, and they seem to be wholly unconscious that they are framing a confederation which is to form a stepping-stone to this final end. It is not that four millions of people might not desire independence if circumstances assured them of being able to maintain it. . . . But the thoughtful colonist . . . fears an attempt to apply to the whole of North America the modern and exaggerated reading of the Monroe doctrine. For British

[3]Foster's articles in the Westminster Review were republished in *Canada First, a Memorial of William A. Foster, Q.C.* (Toronto, 1890).

[4]*Ibid.,* 97.

America there is, therefore, no absolute independence. She must lean somewhere for support, and her inclination, if not her interests, leads her to prefer a species of dependence upon the mother country which shall be something more, though perhaps not much more than a national alliance.[5]

But if the scheme of union, as drawn up at the Quebec Conference of 1864 which was then under consideration, were to eventuate in a new entity, it was to mean not an alien and disassociated state, but "the establishment of a great British power on the American continent . . ." a prospect which had "ceased to be the glorious vision of a remote future," and would "soon be numbered among the most spendid achievements of the present generation." It was not however, entirely for such sentimental ends, that seem implicit in Foster's peroration, that ". . . the men of education, intellect, experience, and position among the colonists were nearly unanimous in support of the proposed scheme. . . ." They knew that small markets had stunted their manufactures, and that "A large proportion of the goods which the Maritime provinces now buy in the States could be supplied by Canada, and the competition would not be with the productions of Great Britain, but with those of the States." Foster thus perceived clearly the pattern of the future, that in which Ontario would become the chief centre of secondary industry. He continued to show his concern for economic matters, notably in his second article in the Westminster Review, published in October, 1866, and devoted to the question of the renewal of the Reciprocity Treaty with the United States. He did not believe that the abrogation of the treaty, an eventuality greatly feared by many, would seriously affect the prosperity of the provinces. Compensation would be found in the new internal, free-trade area to be created by Confederation. Those who expressed alarm had failed to consider the strides made by the provinces in recent years. The coming of the railways and the beginnings of industrialization had prepared them to pursue a goal of development without much regard for the policies of the Republic. There were cases in which the changed circumstances were a distinct advantage. If raw wool were not to be able to enter the United States as formerly, the Americans would prefer the manufactured cloth to their own because of its superiority and in spite of the high tariff which Congress had placed upon it. Indeed, he stated, a commerce in the processed wool had already commenced. The provinces, he concluded, were ready to lay a bold hand on the commerce of more than one continent.[6]

This confident note, not unsupported by the most careful scrutiny of the facts of the case under review evoked, on the whole, a most favourable response. As the editor of the Woodstock *Times* observed, "The writer, if not Mr. Howe, is one equally well acquainted with the history of these colonies. . . ."[7] A little later, at a dinner given in honour of Charles Belford, A. C. Tyner took advantage of the occasion to refer to Foster as "the first of our young Canadian men who had obtained the entree to the pages of the Westminster, the most exclusive, the ablest, and the most influential of English reviews." He had thus been able to influence opinion to such an extent that Canadians were not lightly indebted to him for the success of Confederation.[8]

Not all of Foster's views, however, were equally well received by those in Britain whom he had asked to consider the plight of the colonists. "Far away from the Mother land," he had written, "three thousand miles across the sea, and a thousand miles inland, the Canadian tries to sift from the metropolitan press the real sentiments of the English people; and within sight of the stars and stripes, perceives British journals and British reviews, in which threats, ridicule, unfair comparisons, and even contemptuous distain mark the passages that bear on his case."[9] Foster had made it clear that, not only were the colonies not ready to stand on their own feet, they were positively bound by ties of affection to the old land, an avowal which ran counter to the attitude of self-interest often so baldly stated at the time. Some surprise was therefore expressed that such a vigorous protest would appear in the Westminster Review, a paper generally tainted with the "advanced" ideas of the Goldwin Smith school.[10] Something of what Foster had to contend with is apparent in a letter he received from W. F. Rae in London, dated December 19, 1866. Foster seems to have sought clarification of some matter previously expressed, and Rae replied that he had

[6]*Ibid.*, 157.

[7]W. A. Foster Papers, "Canada First Scrapbook," Woodstock *Times,* November 9, 1866.

[8]W. A. Foster Papers, "Canada First Scrapbook," p. 136. With reference to March 7, 1867.

[9]*Canada First: A Memorial of the Late William A. Foster,* (Toronto, 1890). P. 168.

[10]*Ibid.,* p. 139-168.

tried to get your last communication inserted in a largely circulated paper, I mean the *Daily News*. I saw the editor in person on the subject but he declined my request. He is at present strongly opposed to Confederation, says that one of its conditions is the giving of an Imperial guarantee for the construction of an Intercolonial railroad. He seems to think it possible that the J. A. Macdonalds and others of your public men may hereafter make a bid for popularity by saddling the Home Government with the debt. He distrusts the men who are so eager for Confederation. He regards the conduct of some members of the Canadian Government in the Lamirande Case as so scandalous as to render them unworthy of confidence. Holding opinions of that sort he would naturally object to your article, for granting that it proves your case, yet it does not remove his objections.[11]

He hastened to say that he did not agree with the editor of the *Daily News*. He ascribed the garbling of Foster's previous article to a contributor who was, during the illness of the editor, "under the erroneous impression that the colonial policy of the Review was that of Goldwin Smith." While this explained the excisions and the note of protest at the head of the article, Rae did not believe that any harm had been done to Foster's argument.

His growing reputation as a journalist, and one who habitually spoke with authority on public questions, brought him into contact with leading publicists and men of affairs on both sides of the Atlantic. Foster had become well known, at this time, to the Hon. John A. Macdonald who towards the end of 1866, according to a telegram from Henry Morgan, had recommended that Foster be attached to the Paris Exhibition Commission. Foster went abroad in 1866 and later became Canadian correspondent of the London Times, but with respect to the Paris Exhibition there turned out to be obstacles in the way of an appointment, as Morgan explained to him in a letter dated December 27, 1866. He wrote:

I had a long conversation with McGee when he was in town the other day respecting your prospects of going to Paris with the Canadian Commission. He sent for me expressly for the purpose. He told me of the great difficulties which beset him in his

[11]The writer, William Fraser Rae, 1835-1905, was for a time a special correspondent of the London Daily News in Canada and the United States. He was a widely known journalist, historian, biographer and novelist. He may have become known to Foster through his brother George, who had taken up the practice of law in Toronto.

endeavour to meet your wishes – of the number of influential men in both Provinces who wished to be appointed, and of the dewhision [sic] he had finally come to not to appoint any outside his Department. He was very desirous of serving your interests, owing to your generous and able defence of him in the *Telegraph,* and to the valuable service which you had rendered to the cause of the Union Party. He regretted exceedingly that it was not in his power (for the reason I have stated) to place you on the Commission, but as the next best thing he offered to give you some employment. . . ."[12]

While the nature of the employment to be offered Foster is uncertain, the esteem in which he was held by McGee, and his friendship with Morgan were both facts of relevance to the history of the rise of national feeling in English-speaking Canada at this time.

III

Foster was soon in a position to exert a wider influence, than hitherto, on the course of events, as co-founder, with Hugh Scott, and editor-in-chief of *The Canadian Monetary Times and Insurance Chronicle,* the first number of which came out on August 15, 1867. While devoted chiefly to the concerns of the business community, it sought to bring the whole of the new Dominion within its orbit, and it reflected the spirit of optimism with which many sections of the public were seized as the federal government began to address itself to the tasks in hand. The editor was able to report that the Board of Directors of the Bank of Toronto had "observed with pleasure the increase of business between the Western and Maritime Provinces. . . . This trade though not yet fully developed, has been very satisfactory, and," they stated, "The Directors will take pleasure in fostering it to the utmost of their powers." Referring to his newspaper in his first editorial Foster spoke of the novelty in an undertaking of this nature in Canada, and went on to say that there was now "the absolute necessity of joint action on the part of all the members of the Union," as well as "grave reasons for learning wherein our strength lies, and making the best possible use of the knowledge. We now have a country of which none need feel ashamed, and it is our desire that young

[12]W. A. Foster Papers, H. J. Morgan to W. A. Foster, Ottawa, December 27, 1868.

and old claiming this land as their home, should cherish as an article of faith, the certainty of a splendid future for our new Dominion." He assured his fellow-Canadians that he was not asking them to indulge in vulgar self-praise, or in displays of silly vanity, but rather to cultivate an honest pride, a manly self-respect, having as a solid basis reasons that will stand the severest examination." British Americans had been lacking in self-reliance, and in order to change this "we must cultivate a patriotism that will be something more than inflated verbiage." Writing from England, W. F. Rae expressed hope for Foster's success in the new venture, and that he would make a reputation for himself "as great as that enjoyed by the editor of the *Economist*." As an orthodox liberal he urged support for the doctrine of Freetrade, but stated that he realized that there were obstacles "which impede their adoption in the fullest measure by your Minister of Finance; still they ought nonetheless to be urged in the long run to benefit the nation which unreservedly embraces them."[13]

The almost sacrosanct doctrine alluded to above was, however, not of as immediate concern as one involving a prime assumption of the newly constituted federal union, namely, the viability of interprovincial trade. Troubling questions were being raised by a Nova Scotian correspondent, Robert Grant Haliburton, which, if no satisfactory answer were found, might jeopardize the success of the Union upon which all hopes rested. The possibility of developing an exchange of Canadian tweeds for Nova Scotian coal, sugar, molasses, fish, and oil was noted on September 12, 1867, and on April 30, 1868, the *Monetary Times* published a brief notice of a pamphlet by the son of the author of The Clockmaker entitled "Interprovincial trade our only safeguard against disunion," containing sentiments which the editor found to be "opportune, and calculated to do good at the present stage." It contained, he thought, a good deal of sense, and indicated that Mr. Haliburton had "not permitted popular clamour in his own Province to dwarf his ideas, but endeavours to point out the sources of the existing dissatisfaction in Nova Scotia, and seeks to have these removed instead of advising a return of the old colonial position." The editor was clearly amenable to further treatment of the subject, for Haliburton's article on "How to make the St. Lawrence the Commercial Highway of the West" was printed in the

[13]W. A. Foster Papers, W. F. Rae to W. A. Foster, Rolls Chambers, 89 Chancery Lane, W.C., September 4, 1867.

Monetary Times on July 2. The burden of the argument was that, in order to lower costs, provision should be made for return freights from Nova Scotia to central Canada. The coal deposits of Nova Scotia, he wrote "are destined to do for our commerce what the export of coal has accomplished for the trade of Britain. This system of utilizing coal is the secret of England's commercial and manufacturing supremacy." He pursued the theme further on August 20, observing that the flour of Western Canada had

"to be paid for in cash, and the drain on the Lower Provinces is very heavy, the trade being altogether one-sided. . . . The proposal to encourage return freights of fuel by temporarily giving a bounty to Nova Scotian coal, and taking off canal dues on provincial coal, though at first sight it might appear to be simply a boon to Nova Scotia would have in the long run proved of greater importance to the grain grower and manufacturer of Canada West."

Haliburton noted that at that moment his province was appealing to the Imperial Parliament to dissolve the union, and added that the "adoption of the proposed measure would have cut the ground from under the feet of the Nova Scotian delegation, and would have given the beleaguered friends of union among us, a weapon by which they could have defeated the opponents of Confederation."

Before Haliburton's second instalment had appeared, the *Monetary Times,* to be exact, in its issue of July 23rd, had carried an editorial on the subject of Nova Scotia which might appear to pose a problem concerning Foster's temperament and the nature of the part played by him in the nationalist movement. Foster's editorials had, hitherto, been restrained, judicious, and informed expressions of opinion on public and business affairs; but the editorial in question was hortatory and bordered on the abusive. "If those Nova Scotians who worked themselves into a fury over Confederation," wrote the editorialist, "would only throw into their commerce, their mining and general business habits, a little of the energy, perseverence and enterprise they display in belittling themselves and the Dominion, their Province would be a great gainer." The Province displayed "her want of that mercantile enterprise which has made England what it is. . . . Confederation has not made us all rich, they cry, and then go off into a succession of fainting fits." With the same intent as Haliburton's father had sought through the mouthpiece of his creation, Sam Slick, to spur his fellow provincials to action by contrasting their enterprise unfavourably with that of the New England Yankees, the author of the editorial held up Ontario as an example for Nova Scotians to follow, but not at all in the bantering and good-natured tone of *The Clockmaker*. In short, it seems so out of character that the reader is prompted to wonder whether indeed it could have been written by the editor, or whether Haliburton himself, although referred to in the editorial in the third person, might not have been the author. It could, of course have been a joint product of one of those convivial gatherings in Henry Morgan's 'Corner room' in his Ottawa hotel, which were frequently attended by Foster, Haliburton, George T. Denison, and the poet Charles Mair, in that spring and summer of 1868.[14] Interested as they all were in the pursuit of some personal or professional end, though not devoid of a sincere and unsullied pride in the new political creation and the new nationality, they might as a group have been a prey to excitation and intemperate expression at the prospect of the threat to Confederation posed by the action of Nova Scotia in seeking repeal of the British North America Act. This may have been the effect on Foster and he may indeed, have written the editorial. Especially does this seem possible in light of the fact that a little later on a very different issue, he used the most intemperate language, even, it would appear, calling for the exercise of military power.

It may be that only when he was very deeply moved, when experiencing an intense sense of frustration, or when circumstances of a critical nature seemed to warrant a response well out of the ordinary, did this usually mild and gentle man step out of character in this manner. The case in point was the shooting of the young Ontarian, Thomas Scott, by order of Louis Riel in the course of the Red River Rebellion. The intensity of the response to this act was, as all students of the subject well know, the result of a contingency of factors some of which had been long in the making. All through the fifties the outlook of the people of what came in 1867 to be called Ontario was conditioned by the Toronto *Globe's* advocacy of the acquisition by Canada of the Hudson's Bay Company territories. The idea had become a plank in the platform of the great Reform Convention of 1857. Added to this were the pamphlets of Alexander Morris, the railway imperialism of Edward Watkin, and to cap it all the poetic vision of McGee of a great

[14]It should be clear from what has been said that Foster's nationalism, as was the case with the other participants, predated the Ottawa meetings of 1868 by a considerable number of years.

new nation embracing the north-west and "bound by the blue rim of ocean." The influence on such young men as Foster was inescapable, and when it became evident that the fur company might relinquish its holdings and that the Minnesota frontier was moving menacingly in the direction of Red River, speedy action was called for to fill the power-vacuum which appeared to be forming at that veritable crossroads of empire.

Already on September 24, 1868, Foster had commented in the *Monetary Times* on the mission to England of William McDougall and Sir George Cartier to effect the transfer to Canada of the Hudson's Bay territories.

"Although the matter is of great importance to the Dominion," he wrote, "it is of special interest to the Province of Ontario, and should Mr. McDougall and his colleagues succeed in their mission, they will have earned for themselves the gratitude of every Western Canadian. The fact is, we must annex the North West."

On August 10, 1869, McDougall wrote to Foster to inform him of his acceptance of the Lieutenant Governorship of the newly acquired territory. He stated that he had made up his mind

"to go out to Red River for a year or two at least to start the new machine. It is not improbable that I will retain my seat in the H. of Commons – for the present at least . . . there will I think be much advantage in having a seat at Ottawa, to explain and defend the propositions for opening up and settling the Territory. It will make the people at Red River feel that they are not without some representation although not of their own election. . . . You will agree, I think, that it would not do to give political power to the half-breeds and nomads of the territory just yet. We must wait till we get a settled Canadian population to work upon. . . . I will go out probably in October so as to be there on the day of transfer."

McDougall informed Foster of the plans for telegraph and railway communications, and added that Sir Curtis Thompson, of the Hudson's Bay Company, was "fully alive to the import- ance of the Railway, but the thick headed *Englishers* want to have the geography and capabilities of the country driven in to their pates by a succession of *blows*. Study the western maps and movements in re Railways and give them a *stab* or two in the Times," he urged.[15]

[15]W. A. Foster Papers, William McDougall to W. A. Foster, August 10, 1869.

Something of Foster's involvement in the affairs of Red
River is evident from McDougall's letter, but so far nothing
had occurred to cause alarm. Even when McDougall was
prevented from entering the territory on October 30, 1869 by
Riel's provisional government, and subsequently when the im-
prisonment and escapes of the two Canada First men, Schultz
and Mair, became known, a measure of calm prevailed,
although not without growing apprehension. Even as late as
March 7, 1870, before the circumstances surrounding the
execution of Scott became clearly known in Ontario, the
Toronto *Daily Telegraph* wrote of the capture by Riel of Major
Boulton of the Canadian Party, "We have no fear that the
sentence of death will be carried out. The half breeds are
neither bloodthirsty nor savage. Though they have opposed
Canadian authority they have shown no disposition to shed
blood. . . . Dr. Schultz, who has a peculiar knack of getting
himself and others into trouble appears to have been the prime
mover in getting Major Boulton involved. . . ." "This Schultz,"
it continued, "appears to have done more to injure our cause
than ever was done by Riel himself. . . . Certainly, we have no
right to the country – for we have not paid one copper for it
– and our law and authority have as little right there as in
Newfoundland. If they were to shoot Major Boulton tomorrow
we would have no . . . right to punish them for the outrage."
Such a view of the affairs of the Northwest was bound to act
as a goad to Denison and Foster, and what stuck in Denison's
mind years later was the apathy that he and Foster found
throughout Ontario with respect to Scott's death when it became
known in the last week in March. While the Government press
were trying to cool the public temper, Denison and Foster,
and their associates, as well as the *Globe*, on its own initiative,
were determined to set the heather on fire. A series of inflam-
matory editorials attributed to Foster now appeared in the
Daily Telegraph. On March 31 he wrote that he had been
inclined to consider Riel's offence as trifling, and to advocate
leniency, but now he and his people had carried matters so far
that it could be settled only with the assistance of troops.

"A number of Canadians have been held in close custody for
several months, many persons have been forcibly deprived of their
property, and blood has been shed by these usurpers of authority.
These crimes cannot be allowed to pass unnoticed. The perpetrators
of them must be punished . . . one man they murdered in cold blood.
The only crime of those who were thus made to suffer was that they
were Canadians . . . an armed force must be sent to Red River. . . ."

The note became increasingly shrill as was evident in the editorial carried by the same paper on April 2.

"This foul crime must not go unpunished. This death must be avenged at any cost, at any sacrifice, at any hazard. . . . So intense is the feeling in this city, and so unanimous is the demand for vengeance, that a sufficient force could be gathered together in a day, to sweep Riel and his fellow rebels out of existence in an hour. The people of Canada are determined now that their authority shall be extended over and permanently planted on every foot of the Hudson Bay Territory."

On April 4, the Daily *Telegraph* appeared with its columns lined in heavy black. "We issue this number of our paper in mourning," it was stated, "out of respect to the memory of young Scott, who died a martyr to the cause of our country;" and in reference to what purported to be Scott's last utterance, the editorialist concluded,

"These words must never be forgotten by the Canadian people. They are the last words of one who nobly died, a martyr to his devotion to our flag and our country; the last utterance of a man who faced death rather than turn traitor. And they contain an awful truth; for never was a more cold-blooded or more atrocious murder committed in a civilized country. . . ."

Indignation and exhortation could go no further. These and the earlier editorial on Nova Scotia, to which reference was made above, appear to represent the only occasions upon which Foster was moved to write in this fashion. Recent writers have not, it seems safe to say, always described these events and attitudes with full appreciation of the tenseness of the moment, and the issues that must have appeared to be at stake.[16]

Denison, Schultz, and others were active in trying to prevent Riel's delegates from getting a hearing at Ottawa, and to them it was the "French Party" against whom they had to

[16]Foster remained calm and judicious in his approach to the Red River question until details became known concerning the killing of Scott, after which his indignation knew no bounds. For an authoritative account of the case, see George F. G. Stanley, *The Birth of Western Canada,* (Toronto, 1960), pp. 99-106. Concern over American influence at Fort Garry had been expressed in the *Monetary Times* on January 21, 1870.

contend, as Denison wrote, secretly, to Foster.[17] But things seemed finally to go their way. The Wolseley expedition was despatched to Red River as an earnest of the government's intentions, Riel fled to the United States, and the territory was incorporated as a province. "I think things will come out all right in Manitoba yet. . . ." wrote Denison complacently to Mair on November 10, 1870.[18] In truth, only the first chapter of the tragic story had been written but few, if any, could have foreseen the eventuality.

IV

It was the events at Red River more than anything else that converted a spate of individuals, sometimes isolated but sharing in the diffusive sentiment of nationalism, into a concerted movement. Of the five who had met in Morgan's rooms in Ottawa in 1868, none ever drifted completely away, at least in sympathy, and there were none who did not remain at least fitfully or remotely as participating members; but only Foster and Denison lived in Toronto, which was, and would continue for sociological reasons, to be the dynamic centre of the movement. Soon the group was augmented to the number of twelve – the Twelve Apostles – a nickname for a still unorganized group. But the challenge in the west could be met only by organization, and the response was the North-West Emigration Aid Society under the presidency of Dr. William Canniff, and with J. E. McDougall, William McDougall's son, as one of the secretaries. Perhaps the members themselves could not have predicted the outcome in 1869-1870, but the logic of events would soon render the Society merely a first step towards the entrance of Canada First, as an organized entity, into party politics, a step which was to expose a basic contradiction in the philosophy of the movement.

It soon became almost equally inevitable that a clear statement of viewpoint should be enunciated, and this was provided by Foster's address, printed and published in 1871, but never delivered orally. It seems to have been the first statement affording the public a comprehensive idea of what was in the

[17]W. A. Foster Papers, No. 46, George T. Denison to W. A. Foster, April 11, 1870 (private).

[18]The Charles Mair Papers, (Queen's University Library), November 10, 1870.

minds of the Nationalists. Entitled *Canada First, or the new Nationality,* it opened with a summary of events of the French regime in Canada, exhibiting a point of view which has long since become commonplace, but which must appear nonetheless remarkable to a reader of the sixties and seventies of the Twentieth Century, accustomed as he would be to the slogans of such groups as the Quebec separatists. Foster writes of the conflict between the French and British in the colonial wars, not from the outlook of his own ethnic group, but from that of their antagonists, the French. A careful reading will reveal that this is so, but perhaps it is most evident in his reference to the Expulsion of the Acadians from Nova Scotia in 1755. A sociologist might express the fact by referring to the French, as far as early Canadian history is concerned, as Foster's "in-group," the ethnic element with which he identifies himself nationally, simply because it was the French who then inhabited what came in the fullness of time to be the "national" territory. It seems safe to say that such a "territorial" component of the English-Canadian sense of identity is to be found widely diffused in the thought of this people.[19] No ethnic bias is to be found in Foster's citations of individual achievement gleaned from Henry Morgan's biographical record of the Canadian past.

Perhaps it is because of a third component, in addition to the territorial and political, that Foster felt able to look at the matter in this fashion; for it seems clear that he felt the Norman and Celtic stocks of French Canada to be essentially akin to the peoples deriving their ancestry from the British Isles. The difficulty from the standpoint of modern anthropology is that the "racial" component which Foster believed to be common to both the French and English-speaking peoples of the Dominion, and which went, in his mind, by Haliburton's designation of "the Men of the North," is probably fictional on two counts, since inadequate evidence exists to prove that the various stocks that peopled France and Britain were sufficiently homogeneous to be classed as a racial grouping. A more serious question would arise from the complete irrelevancy of the factor of "race." On the contrary it must be assumed that even if such homogeneity could be found to have existed, it would not account in any way for the nature and quality of linguistic or

[19]Foster's territorial frame of reference differs from that of John Richard Green, for whom the ethnic group provides continuity. The latter's starting point is thus North Germany and Denmark rather than the British Isles.

cultural factors, since there is no evidence of "race" or physique varying concomitantly with mental constitution. Such considerations, however, were far from clear to Foster and his contemporaries, and he was thus not aware of the fallacy inherent in this way of regarding the qualities of Canada's peoples.

He was undoubtedly on surer ground in assuming that a truly national feeling and outlook must involve a careful and altogether appreciative knowledge of the great men and women of Canadian history, and the heroic deeds accomplished within the confines of the nation. He felt also that in an egalitarian country of the New World, such as Canada, the class attitudes inherited from the European past, should be repudiated. It was, he wrote, "not well for us to set up the mummied idols of a buried past as objects of worship. . . ." On the contrary, Canadians should go about strengthening the foundations of their own identity. ". . . strength comes from within . . .", but how can such strength be effectually invoked in the service of the Nation? The answer implies risks that men of courage must run. "When we have grown so wise as to do everything by line and rule, and so discreet as to yield to the demands of force, we shall have attained a degree of perfection incompatible with a free existence." We must not condemn the acts of rashness and daring by which we have been saved and which have been performed on our behalf in moments of crisis as when the invaders were repelled in 1812. For such acts of heroism we must feel gratitude, for, he wrote, "let us not give occasion for the imputation of want of heart." To Foster the supreme illustration of heroism was to be found in what was to him the martyrdom of Thomas Scott, which marked not only the moment of crisis of the Red River Rebellion, but the supreme instant of Canada's new national existence. Modern scholarship has rendered Scott a curious and equivocal candidate for the honour bestowed on him by Foster and by so many of his contemporaries. In contrast there will be few if any who will cavil at the name of Thomas d'Arcy McGee, the name most revered by Foster and his fellow nationalists. It was this man

"who strove with all the power of genius to convert the stagnant pool of politics into a stream of living water; who dared to be national in the face of living selfishness and impartially liberal in the face of sectarian strife; who . . . sowed broadcast the seeds of a higher national life, and with persuasive eloquence drew us closer together as a people, pointing out to each what was good in the other . . . one who breathed into our new Dominion the spirit of a proud self-reliance, and first taught Canadians to respect themselves."

Thus one must not only enter imaginatively, ("thrilling in every nerve," that is by immediate experience), into heroic deeds that exemplify the national spirit at its highest, we must also, as McGee's words implied, cleave to the moral element. "Let each of us have faith in the rest," Foster urged, "and cultivate a broad feeling of regard for mutual welfare, as being those who are building up a fabric that is destined to endure."[20]

It was an expression of nationalism that was saved by that ethical component which has been found to be so uniformly absent from those, on that account, disreputable manifestations that have marred the course of recent history. It was not, however, as should be evident, a manifesto embodying specific proposals such as a political party might seek to implement. Canada First moved closer to such an enunciation when it supported one of its members, Thomas Moss, of whose firm Foster was a member, as Liberal candidate in a bye-election in the West Riding of Toronto in the autumn of 1873. While the nationalists did not merge their organization with that of Moss, they held a meeting on his behalf, at which Foster spoke, and undoubtedly contributed to his victory. No doubt this experience helped to give rise to the question as to whether the movement should be converted into a political party competing for office with the old-line parties. As opposition to party government was one of the chief aspects of its philosophy, it was no wonder that, when the decision to organize as such was made, some members, notably George T. Denison, felt they could not go along with it. Foster, on the other hand, undoubtedly felt that, if it was to be effectual, it had no alternative but to do so, and when the Canadian National Association was finally formed on January 6, 1874, it was Foster who had the chief hand, so it is believed, in drafting its programme.

Many Canadians felt keenly what they regarded as the sacrifice of Canadian interests in the negotiation of the Treaty of Washington between Great Britain and the United States in 1871, and the expressed desire for a Canadian voice in the drafting of treaties affecting Canada is understandably included in the Association's statement of policy. The nativist feeling, embodied in the idea of a militia commanded by officers who

[20]First published in the *Globe*, afterwards as a pamphlet, it is included in *Canada First, A Memorial of the late William A. Foster, Q.C.*, (Toronto, 1890).

were citizens of the Dominion, may have owed something to the snubs which Denison believed, undoubtedly correctly, that he had received on more than one occasion at the hands of British military officialdom.[21] Apart from proposals for constitutional reform, some of which have long-since been achieved, was that respecting the "imposition of duties for Revenue so adjusted as to afford every possible encouragement for Native Industry." Such an idea undoubtedly reflects the concern of the professional and business class of the country for the promotion of industrial enterprise, and has been regarded by some scholars, notably the late William Stewart Wallace, as having anticipated the National Policy that carried the Conservatives into office in 1879.[22]

Such an enunciation of policy was given a wide currency not only by the Canadian National Association, but also through the formation of National Clubs, ostensibly social in intent, and by the founding of the periodical named *The Nation* early in 1874 which, while never an official organ of the new party, as the editor felt called upon so frequently to assert, certainly reflected the views of the Canada First people. Several persons of distinction became frequent contributors including Goldwin Smith, the eminent and former Regius Professor of History at Oxford, who supported the Canada First people after taking up residence in Toronto in 1871.[23] Foster and Goldwin Smith formed a friendship, shortly after that time, which survived

[21]*Ibid.* In the Introduction, Goldwin Smith wrote of the effect of the withdrawal of the socially ascendant British officers on the native-born who rose in the social scale as a result. At the meeting held in support of Thomas Moss's candidacy for a vacant seat in the House of Commons, W. H. Howland raised a storm by attacking the idea of a titled aristocracy which many regarded as anti-British. J. G. Snell, "West Toronto By-Election of 1873, and Thomas Moss," *Ontario History, Vol.* LVIII (1966), pp. 237-257. See also C. N. Hougham, "Canada First: A Minority Party in microcosm," *Canadian Journal of Economics and Political Science,* Vol. XIX (1953), p. 178, where he states Howland was never a member of Canada First, which is difficult to accept.

[22]For the complete platform, see W. S. Wallace, "The Growth of Canadian National Feeling," *Canadian Historical Review,* (June, 1920), pp. 155, 157, 158.

[23]In her *Goldwin Smith/Victorian Liberal,* (Toronto, 1957), Elizabeth Wallace states that as a newcomer to Canada, Goldwin Smith considered himself disqualified from joining Canada First, although he supported it financially and with his pen, as he warmly sympathized with its objectives.

many vississitudes including, much later, a wide divergence of political views, for Foster would never have departed from his original conception of Canada as a self-governing nation associated by strong bonds of friendship with the Mother Country. Commercial Union with the United States, supported by Goldwin Smith, had become a heated political issue by the time of Foster's death in 1888, but in the early seventies Smith seems to have believed an independent Canada a distinct possibility. However, he was accused by the *Globe,* and indeed party newspapers on both sides of the political fence, of favouring Canadian autonomy as a prelude to annexation. The *Globe,* more than any other paper, was particularly fearful that the new political party founded by the nationalists might cause a dangerous split in Liberal ranks, especially when Edward Blake resigned from the Mackenzie Government and revealed a disposition to take over the leadership of the Canada First party, even before delivering his famous speech at Aurora on October 3, 1874, in the course of which he made an eloquent plea for the adoption of the programme of the Nationalists. During all this period Foster continued to ply his pen as a journalist, and to work quietly, as was his custom, through correspondence and informal gatherings, for the cause which was so dear to him.[24] As late as the summer of 1875 he felt optimistic as to the outcome of the efforts which he and his colleagues had made; but failure was in the offing. The bitter and scathing attacks on Smith especially by the *Globe,* the defection of Blake who in the autumn of 1875 returned to the Liberal fold and re-entered the cabinet, the demise of the nationalist-oriented newspaper, the *Liberal,* and of *The Nation* at the end of that year, quashed his hopes and those of his associates. By 1876 he had relinquished the editorship of the *Monetary Times,* and in the ensuing year, following his marriage, he turned his attention increasingly to family and professional matters.[25] Nevertheless,

[24]He was kept informed of the amnesty question by Schultz, Denison, and others. On at least one occasion he addressed the Canadian National Association on the subject. See *Canada First, etc., op. cit.,* (Toronto, 1890), pp. 57-86.

[25]Charles Mair Papers, (Queen's University Library) Henry J. Morgan to Charles Mair, January 25, 1878, "The little corner room is working wonders. Only fancy George Denison going all the way to St. Petersberg, and carrying off the prize! [offered by the Czar for the best work on the history of cavalry]. Foster is married and has become a perfect model for all husbands." But he continued to the end of his life to work in the interest of his friends. For example see the W. A. Foster Papers, J. C. Schultz to Foster, Ottawa, 16

his warm friendship with his original colleagues was maintained to the end of his life. Their correspondence with each other was often jocular, and it is not surprising to find Charles Mair writing to Denison, at one point in the course of it:

"Foster, I have had some letters from full of nerves and hieroglyphics—he has fallen into a sort of Coptic penmanship which I cannot unravel. I suppose it has grown out of incessant pleadings which no one is expected to understand. I have heard of a lawyer who had a hand which only his clerk could understand, another which only himself could understand, and another which neither himself, his clerk, nor anybody else could understand. The latter is the hand Foster reserves for his friends – He will find a more distinct penmanship exists when 'The Books are opened' – give him my warmest remembrances."[26]

The Books were opened sooner than anyone expected. Working under great strain in the autumn of 1888, as solicitor in the liquidation proceedings of the Central Bank, he caught a cold, came down with typhoid, and died on November 1st. Typical of the letters received by Mrs. Foster after her husband's death, was that from Charles Mair written from Prince Albert, N.W.T., on August 13, 1889. "Your husband's death has taken something from my life which can never be replaced on earth — one of its true friendships. We lived apart, but our sympathies and feelings were similar, and my love for him was of a kind deeper even than brotherly love. . . ."[27]

The significance of the career of this man who died on that day in 1888 is difficult to assess, but it is probable that it was far greater than might be thought from the fact that he never held public office, appeared infrequently before audiences, and preferred almost at all times to shun the limelight unless he thought that by going before the public he might advance the

April, 1885 (private) saying he has made his first speech in the Senate, and asking him to get a good coverage of it in the *Mail*, *Christian Guardian* and the *Week*. Schultz wrote to Foster January 22, 1888 from Ottawa, "Sending grizzly bear skin from Rockies for Xmas present to you my old and tried friend." . . . "He is an Elderly Norwester a 'rale old Grizzler' and has head and claws complete. He and Mrs. Schultz send best wishes to Mr. and Mrs. Foster."

[20]George T. Denison Papers, (Public Archives of Canada), pp. 388-399.

[27]W. A. Foster Papers, Charles Mair to Mrs. W. A. Foster, Prince Albert, August 13, 1889. For a full account of Mair's part in Canada First, see Norman Shrive, *Charles Mair, Literary Nationalist,* Toronto, 1965.

cause in which he believed with such a high degree of sincerity. All the evidence seems to indicate that he never deviated from his idea that Canada should remain independent of the United States, maintain the British connection, though autonomous and freely associated with the United Kingdom. Thus, like those of great repute − Baldwin, Howe, Durham, Monck[28] − he was a prophet of the Commonwealth. But it must also be said that, when one probes beneath the florid style in which he sometimes expressed himself, one finds, especially in his Canada First address, a statement in all probability unique in Canadian political literature. We seem to see that to be a true nationalist involved a creative act on the part of each individual, in the course of which the highest attributes of the personality are transformed, the divisive forces within the country are neutralized, the debased colonial status is transcended, and a new man is born. By such means may nations be made, he seems to be saying as we read that half-forgotten address of 1871. Now, when after all these years the existence of Canada is again challenged, one may well feel inclined to the thought that, if Canada survives, it will be because of men such as he.

[28]W. L. Morton, "Lord Monck, His Friends and the Nationalization of the British Empire," in *Character and Circumstance, Essays in Honour of Donald Grant Creighton*, ed. John S. Moir, (Toronto, 1970), pp. 37-56.

9. Canada First:
The Dissident Press
And the Public Image*

I: 1874-1875

The nationalist sentiment, particularly in Ontario, that both accompanied and followed in the wake of Confederation, was brought into sharper focus, than might otherwise have been the case, by a series of occurrences that took place during the early phases of the existence of the new Dominion. The first of these was the Red River Rebellion; but no sooner had the excitement, which this event had engendered, begun to subside than there occurred a by-election in the West Riding of Toronto that revealed the influence of the same nationalist movement that had but recently aggravated the disturbance in the West. It was not, however, until the autumn of 1874 that a sharp controversy in the press of Ontario appeared to many to presage a crisis in the affairs of the Liberal Party and even affect the future of both old-line parties in unforseeable ways. All this was brought to a head by the speech given at Aurora, Ontario, on October 3, 1874, by Edward Blake, as a consequence of which a feeling began to grow in some quarters that a number of those who had hitherto supported the Conservative Party might follow Blake if he should cut loose from the Grits and identify himself with Canada First, as the views expressed by him on that occasion led many to believe that he might. Here, on the lips of one of the most distinguished persons on the Canadian political scene, were most of the policies which the young men of the movement had declared for in their public utterances for several years past: the federation of the empire,

*The best account of the growth of English-Canadian nationalism is that by W. Stewart Wallace, "The Growth of Canadian-National Feeling," *Canadian Historical Review,* Vol. I, No. 2 (1920), pp. 136-165 – later expanded into a book under the same title and published in Toronto in 1927.

compulsory voting, extension of the franchise, minority representation, Senate reform, and above all, the cultivation of national spirit. "We must find some common ground on which to unite," Blake urged, "some common aspiration to be shared, and I think it can be alone found in the cultivation of that spirit."[1]

It was this speech more than anything else that caused widespread questioning as to whether the long ascendency of George Brown over the affairs of the Liberal party might not be threatened by the turn of events, and even be drawing to a close. As to the possible emergence of a new party, the Ottawa *Free Press* observed in its edition of Monday, October 5, that the *Globe* "affects to consider the existence of such a party a myth, and yet the rabid desire which it evinces to prevent the shadow from taking form and substance, shows that it sees in that movement a vitality which is destined to make it a power in the land." Clearly not being an admirer of the tactics of the editor of that newspaper, it added, "The proposed objectives of the societies formed for the promotion of Canadian sentiment are so utterly foreign to those attributed to them by the *Globe* as to make it a matter of wonderment that it should have the hardihood to so grossly misinterpret them."[2] The London *Free Press* saw Canada First as a real threat to the dominance of George Brown, and was quick to discern that the *Globe's* reference to Howland and Goldwin Smith as probable leaders was intended "to conceal another which it dreads to see associated with such

---

[1]This was by no means the first indication of Blake's interest in Canada First, for on April 23, 1874, Lord Dufferin reported to the Colonial Secretary that

He is inclined to put himself at the head of a new party, which has been lately organized in Canada, under the auspices of Goldwin Smith, whose ultimate object seems to be independence. 'Canada First' is the motto they have chosen, and one never knows into what dimensions a political germ of this kind may develop. As yet their manifestations have been very weak and foolish, but they have some able men among them, and the most promising of the rising generation are supposed to sympathize with them – at all events as Blake is both able and honest, and probably at the moment the most able man in Canada, it would be unwise to indispose him unnecessarily to the English connection.

The Dufferin-Carnarvon Correspondence, 1874-1878, eds. C. W. Kiewiet and F. H. Underhill, the Champlain Society, (Toronto, 1955), p. 28.

[2]The W. A. Foster Papers, Scrapbook, The *Free Press,* Ottawa, October 5, 1874.

a movement . . ." No doubt was left in anyone's mind as to the identity of this individual. "Wanted a leader — Edward Blake! What says the *Globe?* Let it consult its inner consciousness, read his Aurora speech — then say!" Under the heading of "The Blake Bombshell" two days later, *The Mail* took due note of a "Recent Mackenzie colleague" avowing his support for Hare's doctrine of the representation of minorities and the doing away with the crown-appointed Senate.[3] Needless to say, *The Nation,* which reflected the views of Canada First, came out on October 8, in support of Blake on Senate reform, noting that what was needed was election of its members by the legislatures of the provinces.[4] There was, as a matter of fact, nothing new in that, Brown having been almost alone an advocate of retaining a crown-nominated chamber. More nearly novel with respect to representation was the system whereby "each voter may vote for anyone he pleases and give his vote, should it not be required for his first choice, to second, third, or fourth candidates in the order of his preference".[5]

This issue was inclined to become technical, unlike the question of future relations with the Mother Country, which evoked heated controversy and gave rise to misrepresentation and invective. It was perhaps a little difficult to know exactly what was in the minds of the members of the Canada First Group on this fundamental question. It may have been partly a question of semantics. Certainly it was not always clear what

[3]The W. A. Foster Papers, Scrapbook, 63, The *Mail,* October 7, 1874. On October 23, 1874, The Berlin *Telegraph* declared that it had little faith in Hare's Theory for the representation of minorities, but claimed that as one of Blake's eminence had broached it, it should be discussed.

[4]See also *The Nation,* November 5, 1874 on the shortcomings of the Senate. In obvious reference to Brown's support of a nominated body, *The Nation* on November 5, 1874, published an editorial entitled "The Nominated Chamber" in which it attributed the nominative principle to Burke and the reactionaries "who took advantage of the French revolution to inculcate arbitrary principles of government with the view of preventing reform. Canada," continued the writer, "was the field in which they first essayed a distant and safe experiment. It was a retrograde movement, in opposition to that which had had course in a majority of the old colonies; which had been better suited to the genius of those colonies than nomination would have been; and which had not, Pitt notwithstanding, been the cause, or a cause of the American revolution".

[5]The W. A. Foster Papers, Scrapbook 99, The Almonte *Gazette,* October 30, 1874.

was meant by "independence" and what by "Imperial Federation". Independence was supposed by some observers, — or at least there were some who affected to believe it — to be a prelude to annexation to the United States. On October 8, 1874, however, *The Nation* scouted the thought. "The only sense", it wrote, "in which Canadian nationality has been said, even by the prophets of evil, to mean annexation is that the Americans would use force to bring about that result. Mr. Blake, while showing the great improbability of any such attempt being made, expresses his faith in the future of Canada as a nation". The frequent references, in the press of the day, to the sacrifice of Canadian interests in the negotiations and terms of the Treaty of Washington of 1871, has long been recognized as one of the roots of nationalist sentiment at that time, and it was rather to counter the danger of annexation that Foster and his associates were intent upon a greater measure of autonomy for Canada. Whether or not this was exactly what Blake had in mind was a matter of speculation. *The Mail* on October 17 doubted that there was a genuine concurrence with his views by the Canada First people, since he favoured Imperial Federation, whereas Goldwin Smith, regarded widely as the mentor of the movement, in addressing "a little Mutual Admiration Society at the Queen's Hotel," came out against it. It was also doubtful, in the mind of the editor of the London *Free Press,* as to whether Blake's national sentiment was identical with that of Canada First. On October 9, he observed that "Every effort has been made to prevent Mr. Blake from allying himself with this party, as such a step would be tantamount to cutting himself adrift from Mackenzie and his incapables, of which he has hitherto been the right bower." But the *Globe,* he believed, has made one of those grave blunders for which it was famous.

While its most strenuous efforts have been directed to keep the followers of Mr. Brown from associating the name of Mr. Blake with the Canada First, it tacitly acknowledges this connection, by greeting Mr. Blake's solemn utterances upon the desirability of a 'national' sentiment as essentially equivalent to those narrow views that have been enunciated as the basis of that new party – Canada First. This is a most serious blunder indeed, as it renders nugatory all the efforts that have been made for many months past to prevent this alliance between Mr. Blake and the Young Canada Party, and virtually acknowledges that Mr. Blake, at Aurora, instead of preaching the pure unadulterated Gospel of the Grits, stood forth as the accredited herald of this soul-destroying heresy – the doctrine of Canada First.

Again on October 18, the same editor denied the *Globe's* allegation that Goldwin Smith and the advocates of the Blake reforms aimed at independence and ultimate annexation. Neither would he admit that Smith was the leader of the Canada First group. The *Globe,* he said, chose to castigate Blake "over Mr. Smith's shoulder." He found it amusing to see the *Globe,* a few days after its savage attack on "Know-Nothingism," sneering at Smith because of his short residence in the country.[6] The *Globe* wished "to summarily snuff out the lights of free discussion," a policy from which he believed there was nothing useful to be gained.

The *Mail* and the *Free Press* were not alone in doubting the identification of Blake's views with those of Canada First. On October 20, the Ottawa *Times* expressed the belief that it would "not be at all difficult to show that neither is Mr. Blake a 'Canada First' man, nor does that party have much ground for hoping that he ever will be," a discerning remark, considered in the light of what was to come. It would be quite wrong for the Conservatives, wrote another observer, to think that Blake meant to desert the Liberals, or that he would become the leader of Canada First, although forward-looking Liberals favoured it. This conclusion that Mr. Blake's political feelings "are estranged from the Liberal Party, and now lean towards the former baby organization, speaks little for their acumen. Since, moreover, Canada First had arisen from a distrust of partyism, how, he asked, could it eradicate the defects of partyism by the establishment of a third party? This was ". . . an application of the homeopathic doctrine at once laughable and absurd."[7] Pursuing the same theme still further, it was noted

[6]To select a Protestant Englishman such as Smith as an object of attack on this score was a curious reversal of the philosophy of the American party that went under this name. With respect to the allegation of "nativism," see the Montreal *Witness,* October 10, 1874, and *The Nation,* October 22, 1874, which indulged in heavy irony at the expense of the *Globe.*

[7]The W. A. Foster Papers, Scrapbook, 84. The Montreal *Witness* felt that "few will be able to see so clearly" as Smith appeared to do "the way our constitution can be worked otherwise than by means of party organization." (W. A. Foster Papers, "Scrapbook," 97). The evils were evident to the *Argus* of Oakville (October 23, 1874), a case in point being the support by the MacKenzie government of the Brown-Fish Reciprocity Treaty. *The Nation* was something less than clairvoyant when it stated on October 8th, 1874, that "A break-up of the old parties is now certain." In 1882 Goldwin Smith was still thinking in the old vein. On June 27 of that year he wrote to

that Blake's support of Reciprocity was genuine, and if he deprecated the public discussion that had taken place in Canada, it was because he feared that the tenor of remarks that had been made on this measure might lessen its chances of passing the United States Senate.

It may here be said that no one who has ever studied Blake's career could possibly suppose that he regarded Reciprocity as a step towards annexation, and it is equally clear that he did not desire the absorption of Canada by the American republic. On the contrary he wished to perpetuate the British connection, but in an altered form; one that provided that Canada would be the mistress of her domestic affairs, but also that she would have a voice in shaping the Empire's relations with other powers. The importance of this question was recognized by the editor of the Berlin *Telegraph* who urged the Canadian public to give ear to the discussion of Canada's position as a dependency, with no treaty-making powers and her "liability at a moment's notice to be plunged into foreign complications which she may have had no part in creating."[8] Public discussion of this question continued into the New Year, and on January 15, 1875 *The Nation* noted Blake's stated desire for open discussion of "independence" as a step towards what he avowed to be desirable, namely a great federal British Empire. Throughout the winter, the *Globe*, in pursuit of its objectives, endeavoured to stifle such discussion, but without success, for, as *The Nation* noted on May 21, "The veto placed by self-constituted authority on the discussion by Canadians of the greatest of Canadian questions has failed to command obedience;" and on June 4, *The Nation* recorded the attack made by the *Globe* on Dr. Canniff who, although a declared opponent of "independence" and annexation, had dared to indulge in a little patriotism. Even Dominion Day was not immune, as is evident from *The Nation's* caustic comments, on June 11, on George Brown's

Foster, "I am sorry that the hold of party should still be as strong, but the end will come. Either the end of party will come, or the end of elective government." Foster had evidently expressed a belief in political preferrment for Smith at the hands of the Conservatives, to which Smith replied, "Can so shrewd a man and so experienced a political observer as you think it possible that John A. should offer a Senatorship to me or to any independent citizen whatever might be his qualification. The appointments are simply a portion of the party bribery game and will never be given on any other ground." (W. A. Foster Papers, Smith to Foster, Buxton, England, June 27, 1882).

[8]October 23, 1874.

ridicule of the idea of celebrating the birthday of the Canadian Union. As stated on July 9, *"The Globe* kept up its benevolent efforts to produce a fiasco, clearly perceiving that patriotism must be the death of Gritism, and the firemen were withdrawn from the celebrations as a result of pressure from those who preferred celebrating the mutual butcheries of Irishmen two centuries before to the union of Canadians in a common country at the present day." Nevertheless the events of Toronto's Dominion Day celebrations did not go unnoticed in far away Saint John, New Brunswick, where the *News* of that city remarked that "The Torontoese of all classes and creeds came out strong on Dominion Day. They had processions, orations, pic-nics [sic], and open air games, and a good time generally. The orations were delivered outdoors in the Queen's Park. Mr. W. H. Howland, the President of the Canada First Club, presided on the occasion and delivered a speech. He pronounced very strongly against annexation and for the British connection," as long, adds the reporter, "as it might seem convenient – at least so we interpret the tenor of his remarks as reported in the Toronto papers."[9] Some of the ostensible ambiguities in the Canada First programme were bothersome. It was a little difficult he wrote, to understand what these Canada First patriots would be at. "On some points of their creed they do speak out with clearness. In respect to others they seem to hold the doctrine of reserve, and speak with studied vagueness." This vagueness left doubts as to whether "independence" might not mean increased, perhaps complete, autonomy, but nevertheless a condition not incompatible with "imperial federation" if autonomous powers were exercised in such a way as to develop an intra-imperial structure as an agency of the various sovereignties. The ambiguities that appeared to many to exist in the professions of the new movement stemmed, it would seem, from divergent views on this question, that is to say, as to whether the British nations would form a concert or association such as was to devolve, in due course, in the form of dominion status, or develop a more closely-knit structure in the interest of common action in international affairs.

In the realm of imperial relations one cannot say that Goldwin Smith's views were either unvarying or exactly similar to those of the founders of the Canada First Movement. It is certain that at a later date a wide cleavage existed between Colonel George Denison and himself on this question. For the

[9]St. John, N.B. *News,* as reported in *The Nation,* July 16, 1875.

moment it is necessary to enquire further into the *Globe's* decision to attack Smith rather than Blake, in the months following the Aurora speech, and to try to determine as precisely as possible the relationship between Smith and the Canada First men at this time. In relation to these questions it has already been intimated, that the *Globe* had chosen to attack Blake indirectly, that is, through Smith, according to widely held opinions, although they varied somewhat as to the precise motives that underlay such a lavish expenditure of printer's ink. To the *Home Journal* it appeared to be because of Blake's "unpardonable offence of declaring himself in favour of a reform of the Senate," in spite of the fact that a majority of the Reform party supported such a policy. One observer expressed puzzlement as to why "certain journals" handled Blake with such extreme caution "while at the same moment the vials of personal vituperation are poured out upon the head of Prof. Smith." Earlier in the year Canada First had been almost beneath the notice of the *Globe*, and on October 19 came the frank admission that the nationalist movement was not a danger in itself, but only because of the uses to which it might be put. It was not originally, so the argument ran, an offshoot of a scheming brain, but it had become so. It had ceased to be harmless when adopted by Goldwin Smith, "and adopting him as its high priest means action at once aggressive and dangerous." Friends had said that he had recanted his views in favour of Canadian independence on his coming to Canada, and that he no longer believed that the Empire was disintegrating and that the colonies should go their separate ways, free to form other alliances. But now as president of the National Club he reaffirms his belief in independence, and opposes Imperial Federation. Thus is Canada First unmasked as a proponent of Canadian independence from Britain, a stand denied, the editor noted, by many supporters of the Nationalist movement.[10] In commenting on the *Globe's* contention that Canada was not a nation "except by a mere play upon the words," *The Nation* whose very name implied the existence of such an entity, harked back to the statement in the *Globe* of September 4 that "The nation as now constituted is still so young that no previous Governor-General had the opportunity Lord Dufferin has had of witnessing the 'confederated commonwealth' throb with a consciousness of its own nationalized existence." This sense of nationality, the *Globe* had written in

[10]W. A. Foster Papers, "Scrapbook," 105.

that pre-Aurora era, had had the effect of making Canadians aware of the advantages of being part of a greater nation. When the *Globe* then stated that "we are a nation with an individuality of our own," how can it accuse distinguished men, who say the same thing, of being annexationists? How could it, within a little while, hint at revolution? Canada First, the *Globe* had asserted, "might be the fathers and founders of a new nationality, but they might also be simply mischief-makers, whose insignificance and powerlessness were their sole protection. . . ."

On October 24 the *Leader* rendered its own version of the affair. Brown, in alarm at the evident menace to the Brown-Mackenzie ascendency over the Liberal Party, was studiously playing down the causes of division between himself and Blake, and was turning his guns on Smith to divert attention from the rift in the Liberal ranks, although in truth there was little difference between the views of Blake and Smith, except perhaps as to the form that changing intra-imperial relations might take. The *Globe,* it was said, had just discovered that "independence" was an evil, certain to lead to annexation. L. S. Huntington, who was stated to be an annexationist, had been approved by Brown when a cabinet minister; and Senator Christie, whom the *Leader* clearly regarded as another of the ilk, "had become all but a citizen of the United States."

II

With Smith's election as president of the National Club the attack upon him mounted in intensity. In a long and detailed *Globe* editorial on October 27, it was noted that the Canada First people had

carried – in a vote on their programme – British connection by a vote of four only . . . they had chosen as their standard bearer . . . one whose all but exclusive claim to political prominence or place lies in the persistency with which he has advocated the up-break [sic] of the British Empire. . . . Mr. Smith has come into a peaceful community to do his best for the furtherance of a course which means simply revolution.

Only the insignificance of Canada First would save Smith and his colleagues from being tried as traitors, and from a traitor's doom. "Mr. Goldwin Smith as leader of an armed revolution would not" in the opinion of the editor, "be a very heroic spectacle, but to witness this Canada is now invited, with what result we shall soon see." Smith, who happened to be in Montreal, wrote to W. A. Foster on the following day in an optimistic and derisive vein. "The madness of the *Globe* is about the most cheering sign I have seen. *The Nation* has a fair opportunity of showing up a *Liberal*, and an old demagogue who incites to personal violence against another Liberal for differing from himself." He suggests that the best reply to the *Globe* might be to reprint the speech which he himself had recently given on the current issues, adding "We must be temperate and cautious of course, but we must show no want of spirit or the enemy will get the better of us." "Though Goldwin Smith had been proscribed," wrote *The Nation*, "it was the dawn that broke from Aurora that first disturbed the sleepers." But the independence that was preached was independence from the tyranny of the *Globe*. We are not advocates of independence from the Mother Country, *The Nation* stated, but if its advocacy be a crime, that crime was licensed by Queen Victoria who knighted A. T. Galt "with the express understanding that it should not interfere with the liberty he claimed in advocating the independence of Canada."[11]

It is difficult not to conclude that the *Globe* was deliberately trying to goad Smith into some rash statement which would condemn him out of his own mouth. Its failure to do so may well have prompted the excesses to which it became increasingly prone throughout 1875. On February 20 the allegation that he had preached treason was repeated, and, observed that organ, "were he logically consistent and physically brave . . . he would be looking to 'armed revolution' if necessary for the accomplishment of his purposes. No one could dream of his taking the field, but he might invite others to do so."

Having asserted so often that Smith was the founder and leader of Canada First, the *Globe* may have come almost to believe that this was so. But it could not seem altogether to dispel a lingering doubt, and it must have been a very aggravating thing to find oneself in a prolonged bout of fisticuffs with an unidentifiable opponent. In the circumstances it seemed necessary to assume much that was not susceptible of proof and to spice its assumptions with what it no doubt deemed to be the requisite amount of *argumentum ad hominum*. In illustration it may be noted that at one point the public were confronted with the remark that national sentiment

[11]*The Nation,* October 29, 1874.

originated with a man who is not a Canadian, who is not satisfied with England, and who has abandoned the United States. He began this discussion. He indoctrinated a party of young men. He has had influence in some measure upon Mr. Blake. He has been instrumental in founding the new Journal. He has been made president of the National Club.

Such assertions continued to be made notwithstanding repeated denials. On December 3, 1874, *The Nation* stated categorically that Goldwin Smith was not the founder of Canada First, and *The Nation* was not his organ.[12] *The Nation* however, seemed somehow to imply that it was privy to his mental processes when it denied that the distinguished professor wished to sever ties with the Mother Country. Be that as it may, it recorded on December 31 the *Globe's* accusation that Smith was a "covert traitor" for writing an editorial which in fact he did not write; and as late as August 20, 1875 it still felt it necessary to deny that Smith was its editor, and that he was responsible for the articles that appeared in its pages, as the *Globe* continued to assert in the face of repeated statements to the contrary. "The conduct of the *Globe* in this matter is simply contemptible," wrote the Orangeville *Advertiser*.[13]

As personal abuse is often inclined to be repetitious, there would be little purpose in following the course of the *Globe's* utterances on Goldwin Smith for the balance of the year 1875 were it not desirable to indicate how widespread were the adverse reactions on the part of a large number of newspapers from all over the province. There were perhaps some minor variations on what had become a shopworn theme. The Berlin *Telegraph* on June 18, 1875, in reference to a pamphlet by Dr. Caniff, a well-known member of the Canadian National Association, cited the *Mail's* faint praise of that publication as a "pleasant and harmless" contribution to the national literature of the day. But, wrote the commentator, were it even seditious as a Fenian Manifesto, there would be no excuse for the *Globe's* assailing Goldwin Smith over Dr. Canniff's shoulder, "dragging his name and antecedents through two or three columns of spiteful criticism" and charging him with

[12]It had already, on October 22, 1874, been equally categorical in denying what some students of the subject have continued to the present time to assert, namely, that *The Nation* was the organ of Canada First. On that date it stated that it was "not the organ of Canada First, the Canadian National Association or the National Club," and that it did not assume to speak for Blake or Smith.

[13]Quoted in *The Nation*, August 20, 1875.

offences wholly foreign to the subject under discussion, which were in any case, gross exaggerations, such as that he had conspired against the peace of the Canadian people and was "confessedly guilty, in words at least, of everything short of high treason." Apparently the Berlin *Telegraph* considered a note of levity in order, when it observed that far from being the revolutionary alleged by the *Globe,* when Smith visited Berlin, Ontario, "No one heard of his inciting the people to revolt, of his mining the Court House, robbing the bank, lying in wait for the Royal Mail with a sixteen shooter. When he walked the streets he was not observed to trail a British flag in the dust with one hand and bear aloft a glittering American eagle in the other." Disclaiming any sympathy for Smith's views on parties and on certain abstract political questions, the editor nevertheless defended his right to hold and express his opinions freely. He called for fair play in place of spiteful persecution of a "gentleman of splendid abilities and high literary culture" who had contributed much to the ascendency of liberal principles and good government. The attacks on him were nothing less than degrading to the journalism of Canada. As for Dr. Canniff the *Globe* was said to have mixed up his views with those of others that were not his, as well as censuring Smith for an article with which, as it was afterwards shown, he had nothing to do. The *Globe* wound up, in the words of *The Liberal,* "with a mad bull-rush at the latter gentleman in the shape of a charge that his talk (though it has no evidence that it is his talk) means nothing but dismemberment and revolution. . . ." The Supreme Court Bill, then before the House, was supported by the *Globe,* although it embodied a principle that was equally revolutionary in character "being a sudden renunciation of one form of connection with the Crown." The *Globe,* stated *The Liberal,* was open to the charge of having done what it had accused Canniff and Smith of doing.[14] According to the Brockville *Recorder,* Smith had offended because of his view that party should not stand before country, that personal vituperation should give way to reasoning and logic, that as the Dominion grew in wealth and population, it might well be called upon to assume the responsibilities of an independent state. That the press should be argumentative rather than abusive, that a broader and more enlightened range of statesmanship should replace sectional prejudice, was to the *Globe* nothing but heresy and treason. The people would not believe

[14]Reprinted in *The Nation,* June 4, 1875.

this, and would no longer bow to Sir Oracle of any political stripe. Not that the editor of the *Recorder* had any objection to the annihilation of Smith's opinions, but it did state that it could not agree to the annihilation of the Professor himself.[15]

By late June, 1875, it was evident that some editors had begun to find the whole argument increasingly unrealistic. "A hundred years after every man now living in the Dominion shall have been consigned to the dust," wrote the Perth *Expositor*, "it is more than probable that British North America will still be part and parcel of the great Empire." The Grand River *Sachem* believed that the day when character could be blasted by *Globe* editorials had passed away forever.[16] This was all very well, but as W. A. Foster wrote to Charles Mair on August 10, 1875 "the fight hurts us as we do not trust our existence as a party to the Independence question. That question may be discussed ad nauseam but we do not wish to be bored to death with it."[17] By this time something like a score of major *Globe* editorials had been devoted to Goldwin Smith, and influential Liberals were reported to be endeavouring to induce the *Globe* to desist from its attacks.

III

On the basis of the foregoing survey of press coverage of the *Globe's* assault on Goldwin Smith and the Canada First group, and in the light of other well-known facts relating thereto, it may be possible to draw some tentative conclusion with respect to the whole matter. It is clear that Goldwin Smith was widely regarded as having initiated many of the ideas to which the Canada First group subscribed. Some observers moreover persisted in asserting in the face of repeated denials that the ex-professor had been the founder of the movement, and that he continued to be the paramount influence upon it. These views however must be set against Smith's own statement, made years later, which is quite categorical.

I was never a member of the "Canada First" Association, and the National Club, of which I was made President, was social, and

[15]Reprinted in *The Nation,* June 25, 1875.
[16]Reprinted in *The Nation,* July 2, 1875.
[17]Mair Papers (Queens University Library), W. A. Foster to Charles Mair, August 10, 1875.

intended to bring together Canadians of all parties. Nor had I anything to do with starting *The Nation,* though afterwards, when that journal was in difficulty, I was persuaded by some to help it with my pen. I also contributed a few articles to the Liberal.[18]

It is essential to enquire as to the degree to which it is possible, if at all, to square this statement with what was widely held to be the case by large sections of the Ontario press in the years 1874 and 1875. Could it have been technically true while at the same time misleading as to the actual role played by Smith in the Nationalist movement of that time? A question such as this suggests that the problem may be one of defining the sense in which something can be factually accurate, but at the same time exclusive of large pertinent realities. It would appear to be so with respect to Smith's influence on Canada First. He did not found, as no individual could, a political and cultural movement which resulted from a relatively widespread ferment in the Ontario of the Confederation era. The socio-political maturity of which it was an expression was the product of social forces long at work among the peoples of that province. In attributing so much to Goldwin Smith the *Globe* was guilty of having repeatedly uttered what was at best a half-truth. It must be admitted at the same time that a creative personality may exert such a profound influence upon his environment, especially if it accords well with his own temper and intent, as to impart to it an indelible stamp in terms of which it will tend strongly to be identified in the public mind. In his case he defined the problems which he believed to be paramount with a felicity of expression unmatched by his contemporaries, although the solutions which he proposed were unacceptable to many, perhaps a majority of the population of the province in his day. Nevertheless he raised the whole intellectual tone of the debate on the aims of the nationalists to such a height that he seemed to be the founder and editor of the periodical called *The Nation* when in fact he was not. He contributed to its effectiveness as a political journal although his name may never have been enrolled in the membership of the Canadian National Association. He became the President of the National Club in the autumn of 1874, but in his old age he no longer seemed conscious of the political implications attendant upon membership in the organization

[18]*Reminiscences by Goldwin Smith, D.C.L.,* Edited by Arnold Haultain, M.A., (New York, 1910), p. 443. See also his statement in *The Week,* November 4, 1886.

over which he had presided. He displayed throughout his life a curious ambivalence with respect to the measures that he tried to effect and the movements that he was concerned to promote. Perhaps it was a kind of perverse egotism that prevented him from identifying himself with his own chief concerns. He was fond of drawing attention to what was appropriate to the status of an English gentleman, while consorting with colonials whom he did not think of as possible aspirants to that condition, but who should none the less pursue a course that would culminate in a national character and status of their own.[19]

He thus gave encouragement to a development which was already current, to some extent, at the time of his arrival in Canada in 1871. The fact of Confederation itself proclaimed the existence of such a sentiment, inchoate and partial as it may have been in the years immediately preceeding the union of 1867. When the men usually credited with founding the Canada First movement namely W. A. Foster, Henry Morgan, George T. Denison, Charles Mair, and R. G. Haliburton, joined forces in the spring and early Summer of 1868, they were impelled by a sentiment which was entertained by an unknown number of citizens of the new country, besides themselves. The strength of their convictions, and the degree of maturity with which they addressed themselves to the realization of their objectives were recognized widely throughout the province. "The class of men who have unfurled the banner of the National party," wrote the Brantford *Daily Expositor* just a week after Blake's Aurora speech, "are not those who can be awed by sarcasm and irony. Talent of no inferior order is at their command. . . ." *The Nation,* which was regarded by this paper as the organ of the movement, "commends itself to many of the educated and intelligent classes of the country."[20] It regarded Blake, and not Smith, as having given life to the association.

[19]See for example the article in *The Nation,* May 28, 1875, in which an attitude of condescension is evident, and which may well have been from Smith's pen. A colonial intruder in English society would always be doing or saying something that would remind his companions that he was not one of them. "Canada," concludes the writer, "is raw, rough, and democratic, but she is your own."

[20]See also the Dufferin-Carnarvon Correspondence, 1874-1878, (Toronto: The Champlain Society, 1955), page 28, Dufferin to Carnarvon, April 23, 1874, in which he states of Canada First that "the most promising of the rising generation in Ontario are supposed to sympathize with them. . . ."

"Mr. Blake has touched a spring which will give the new party an influence and a status, and whether he identifies himself with them or not, having got the start they want, they will be sure to work up." But Smith, for all his aloofness, seems to have arrived at a closer intimacy with the inner circle of the Canada First men than had Blake. Of this there are some indications in George T. Denison's publications, and even more in the Denison Papers in the Public Archives of Canada. Smith gave Denison the run of his library at the time when the latter was engaged in the writing of the *History of Cavalry* that won him the prize in the world-wide competition for the best book on this subject, instituted by the Czar of Russia. Denison and Smith discussed their common interests when they were together, and continued their discussions by correspondence when either the one or the other was abroad. If both were apostles of Canadian nationhood, both nonetheless sought to strengthen the ethnic tie between Canada and the Mother Country.[21] With respect to his pursuit of this objective, Smith wrote to Denison from Sheffield on January 20, 1874,

In your absence I do what I can to advocate emigration to Canada. But it is uphill work; the employees, both manufacturing and land-owning are averse to emigration, which they fear will raise the price of labour; and these strange people are so enamoured of the Yankees for having kicked and plundered them that they will not even let one say that an Englishman will find a more friendly home in Canada than in the States. A few years ago they were launching Alabamas and pouring out the most insincere abuse of the States! They go round like a weather cock and seem quite to have lost the old British solidity of character. The only way is to appeal direct to those who are likely to emigrate; and this, when I have a chance, I shall do.

In thus expressing himself Smith revealed not only an English sentiment compatible with the idea of a new trans-Atlantic nationality, but the degree of intimacy and cooperation that characterized his relations with the men of Canada First.[22]

[21]It was Smith who gave Denison a letter of introduction to Lord Salisbury when he went abroad in the Spring of 1873 with the purpose of encouraging British immigration to Canada. See the George T. Denison Papers, Public Archives of Canada, Paper 284, Smith to Denison, April 1873.

[22]The George T. Denison Papers, (Public Archives of Canada) Smith to Denison, Sheffield, England, January 20, 1874. Their friendship continued after 1877. On June 1 of that year, Smith wrote, "My Dear Denison, I am delighted to see that you are appointed Magis-

The close personal relationship between Goldwin Smith and the members of Canada First emerges most clearly from a perusal of the Foster Papers, for it was undoubtedly with Foster that he felt the most intimate tie and to whom he gave his confidence most unreservedly. Their friendship and correspondence stretched over a considerable period. On January 15, 1874, we find Smith addressing Foster from Sheffield in the most familiar terms. "I venture to address you with a familiarity which I would fain see you sanction by doing the same. My Dear Foster you may judge with what interest I have read your letter and watch the 'launching', of which I got a sort of account, though through a hostile medium, in the *Globe*." He proceeded to give advice as to the line that he thought should be followed, which Foster seems to have heeded.

I doubt however whether it would be wise at present to put forth a regular programme. Any programme which could be put forth without raising a storm dangerous to your bark would, it seems to me, be hollow, inadequate, and disappointing. It is better, I should say for the present to be content with treating such questions as may present themselves in a national sense and thus developing the principle and propagating the sentiment. Questions relating to our power of making commercial treaties in our own interest, and to commercial self government generally, might be good ones to begin with.

The recent disallowance of a Canadian Bill might afford the occasion for a demand for greater liberty for Canada in commercial relations with other countries. He would act on a suggestion made by Foster with regard to influencing the British press

but you may imagine that I have little access to the papers which would influence Conservatives. Our Conservatives are alien to Canada. They not only cling to the political connection, but they plume themselves on their fancied moral and social superiority, as Englishmen, to the people around them. The justice of their pretentions are illustrated by their universal preference of party to honour in the case of the Pacific Scandal.[23]

The same source reveals Smith's concern to promote the trate in place of McNab. To have men of honour on the bench of justice is of all public objects the most essential to the welfare of the Community. George T. Denison Papers, (Public Archives of Canada) written from Richmond, Surrey, pp. 580-583.

[23]The W. A. Foster Papers, Smith to Foster, Sheffield, January 15, 1874.

cause which he and Foster had most at heart, and his willingness to afford material support for undertakings that might serve to advance it. A controlling interest in the *Sun* newspaper having appeared to be desirable, Smith offered to assist in the amount of $200.00. "Care will of course be taken," he wrote on October 21, 1874,

that in changing its course, the paper does not brush its tail off. It has only to abstain from saying anything against us, keeping its present opposition line in other respects. No doubt it will be useful for the Toronto elections, with regard to which, however, I would say that my candidature must be regarded not only as an open question but as quite a secondary matter compared with other considerations, the first of which, on all accounts, is obviously to break the present yoke. It may very likely be better for us to get a voice in the nominations than to put forward a candidate ourselves . . . if I came out after these attempts of the *Globe* to crush me, it must be in a decided opposition to the Government.[24]

In a letter written four days later he again offered an opinion with regard to the policy of the *Sun* ". . . I did not mean that it should go into opposition, but understanding from you that it was an opposition paper, I suggested that it should not change its line too suddenly, for fear of losing its constituency." And he adds significantly — "Pray let nothing be done that can in the least degree embarrass or compromise Blake."[25] Writing from Oxford several years later he mentions some problems arising from a somewhat similar financial commitment which may serve to throw additional light on his motives during these years. He was inclined to offer Robertson, a well-known newspaper proprietor, the privilege of repaying the principle on a loan which he had made, *without interest*, as he had provided the money in the first place to enable the paper to get started, and not to make any profit for himself. He stated that he had been concerned to provide a sound project since "to make it an organ I have no desire . . ." Five years later, he wanted to support a sound candidate in the same spirit as the nationalists had once supported Moss. "I shall not be there to vote", he wrote from Oxford on May 19, 1882,

as I do not sail till July 1. But I am good for $100 towards the Elec-

[24]The W. A. Foster Papers, Smith to Foster, Montreal, October 21, 1874.
[25]The W. A. Foster Papers, Smith to Foster, Montreal, October 25, 1874.

tion Expenses of any worthy candidate of the Independent Liberal stamp. You and Howland know the sort of man I should like to support. I look to general character and ask no inquisatorial questions about particular opinions. I want the man to say that he will not be the slave of either party but will act solely with reference to the good of the Canadian people.[26]

Although he had once considered seeking election to a seat in the Canadian house of commons, he had evidently foresworn any idea of a political career, for as he confided to Foster on June 27, 1882 that

Far from seeking a Senatorship or anything else in the gift of politicians, I have made up my mind never to accept any appointment, office, or distinction of any kind, great or small, in Canada. They bring me nothing but annoyance and abuse. I am quite content to be an Englishman living in Canada, and to make my library my only sphere of action. Party has no domination there.[27]

Of abuse, in truth, he had had enough to last most men a life time. The *Globe's* castigations which had commenced so long before were as vigorous as ever, and it was in this connection, perhaps more than any other, that Foster was regarded as a friend, a confidant, and an equal. Thus we find him writing on November 21, 1881, that if he should decide on criminal proceedings against the *Globe* he would avail himself of Foster's professional advice and knowledge.[28]

As an indication of the *Globe's* continuing animosity towards him he sent Foster on December 2, 1881, a clipping from that paper which stated

The most wretched of all countries is, in the opinion of Mr. Goldwin Smith, that one which has the ill-luck to be the temporary place of his abode. This unfortunate man has been, all his life through, a confirmed scold, a makebait, a carper at everything which other men hold worthy of reverence a combination of the snarling of Thersites, the cunning of Ulysses, and the malice of Voltaire. England he hates; with the States he was displeased. During the decade of his residence in Canada he has lost not a single opportunity of doing injury to the country.

This sort of thing, as Smith saw it, was of course "beneath any kind of notice. But this man who is so transported with

[26]The W. A. Foster Papers, Smith to Foster, May 19, 1882.
[27]The W. A. Foster Papers, Smith to Foster, June 27, 1882.
[28]The W. A. Foster Papers, Smith to Foster, November 21, 1881.

malignity as to write it, because he fears that I am being received in England may . . . be someday betrayed into an indiscretion which would place him within the reach of the law. . . . A direct attack on character, or a mistatement clearly involving one, is the thing wanted, as a basis of operations. I should not much wonder if it were to come."[29] With some measure of detachment he reviewed the long record of acrimomy and denigration in a letter from Brighton addressed to Foster on January 9, 1882. It appeared to him that

> The attacks commenced as soon as I began to play the part of an independent journalist, and their object, I have little doubt, was to protest against independent journalism, the monopoly of the *Globe*. This is not a game which the community can afford to allow anybody to play with success. George Brown thought, and boasted in England, that he had driven me out of Canada. He was right in thinking that an English gentleman dislikes blackguardism. He was wrong in thinking that an English gentleman does not still more dislike giving way to attacks of a blackguard.[30]

IV

We have been endeavouring by means of a liberal use of quotations from contemporary sources to provide as clear an idea as possible as to the nature of the issues that stemmed from Blake's proclamation, in 1874, of much of the programme of Canada First. Likewise in order to attempt to define with some degree of exactitude the kind of relationship that actually existed, whatever it may have been publicly alleged to be, between Goldwin Smith and the leaders of the nationalist movement, passages from his correspondence with those with whom he appeared to be most involved have been cited. It should be evident that whatever influence Smith exerted, it was not that of a wily and dominating mentor upon the malleable minds of a group of callow young men. Youth in any case was not a liability, for, as *The Nation* expressed the matter on one occasion, the sneer that Canada First was formed by a set of mere boys "has been repeated under the cover of journalistic impersonality by critics who have not attained either the age or the wisdom of a Nestor." In pleading guilty to the charge the editors of *The Nation* observed that the rational and practical

[29] The W. A. Foster Papers, Smith to Foster, December 2, 1881.
[30] The W. A. Foster Papers, Smith to Foster, London, January 9, 1882.

sentiment of nationality could not find a place in hearts in which all sentiment was dead. It could not find "a place in the heart of an old political hack or of a party journalist who has written for twenty years without conviction." It was, in any case, a cause in which an element of feeling was likely to attract the young. "German unity," they continued, "used to be called the dream of boys. Italian independence used to be called the dream of boys. And so, in a certain sense, both were. But the German students have marched into Paris as Bismark and Moltke; the youth who in the dim dawn of Italian Independence burned and bled for Italy, are now sitting as gray-haired senators in the Roman Capital."[31]

The reasons why Canada was not destined to witness a like outcome may seem obvious, but nevertheless have never been fully set forth. If Canada First had been a purely political movement, some of those who have written on the subject would have been justified in recording its demise at some moment during the second half of the decade of the seventies, perhaps in 1876. That it should have developed at all was evidence of a degree of societal maturity reached by Ontario in the decade of Confederation. By the same token it may well be that it failed, in anything like full measure, to meet the type of challenge with which it was confronted because the formative influences in terms of which it had emerged were of insufficient force to enable it to do so. It was, in short, somewhat in advance of its time, lacking, as clearly was the case, a widespread and deeply felt popular response. Hence it succumbed to the adverse pressures that were brought to bear upon it. On the other hand its weakness stemmed, in part at least, from an inability to translate its too vague aspirations on behalf of the new Dominion into concrete and unambiguous statements of policy representing a clear consensus among its members. This was particularly true with regard to the concept of "independence." What this seems to have meant in contemporary terms was that Canada should fully participate with the Mother Country in decisions affecting its own interests and destiny; or, alternatively that it should enter into a voluntary and fraternal association, based upon a sentimental attachment and common objectives, rather than upon coercive instruments. When, however, they called the second of these alternatives "independence" they left themselves open to misunderstanding, and severe criticism put

---

[31]*The Nation,* February 26, 1875.

[32]For this impression, see *The Mail,* October 17, 1874, contained in the W. A. Foster Papers, Scrapbook 63, 64.

forth in the name of the ancient loyalty to the Crown which was so deeply rooted in large sections of the provincial population. The *Globe,* for its own reasons, took advantage of this situation to try to destroy Canada First, and it seems reasonable to suppose that the thundering of the influential Toronto daily against the movement was a potent factor in bringing its public phase to an end. While the *Globe's* intransigent attitude may well have lost it some popular support within the ranks of the Reform party, especially in that section which was inclined to adhere to Blake's leadership, it was not without such redoubtable allies as Oliver Mowat, and Blake himself from the beginning had displayed some hesitancy in casting his lot fully with the Nationalists. In this connection it is worthy of mention that the Ottawa *Times,* within a few weeks of the delivery of the Aurora speech, was, in spite of the clear and forceful terms in which it was delivered, skeptical as to whether Blake was in truth a Canada First man. His views on the Pacific railway and the importance of bringing British Columbia into viable relationship with the Canadian Union seem hardly to have accorded with the unrestrained expansionism of the Canada Firsters.[33] Also doubtful as to Blake's political intentions was the observer who wrote that by enunciating a reform programme, Blake "steps out, as a great mind like his naturally does, in advance of the Liberal body, and seeks to lead it upwards and onward, but he does not desert it for another."[34]

Such doubts, however, did not allay the optimism of the Nationalists, for we find Foster confidently anticipating the breakup of the old parties in his address to the Canadian National Association in February, 1875. It is noteworthy also that in writing to Mair on June 10th the same year he was still unshakeably buoyant, presuming that Mair had read Blake's speech, and adding, "Good boy Blake! He will go on to perfection. As for the Grits, I do not object to your valedictories on 'em. The National Club is in full blast – about 400 members – . . . ." It was ominous however, that *The Nation,* on July 2, 1875, should have had to record the end of the *Liberal* which had also reflected the views of Canada First. It was an even worse omen when *The Nation* itself ceased publication in the following year. When Thomas Moss, whom they had helped to elect to parliament in 1873, was appointed to the

[33]Compare D. G. Creighton, *The Old Chieftain,* p. 191, and The W. A. Foster Papers, "Scrapbook," 66, and 68, The Ottawa *Times,* October 20, 1874.

[34]The W. A. Foster Papers, "Scrapbook," 84.

Bench, it was but a prelude to the greatest blow of all, namely the return of Blake to the orthodox Liberal fold in the autumn of 1875 and his acceptance of a cabinet post in the Mackenzie Government. There is no doubt that a good deal of the heart went out of the movement; and it was not surprising that the National Club began to lose its political character, and that the Canadian National Association should have ceased to be a strong force in the community. In writing to the Colonial Secretary on January 19, 1877, the Governor-General reported categorically that "The Canada First Party as it was called has in fact disappeared."[35] In his disillusionment, Goldwin Smith soon turned to annexation as to what seemed to him the only practical alternative. In 1884, Denison expressed his opinion to Charles Mair as to why they had failed. "But for Blake, I believe the Canadian party would have had great and perhaps controlling influence today, and perhaps Goldwin Smith's support did injury at the time and before he was understood." But he added that though the movement collapsed "the spirit is more vigorous than ever."[36] Graeme Mercer Adam, who had been close to the national movement from its inception, expressed himself in a like vein a few years later when he wrote that "Though the movement waned and died its influence was by no means lost . . . it awakened youthful desire for intellectual freedom, and for an increased measure of political independence."[37] If the idealism to which he referred was too frail to contend against the pressing concerns that absorbed the thoughts and energies of Canadians so increasingly during the decades of the Great Depression, it was not entirely lost. Many years ago W. S. Wallace noted how something of the spirit of Canada First passed over into the work of the poets. Even the National Policy that carried Macdonald's Conservative party to power in 1879 may have been in part a legacy from the Nationalist ideals of the earnest young men of Canada First. The movement had not in fact come to an end. As has been suggested, there were some contemporaries who discerned that the political enter-

---

[35]The Dufferin-Carnarvon Correspondence, 1874-1878, eds. C. W. Kiewiet and F. H. Underhill, (Toronto: The Champlain Society, 1955), p. 331, Dufferin to Carnarvon, 19 January, 1877.

[36]The Denison Papers, 882, (Public Archives of Canada) G. T. Denison to Charles Mair, April 10, 1884.

[37]The W. A. Foster Papers, "Scrapbook," Review by G. Mercer Adam of Goldwin Smith's volume of memorials to William Alexander Foster, recently deceased, who, if anyone did, deserved the name of founder of Canada First.

prises that seemed to have failed of their immediate objective, were merely limited aspects of what was in fact a larger movement than could be subsumed under the political rubric, and that there was a sense in which its effects were felt long after the supposed day of its demise. It had an epilogue, indeed, several, if the truth were told.

V | IDENTITY AND DUALITY

10. Evidences of Culture Considered as Colonial

When in 1867 the province that was to become Ontario and Quebec was federated with New Brunswick and Nova Scotia to become the new Dominion of Canada, a formal act was performed which was one day to appear to many citizens of the country as symbolic of the emergence of a new nationality. At the time, this implication could hardly be said to have existed outside the minds of a few statesmen, and only time would tell whether the new country would come to claim the allegiance of its people. Apart from visionaries like Thomas d'Arcy McGee, few of its inhabitants felt any glow of pride at the birth of a state which was so evidently a child of expediency. Most of the lands which were to make Canada, territorially, one of the largest countries in the world still lay beyond its borders. In the east Prince Edward Island and Newfoundland remained aloof, and the western prairie, the region of the cordillera, and the remote Pacific settlements had yet to come in if the promise of the new state was to be fulfilled. To the north, fur-trader and Indian trapper pursued their quarry over a land of rock and tundra that lost itself in the wastes of the Arctic. Even when most of these territories had become legally incorporated, it remained difficult for Canadian citizens to encompass mentally the extent and variety of their country or to discover an identity with each other in the absence of the emotive symbol that the imagination was one day to make of its map. Only along the southern border was it possible to experience a sense of neighbourhood, but this was made difficult by the momentary unfriendliness of the United States, partly in response to which the new Canadian political structure had been designed.

The scattered settlements of fishermen, farmers, lumbermen, and traders which made up the bulk of the population from the Atlantic to the Great Lakes had but slight contact with each other and, apart from the French in Quebec, most of them still felt a strong attachment to the parent state. As the population of the provinces was constantly being depleted by emigration and replenished by new arrivals from overseas, it was difficult for them to develop a sense of community, with roots in their own soil. It may be that few of them had any strong desire to do so, and were content to hope that through the federal union of 1867, a solution would be found for the political and economic problems that had vexed the provinces for several decades. Moreover conditions of pioneer life during the first half of the nineteenth century had not been conducive to the expression of profound thoughts and emotions in literature and the arts. It is true that, for some time, isolated individuals and coteries had been attempting to formulate through the appropriate media the novel experiences of life on the northwest fringes of the Atlantic world, but these attempts had largely failed to achieve any adequate artistic expression of the pattern of Canadian pioneer society itself. This was in the nature of things since it was in reality an aggregation of outposts, incomplete and fragmentary in themselves, of that larger community of which Great Britain, and the United States, and less directly, France, were the cultural citadels.[1] The religious cast of the provincial mentalities, both French and English, was not encouraging, though it was not utterly inimical, to the inception of an aesthetic tradition. There were few evidences of spiritual uncertainty, and the hazards of life were largely conceived as economic in character.

In comparison with developments in the arts in the years since Confederation, and especially after the turn of the twentieth century, the cultural assets that had accrued from the local past were meagre, though they were not entirely negligible. Nevertheless the more impressive quickening of the creative impulse that marked the national period of Canada's development in the aftermath of Confederation did not occur, *sui generis*, as a response to the internal tensions of Canadian society. It came as a result of the relationship that had obtained between the culture of Canada and that of the larger world of which it had formed a variant part. The colonial relationship, broadly conceived, does not necessarily involve political subordination, nor can it be defined entirely in terms of tribute rendered through an unfavourable balance of trade. The cul-

[1]When political disruption of an imperial system takes place as a result in part of the formation of a subsidiary metropolis, cultural emulation of the former centre of power is likely to continue, the results of originality being almost negligible. On the degree of imitativeness of the human mind, in general, see G. Spiller, *The Origin and Nature of Man,* (London, 1935), pp. VII, 194, 195, 205, 261, 347.

tural process of a colony, whether the term "culture" is construed broadly or in the narrower sense of mental attributes,[2] it owes almost completely to its centre of reference in the homeland. The currents of thought and feeling that course through and invigorate the colony's diminutive life are emanations from the heart of the society of which it is a peripheral member. Little does the inhabitant of a far-flung frontier of a growing *imperium* see that is uniquely his. That the culture of Canada has stood in this relationship to those of the British Isles, France, and the United States, and through them to the great Hellenic and Christian sources of Western Culture, a cursory enquiry into the facts would be sufficient to confirm. Thus the volume and pressure of the external influences upon the population of the Dominion and its antecedent provinces have always exceeded those impinging upon it from its "own" historic past, though that past has helped to determine the way in which the influences have been received, whether full-blown, modified, or largely rejected. Moreover, these influences have proved in the long run even more potent than the nonetheless formidable impact of the Canadian environment upon the consciousness of its people. It is certain that Canada, even through the most recently developed phases of its existence, could have approached only remotely to the condition of being a "world-in-itself" like the great metropolitan centres of France and Great Britain which in early modern times became the foci of complex politico-economic systems, centralized, differentiated, and dynamic, from which mounting cultural pressures sporadically discharged in radiations that renewed the cultural modes prevailing in all the regions that paid tribute to them, and from which the dependent people's sense of the meaning of life was derived.

Canada was, and to a large extent still is, in a non-political sense, an aggregation of such dependent regions, and in consequence the most salient features of its culture have more closely represented a reflection of the existent modes of the metropolitan areas than a growth of that problematical internal soul for which Canadians have come to search, with a view to calling it their own. Paradoxical as it may appear to the unthinking nationalist, the nation's culture can approach fruition as the unique expression of its "genius" only through the intensification of those influences which bear upon it from

---

[2]The term "culture" is generally used herein in the broad anthropological sense, after Tylor.

without, and constantly enrich and refine its content. The maturation of Canadian society and culture through the internal growth that has taken place to such a large extent in response to external stimuli, has posed new moral and aesthetic problems, at the same time that it has provided the conditions for their solution on progressively more integrated levels as the process of cultural growth has continued. Recent Canadian scholarship has revealed the emergence of a characteristic temper in the spirit of which Canadians have sought solutions for those recurring political and economic problems to which the complexion of the arts must ultimately be related.[3]

The definition of national character, even in the case of the long-established and relatively integrated nationalities of western Europe, has seldom been attempted with success because of the diversity of personal types resulting in great measure from social differentiation, and because of the subjective hazard of generalizing from partial and fragmentary experience. The growth of a discrete and pervasive character in a country divided, as Canada is, by geographic barriers and distances, conflicting economic interests, political particularism, diversity of religious beliefs and practices, language and cultural traditions, has been slow and tenuous; and the number of crucial traits which it has shared with kindred nations has been so great that the isolation and definition of distinctive characteristics have been fraught with the greatest difficulty, and have indeed only recently been attempted by Canadian students of their country's art and literature. Nevertheless, concomitantly with the development of political autonomy, and as one manifestation of a retarded but persistently growing national consciousness, there has been an increasing concern, at least on the part of small but vocal groups of writers and artists, for the promotion of a distinctive culture which would be worthy of Canada's international status as achieved in the aftermath of the First World War. Unfortunately for the cause which certain organizations have been founded to serve, there has often been little understanding of the subtle properties of cultural distinctiveness, which has tended to be equated with such purely objective content as local names and events in the country's history, and with physiographic data. More imponderable but less superficial are the configurations of beliefs and attitudes, hierarchies of values, and the peculiar sensitivities and nuances

[3]See, for example, Edgar McInnis, *Canada: A Political and Social History,* (New York & Toronto, 1947), Preface, p. viii.

of feeling with which they are invested. Springing from the interaction of climatic and physiological factors with the forms of social and ideological life, as well as with the aggregate of temperamental traits which are inherited in individual family lines, but in themselves have no identity with national characteristics, these phenomena, considered in any degree as distinctive products, have eluded precise definition and are but ill-understood by the mass of Canadians, and even by those persons who have reflected deeply upon them. A unique and pronounced national character could not be expected to arise and stand out clearly in a country of dual culture upon which the weight of the French and British traditions and the impact of the United States have been so strong, and whose most thickly populated sections share with the northern States a terrain which in the two cases is almost identical in type.

It would be begging the question to assert at the outset that such a character exists, but it would be miraculous if a people who achieved a considerable measure of internal self-government in the *annus mirabilis* of 1848, and who laid the basis for a new federal state in the same year that the Habsburg empire was converted into the dual monarchy of Austria-Hungary, should have been strangers to that impulse towards territorial and political nationalism which assumed such explosive violence in revolutionary France, spread in the wake of Napoleon's armies, and ultimately encompassed the globe. The conception of the nation, coloured by some of the empirical manifestations of the *Weltanschauung* of nineteenth-century Romanticism, when applied in the cultural field, gave rise to a profound misunderstanding concerning the nature of historical causation. Institutions, ideas, and modes of expression, came to be looked upon as the mystical exfoliation of the genius of particular peoples. The belief in mysterious creative forces working in the souls of nationalities, often regarded as the unique properties of races with which those nationalities were mistakenly equated, and which was at least implicit in the writings of some of the most eminent historians of the time, blinded them to the extent to which the evolution of nations was causally involved with social forces of wider provenance than national localities and their inhabitants. The idea of the independent development of a people's culture, to which the contribution of traits from external sources was minimized, became a basic assumption of Victorian ethnologists. Events that occurred in a particular territory were chronicled without regard to their true causal relationship, which was often indirect. This was more justified with respect to mature national states which, within strict limits, had achieved a life of their own, but it was impossible to apply it to an immature and marginal country like Canada. Nevertheless it has served the time honoured purpose to begin the history of Canada with an account of events of only local importance rather than with the evolution of those European ideas, institutions and processes whose causal import for modern Canada is so much the greater.

There is however another sense in which the growth of a national consciousness has placed a peculiar emphasis upon the home territory, and in which the political boundary has become a cultural determinant. If history could be considered as "the world the spirit makes for itself," each moment of historic time would involve the recreation of those elements of the past which serve to fulfil a contemporary purpose, and which are caught up and transmogrified, and assume a significance that might be quite alien to their original character. In the light of Croce's meaning of the contemporaneity of history, we may observe how the spirit of enquiry, permeated by nationalistic bias, or even by the sentiment that has sometimes attached itself to the past history of familiar places, has preferred the selection of local content to that unconnected in outward mien with the territory embraced by the national state. This motivation has sometimes dictated an interest in the Indian, but not to the extent of incorporating traits of his culture ino that of modern Canada, beyond imitating and reproducing some of his art-forms which have generally been lifted out of their context and employed in ways that the Indian himself would hardly understand.

II

When one turns to the examination of specific Canadian traditions one notes that there has been a singleness of purpose in French-Canadian culture that contrasts somewhat with that of English-speaking Canada, the development of which has been subject to a measure of discontinuity, dispersion, and division. In seizing upon the amenable aspects of their colonial heritage and reworking them into the fabrique of their emerging national ideology, the French-Canadians established an internal continuity, on their own soil, which has not been nearly so marked among the English Canadians, whose sense of national enterprise after 1867 was qualified by their adherence to what to some observers appeared to be an incompatable imperial ideal. The time came, however, when it might be said that through a unique formulation, English-Canadians were able to reconcile their national feeling with a revised and unusual imperial allegiance which tended to put a period to the doubts and hesitation that until then had characterized what can only be described as a divided mind. But whatever the future might hold in store, the effect of that imperialism in those days was to preserve an attitude of dependence upon the Mother Country which accentuated an imitation of her cultural precedents and prevented Canadians in their creative undertakings from rising to the heights which the English themselves were able to reach, not only through their higher degree of social "frequency" and the richness and intensity of their cultural inheritance, but because of their sense of unlimited possibilities, expressive of the certitude inherent in their metropolitan status. Thus the imperial tie in a certain sense served to retard the reception by the fragmented societies on its periphery of the fullness of their metropolitan cultural heritage, because what they were not able successfully to emulate they could hardly succeed in making their own. This tie has thus facilitated the flow of cultural traits from the imperial centre, to the partial exclusion of those from other centres, but paradoxically it has decreased the capacity of the populations of the outlying areas to profit, culturally, from the relationship. They imitated but they could not duplicate the achievements of the Mother Country. Moreover the measure of political centralization that has until recently existed has prolonged the tendency to look to the metropolis for guidance instead of back into the past developments within their "own" national territory, and while this, as has already been suggested, can be self-defeating if carried to extremes, at the same time, it tends to render slight the force of internal continuity. Successive creative impulses have prompted developments which have usually turned out to be culs de sac, each living out its limited span, and failing to flow together with others to form a vital and continuous stream. Poets and artists were either unaware of predecessors or thought that nothing was to be gained by exploring their precedents. Charles G. D. Roberts, who, perhaps more than any other, fathered the national movement in English Canadian poetry, considered that he was writing on a tablet where no one had written before. He showed little awareness of the work of Sangster and Heavysege, nor of that of Jonathan Odell, the Tory poet of the American Revolution who had been among the founders of his own city of Fredericton.

Perhaps indeed the writers and artists of the last quarter of the nineteenth century had little enough to learn from those of the colonial communities that had come into existence at the close of the American Revolution. Separated politically from the United States, and by the antipathy which many of them felt, or forced themselves to feel, for the institutions of the triumphant Republic, they were separated by distance from Great Britain and from each other. Each coast and watershed of the Maritime Provinces was isolated from the others, and Quebec intervened between them and the distant and attenuated settlements that spread across the southern area of what later became the Province of Ontario. In the days before Confederation it was impossible for these fragments to coalesce into a single society with a pattern and rhythm of its own, from which might emerge an art form which expressed its insistent and significant truths in terms comprehensible to its people. Time has lessened but never entirely removed this initial source of weakness. It would be a mistake to suppose that this weakness was augmented to any great extent by the diversity between the different Protestant churches and sects, or between the Yankee, Scotch, Loyalist, and Irish elements, since in both cases they were subject to the solvent of a common language, and if they had not tended towards geographical segregation, they might have reacted as something approaching a unit to the intellectual forces that belatedly and weakly impinged upon them. There was, however, another handicap from which they suffered in a cultural sense, in addition to the attitude of dependence upon a distant mentor. They could not invoke moral and aesthetic sanctions which had been worked out in their "own" communities within their present territories. This, as has been said, is the paradox of the position in which all dependencies find themselves. Though the Loyalists could pride themselves upon their membership in a great imperial community, they were Americans who had been wrenched out of a relatively mature social context by the catastrophe of the American Revolution and set down on unfamiliar and primitive ground that had none of the associations which generations of living had established with the lands they had left behind. Much of the continuity with their colonial past had thus been broken. A rootless and bitter people could cherish habits of minds which had been formed in the relatively sophisticated society from which they came, but they could not with ease perpetuate them in their place of exile where the conditions that had produced them were not to be found and where the majority were compelled to relive the primitive conditions that had challenged the ingenuity of their ancestors. Many had to forswear the occupational specialization which is characteristic of a differentiated society and which is favourable to the achievement of eminence in creative fields of endeavour. Moreover the sense of intellectual mastery that lifted up the hearts of men like Franklin and Jefferson, and made them capable of high achievement, was lacking in the new British North American communities, with the qualified exception of Nova Scotia, in the first quarter of the nineteenth century. To colonialism, isolation, and dispersion, and the low emotional and intellectual tension characteristic of peripheral regions that lack the saving presence of a crucial challenge, must be added the nature of the society which the Loyalists, with later recruits from overseas, sought to establish on the new soil.

Although there were many shades of political opinion represented among those who had fled north from the United States to British territory at the close of the American Revolution, the reactionary elements among them, who sought and often secured positions of influence in the British provinces, shrank from novel ideas which might harbour the taint of democracy and what was soon to be called Jacobinism, and they were in consequence responsible for initiating a tradition that was unfavourable to the free-ranging mind. It was natural that they should have looked with disfavour upon social and political experimentation, and that they should have sought to foster a social structure that would be an image and transcript of their conservative ideals. Their tendency to repress political opposition and to curb the free expression of ideas was not conducive to the development of a broad and vigorous culture. They attempted in their literature to cling to the out-worn neo-classicism of the Revolutionary period, but when the Revolution was over, no other event of similar magnitude arose to stimulate literary effort. There ensued a deterioration among those who clung to the spirit of the eighteenth century. Moreover the antipathy to the United States, which after the War of 1812 grew rather than diminished, together with the class attitude of the time, exercised a baneful and stultifying influence on the arts. It is true that democratic sentiment was not lacking among the unprivileged mass of Loyalists and other elements, and was reinforced by intimacy with the neighbouring States until the American invasion of Canada in 1812 temporarily closed the ranks of Canadian society and forced the populace to seek refuge in the reactionary oligarchies which then controlled the provinces. Later with the sharpening of domestic conflict preceding the Upper Canadian rebellion of 1837, the radical political press crystallized opinion against the ruling clique of that Province, but it could not stimulate significant expression among a semi-illiterate and socially dislocated people. The radical Scottish Canadian poets, of the school of Burns, wrote in a crude, tangy, and realistic style, but they were too few and too dispersed to establish a Canadian tradition in this vein, and too unmindful of an emerging trans-Atlantic nationality to be concerned with doing so. Thus no contribution to the arts of permanent significance was forthcoming from the inchoate masses or from the provincial "Family Compacts" and their adherents, although that the latter were not without a sense of style in their daily living is attested by the spacious and dignified Georgian houses that may still be seen in parts of the Maritime Provinces and southern Ontario. Some of them made sketches, without noteworthy merit, of local scenery and settlements, and some, like the old Toronto families, patronized the work of George Berthon whose portraits of the colonial dignitaries reflected the courtly tradition of Van Dyke and Lawrence which accorded completely with the eighteenth century social ideals of the patrons.[4] Yet the efforts of J. G. Howard to maintain a "Society of Artists and Amateurs" under appropriate sponsorship during the period of the Rebellion were doomed to failure.[5] Canadian subject matter was not utilized with any effectiveness before Paul Kane and Cornelius Krieghoff discovered the "quaint" and "picturesque" properties of Indian and habitant after the century was far advanced.[6] The musical clubs and choral societies formed at the same time in the small urban centers were noteworthy only for the developments in music to which they later gave rise. In the literature of early Ontario John Richardson is today recalled for the competence with which he depicted the pomp and circumstance of war; and the sisters Suzanna Moodie and Catherine Parr Trail, though they began by execrating their colonial existence, introduced

[4]Berthon was a Viennese who migrated to Toronto in about 1841.

[5]John George Howard settled in Toronto (then York) in 1832, became the city's first surveyor and in 1880 a charter member of the Royal Canadian Academy.

[6]Kane, an Irishman, came to Canada in 1819, and wrote *Wanderings of an Artist among the Indians of North America.* Krieghoff arrived in Canada in 1846 and became the chief painter of scenes from French-Canadian Life.

the first strong note of romanticism into English-Canadian writing, and lived to celebrate the promise of a new British nationality in the New World. In the decade before Confederation, Charles Sangster was hailed as a "national" poet, but he was too imitative of Byron and Shelley, too lacking in depth of feeling, and too beclouded by the vague and general imagery of the current Romantic mode to see the exact curves of the variant Canadian scene. Jonathan Odell carried the literary canons of Pope, Dryden, and Churchill into New Brunswick at the end of the Revolution, but in that province and in this outmoded genre he had no successor.

With the exception of the United States there was only one place on the western periphery of Britain's cultural domain where conditions were in some measure favourable to the production of creative writing of high literary merit. That place was Nova Scotia. The province was conquered by British arms and settled by Yankees from New England before the conquest of the main French strongholds on the St. Lawrence, and therefore had had a longer time than the other areas to develop the features of a community. Its location as a peninsula near to but separated from New England, and the nature of its economy, together with the changes wrought in the character of its Yankee, Scottish, and Loyalist settlers by these conditions, were favourable to the production of a distinctive provincial culture and a measure of social and intellectual maturity beyond anything to be found elsewhere at that time in British North America. By the middle of the nineteenth century it had almost come to experience a sense of nationality within the larger imperial community. Its leading minds were able to transcend the conditions that gave them birth, and in place of interpreting, create. The fact that Haliburton's The Clockmaker exerted some influence on the literature of the United States and Great Britain, but contributed virtually nothing to later Canadian writing, is indicative of the folly of attempting to treat the culture of a country like Canada as though it were a discrete development, detachable from the North Atlantic context. Nevertheless it might well be that Howe and Haliburton, and the historians Akins and Murdock, would have foreshadowed a provincial literature of general significance if the course which then seemed set for Nova Scotia had not been profoundly altered by the Confederation of the provinces in 1867, and the economic and political forces of which that event was in part an expression.

III

Although the union of the provinces in 1867 promised an enlargement of cultural possibilities and some abatement of the kind of colonial attitudes that had not been uncommon in many quarters for several generations, it did not signify, in the field of literature and the plastic arts, any immediate recrudescence or change in the tone of the Romantic naturalism that had already achieved a local vogue with the paintings of Jacobi, Krieghoff, and Kane, and in literature with the novels of Richardson, and the poems of Charles Sangster and Isabella Valancy Crawford.[7] In the influence which Constable and Rousseau came to exert on Homer Watson and other Canadian painters it is possible to discern merely an intensification of the romantic naturalism that had everywhere been found throughout the western world for some time past.[8] The varieties of the romantic sensibility current in Canada towards the end of the nineteenth century were due in part to the emulation of the different individual styles of the creative spirits of western Europe or, more accurately, to the peculiar permutations which the Canadian artists themselves made from the assortment provided by their own and previous phases. Sometimes it was the rhetorical style of Delacroix or David that suggested a fitting means of rendering homage to a national hero, as in the monument by Hébert commemorating the founder of Montreal; to others like Horatio Walker, it was Millet who revealed the subdued and simple lyricism of the peasant life.[9] Although no two Canadian poets read the Romantic literature of England and America in exactly the same way, or took from it in equal kind what was necessary to their own fulfllment, it is certain that the poetry of Keats was the paramount spiritual force in the work of Charles G. D. Roberts, Bliss Carman, Archibald Lampman, and Duncan Campbell Scott in their most formative years. Of all the writers

[7]Otto Reinhold Jacobi, a native of Konigsberg and a founder in 1867 of the Society of Canadian Artists, became a charter member of the Royal Canadian Academy.

[8]Homer Watson, a native of Upper Canada, was noted for his paintings of the Ontario countryside. None of the nineteenth century artists, and only Haliburton in literature, seems to have escaped the vogue of romantic naturalism.

[9]Nevertheless Hébert became the foremost Canadian sculptor of his time. Walker resided for most of his life on the Ile d'Orleans, and was famous for his human and animal figures.

of the last quarter of the nineteenth century it was these who best represented what English Canada had then to give. What distinguished them from their predecessors was not a greater emotional depth so much as a surer grasp of the technical requisites of their craft, and a larger sense of aesthetic possibilities than in earlier generations. This was because Canadians now wrote from a fuller, more complex, and more subtle social and cultural background than ever before. It was because the Romantic mode now came in fuller flood into an area which by 1880 was better prepared to receive it. It is possible, however, that the very success of their response may have made them less adaptable to the new disturbing currents already working in the body of English thought. England had already moved on to new modes by the time its early Romantic sensibility had become habituated in Canada; but the increasing effectiveness of the Canadian response and the technological improvements in communication combined to reduce the time lag that had been one of the striking features of the period of political colonialism. It is undeniable that the growth of national feeling in the aftermath of Confederation further increased the effectiveness of the response.

Greater competence could have enabled Canadian writers and artists to render their milieu more effectively than had been earlier the case, but it did not make certain a revision of the way that they saw and felt about the Canadian environment.

The question of the character of the artists' response to nature in this country is one which must necessarily concern the student of Canadian cultural development. It is evident that traits of French and British culture, lifted out of native contexts, attenuated by the passage of the Atlantic, and implanted in the new world, survived the process only through coming to terms with the sociocultural and physical conditions already prevailing there. In the long run the immigrants met the challenge of the aboriginal cultures by shattering them, and obliterating the remnants or thrusting them aside, incorporating almost nothing of permanence. The colonial communities of both French and English language and culture grew by habituation to the physical environment of North America, in the act of expanding through the direction of their own energies, and the reinforcement of those energies especially in the case of the British, by continual recruitment from overseas. Colonial society grew in scale and complexity also by virtue of the incorporation of ideas, attitudes, and institutions radiated from the metropolis, whose pressure upon the colony was always importunate. But whether acceptance by the colony of novel traits was forced or not, they had to achieve some "permanent natural right in the place" by mutual accommodation with the pre-existing cultural configuration. In view of the discussions that have taken place in Canada concerning the character of the impact of nature upon the Canadian consciousness and expression in the arts, it is most important to bear in mind what sometimes seems to have been forgotten, namely, that man since the advent of his species has never lived in a state of nature, but has always lived in a physical environment modified by human artifice. No man can step out of the cultural milieu in which he has his being; but if it were possible to do so he would cease to be himself; and if he stepped not out of one culture into another, but from the world of culture into the world of nature, he would cease to be human. He would become unclassifiable like Caspar Houser before that being's re-entry into the world of man.[10] It follows that man by virtue of his humanity can give only a conditioned response to the sensory stimuli of the physical environment, a response which is made through the exercise of an already formed pattern or *Gestalt*. Such patterns may be likened to a transparent and figured screen hanging between the eye and the object, so that the eye of man is never naked and the object never seen as it really is. It is subtly blurred and distorted by the mental preconceptions of the observer who tends to read into the object something that is already in his mind. Allowing for the existence of individual vagaries, persons living in a particular culture will tend to share the patterns or preconceptions which are that culture's stock-in-trade, and which through repetition will always tend to become stereotypes until they are shattered and reassembled into new conformations by novel impacts from the socio-physical world. While a particular preconception, and the emotional tone with which it is invested, is dominant, it constitutes the mode of the time and place, and the impact of nature on the senses is registered in the terms which that mode dictates. The Romantic mode which dominated Europe and America, throughout most of the nineteenth century, might be described as an affective attitude of man towards himself as reflected in his attitude towards nature. Since the mode was not static in its western European habitat but followed a curve

[10]The consequence of reduction to a sub-human level as a result of being deprived of contact with other human minds is best illustrated by this case. See R. M. MacIver, *Society: A Textbook of Sociology,* (New York, 1937), p. 40.

of development in accordance with a logic of irrationality, it will be found that when diffused beyond its place of origin only certain of its phases gained adherence in Canada during the period of its dominance. Because of the many diverse currents of thought and feeling at play in Canadian life, the range of temperamental variations, and the structural differentiation of Canadian society, no dominant and pervasive attitude to nature peculiar to successive epochs of Canadian history, is likely to have existed. Nevertheless it is true that nature and man's relation to natural phenomena have engaged more fully the attention of the Canadian artist, and have been dealt with far more effectively by him than the relations of man and man.[11]

IV

There were many reasons why Canadians during the half-century following Confederation were unable to produce memorable works in certain fields, notably the drama and the novel. The low degree of social cohesion, the absence of an aesthetic concensus, both in part a consequence of a widely scattered population, had denied to the Canadian artist both the personal

[11]As has often been said, the Canadian concern with Nature results from there having been so much of it. On the other hand the experience of the natural environment was conditioned in great part, it might plausibly be argued, by the successive climates of thought and feeling given off by the metropolitan centres of Western Civilization. As the echoes of neo-classicism died away, Nature came to be regarded quite widely in the Wordsworthian sense as beneficent, especially in the heyday of Romantic naturalism. Gradually, because of the emergence of new forces, the idea of nature as "red in tooth and claw" supervened, to give way in turn to the sense of a universe indifferent to the human lot, as in Hardy or Earle Birney's David. T. E. Hulme experienced the impact of this third phase in an acute form on visiting the Canadian prairie where he was "haunted by the vast image of space," and conscious of "the separation of man in the face of Nature," in a way that was, I believe, impossible to the Romantics. Michael Roberts, *T. E. Hulme,* (London, 1938), p. 226; Alun R. Jones, *The Life and Opinions of T. E. Hulme,* (London, 1960), pp. 23-24. Professor Northrop Frye ("Canada and its Poetry," *Canadian Forum,* December, 1943, p. 209) found "the evocation of stark terror" as a characteristic response of Canadian poets to the physical environment of their country. I believe that this response is likely to be found much more frequently and more pronounced in the Moderns. – A.G.B.

means and the social field for divining and resolving subtle and complex human conflicts with passion and imagination. Among the reasons for the weak development of the novel in Canada has been, with rare and recent exceptions, the unwillingness and perhaps the incapacity on the part of Canadian authors writing in both French and English to subject the prevailing social standards of their country to fearless analysis and corrosive criticism. In this, and in other less obtrusive respects, the political boundary between Canada and the United States has been a cultural barrier insulating Canadian society against the boisterous and disturbing consequences of the American popularization of Darwinism, and the "progressive" relativism of the pragmatic philosophy of Pierce, James, and Dewey, both of which combined to shake the faith of millions in the "eternal" truths of traditional religion, law, and ethics. Although something of all this filtered through belatedly to remould the outlook of isolated Canadians, its impact upon Canadian thinking as a whole was hardly perceptible before the nineteen-twenties when, merged with the searing message of Marx, it began to work in the consciousness of some of the young men and women who came of age in the decade following the First World War.

Thus there was hardly anything in Canadian letters comparable to the extensive literature of social protest and exposure that sprang into existence in the Republic as a reaction to the stark poverty and debasement of the masses that attended the spectacular development of industrial capitalism in the eighties and on into the "era of the Muckrakers" in the first decade of the twentieth century. *The History of Canadian Wealth,* by Gustavus Myers, one of this company who turned momentarily to the exposure of the corrupt bargains that sometimes marred the politics of business enterprise in Canada, was for many years banned by the customs with a view, no doubt, to forestalling awkward questionings. It was not until the vogue of such writers as Hemingway and Steinbeck sharpened the awareness of a people whose traditional stability was shattered by the Depression of 1929 that almost the first evidences of social realism and protest appeared in Canadian fiction.[12]

---

[12]The spirit of critical realism was evident to some extent in a few writers of an earlier period, such, for example, as Sara Jeannette Duncan and Robert Barr, the Scottish immigrant, notably in the latter's *The Measure of the Rule,* 1908. Writers like Morley Callaghan and Irene Baird were evidence of the sharp break with the Canadian past that occurred later.

The failure to deal frankly with many disturbing social problems can be explained also, at least in part, as a result of the middle-class Victorian prudery that so fully characterized the incoming peoples in the nineteenth century, and fastened itself also upon the moral sensibilities of the descendants of the Loyalists, the French-Canadians, and other earlier groups, becoming in Canada as elsewhere the norm of the Anglo-American world. As time went by it became more difficult to escape its restrictive influences in the small and marginal Canadian communities than in the larger, more diverse, and more resilient societies of the United States and Great Britain. Thus the limitations that it placed upon the creative spirit in Canada were more persistent and severe than in those other countries, and consequently more devastating to the writer and the artist who could attain to full stature only in an uninhibiting milieu.[13] The prudery served to reinforce the mulish conservatism of a society which had become "mildewed with discretion" because it possessed no tradition of successful popular insurgence on its own soil comparable to the English tradition of 1689 and the American heritage from 1776. Indeed the initiation of social and cultural change has rested less in Canada upon a popular basis than in the other two North American countries, Mexico and the United States. Mexican art draws spiritual sustenance from the ancient folk culture which the Conquistadores and their successors failed to destroy, and which had no real Canadian counterpart, even in Quebec. The American epic of westward migration was the work of individuals and families who fought their way into the wilderness on foot, on rafts, and in covered wagons, a generation or two ahead of the railroads, and beyond the reach of the protective arms of paternal government. The Canadian trader nearly always wore the badge of authority of a great fur company, and the later mass migration into the Canadian west enjoyed the sponsorship of government or corporation, and followed the building of the transcontinental railroad and the establishment of the reign of law by the Northwest Mounted Police. Paternalism, and official initiation and sponsorship by a strong central authority have thus been characteristic of the Canadian configuration, and have sometimes made for a conservatism in the bad sense of the word, defeating benign and progressive intentions. The history of the Royal Canadian Academy, and for a time of the National Gallery of

[13]It would however be a mistake to overestimate the effects of prudery, stemming from the emergence of revised forms of puritanism in the nineteenth century.

Canada, both initiated by official action, in 1880, accorded with the historic pattern. Because of its prestige the Academy was able to impose its moribund standards on artist and public with such success as to prompt the Canadian painter, Sir Wylie Grier to remark in 1913, that if an artist were any good he could not paint acceptable Academy pictures. Such official domination, in conjunction with the survival into the twentieth century of the "practical" and unimaginative mentality of the frontier, and a rigorous puritanism, merely served to reinforce the materialistic outlook of a bourgeoisie whose single-minded exploitation of the natural resources of the continent was destructive of authentic cultural values.

Such an environment was insufferable to creative spirits like the poet Charles G. D. Roberts, who fled to New York in the nineties, and to the painter James Wilson Morrice who escaped from the stuffy Victorian atmosphere of Montreal to the banks of the Seine. There may have been something of the "Romantic flight" about these movements which would link them in that respect with Rimbaud,[14] but the impossibility of achieving self expression in the kind of half-world in which they had been compelled to move may be sufficient to explain their actions. It might be claimed, and indeed there is some evidence, especially in the case of Roberts, that they were condemned to fail in the fulfilment of their potentialities, for through exile they cut themselves off from a limited but genuine source of vitality, without attaining to true metropolitan stature. The *déraciné* individual is always poised between two worlds, and belongs wholly to neither, as is clearly reflected in his consciousness. Though he may find companionship with other uprooted souls, it is in a community of fugitives, not only from colonial straits, and from those very materialistic mores which have come to dominate the entire field of his society, but which he can escape because the metropolis can embrace within its broad bosom a brood of half-acknowledged outcasts who make of it what they will, which is always a world apart. A further reason why the artist, increasingly within the last century, has failed to find a "useful" place in Western bourgeois society, is to be found in the consequences of the industrial revolution which has sepa-rated him from the "great audience" without which he cannot hope for fulfilment. The artist is a skilled craftsman who has lost his function in the face of mechanical and mass production, which has vitiated the general sense of style by rendering the

[14]Wallace Fowlie, *Rimbaud,* (New York, 1946), pp. 45-52.

public insensitive to aesthetic qualities and incapable of responding to the spiritual insights which the artist's work should provide. Moreover the industrial revolution had accelerated the processes of social differentiation, making for specialized ways of living and working, with a corresponding loss of sympathy among different classes of persons and the emergence of technical terminologies, both literary and plastic, which have narrowed the artist's audience to his own immediate circle and prevented him from recreating a collective vision for his people. He has tended, except in moments of rapprochement, to substitute his personal vision, which, within the last half century, has often become detached and abstract, leaving him open to the charge of subscribing to a cult of unintelligibility, such as has been leveled against many modern poets and painters. The removal of the artist beyond the limits of public credibility was a factor in the rise of Impressionism, and left the uncreative element to exploit the technological inventions of the age, with almost no consciousness of a need for a clarification of the meaning of existence through the visions of their creative spirits. The consequent incapacity of society to assimilate and give form to the inchoate phenomena of the industrial revolution has been advanced as a reason for the loss of a sense of style in the Victorian period which, unhappily for Canada, coincided in time with the great expansion and settlement of this country, with the result that the Canadian landscape is crowded with buildings illustrative of the various revivals of Romanesque, Greek, and Gothic styles, all jostling each other in a chaotic and formless manner, proclaiming the nemesis of creative conviction.

Such an explanation of the confusion of forms in existing Canadian architecture is not incompatible with the notion that the cause is partly to be found in the logical progression of a self-defeating Romanticism which has required the abandonment of a no longer creative centre of reference, and a flight in quest of renewal of its incipient vision. Each failure to recreate that vision further excited the appetite for novelty, and drove the Romantic spirit on through a succession of flights to embrace exotic forms, exhausting its energy and rendering itself increasingly incapable of achieving a form of its own. Intensity was lost in dispersion and it could do no more than imitate through "revivals" the forms that were symbolic of other historic moments. Whether the execrable taste of late Victorian architecture, which, as has been said, had tended to persist to some extent in Canada, the withdrawal of the artist from an audience, and his recourse to a personal vision requiring expression in the geometric and the abstract, are significant of one of the not infrequent changes of rhythm within the span of Western society, or whether they are symptomatic of the subsidence of the great ground-swell that first made itself felt in the humanistic renaissance of the sixteenth century, as writers like T. E. Hulme and Pitirim Sorokin appear to have suggested, it may be impossible to determine with accuracy at such close range; but whichever the case may be, the effects in recent art and literature may nonetheless be clearly traced.

The romantic mode, refined by the Barbizon and Dutch schools of painting, which had determined the character of Canadian art throughout much of the nineteenth century, gave way, long before that century was over, for reasons outlined above, to an impressionism that was akin to the literary aestheticism of the era of "art for art's sake," in which deep feeling, with an ethical content, was eschewed for a refinèd record of sensations derived from the play of light on the surface of objects. Although the valuable technical discoveries of the Impressionists were not balanced by an expressed awareness of the fullness of life, their work gained gradual recognition as the mirror of a generation that could no longer see itself in the "natural" landscapes that had been the sign manuals of its immediate forebears. It was partly because Canada and the United States were slow to react favourably to this new mode, as it diffused over the field of Western society, that artists like Whistler and Morrice, whose creative impulses were quickened by it, found congenial fellowship and aesthetic stimulus only in the metropolitan atmosphere of London and Paris. Morrice, however, returned not infrequently to Canada, and he and his friend Maurice Cullen were chiefly responsible for overcoming the Canadian hostility to Impressionist painting. By 1913 their work was no longer the chief target of attack by the pundits. Morrice, who was the most outstanding Canadian artist up to that time, painted the sentimental spirit of his subject, rather than its precise character and contour, but achieved a rhythm and a design that went deeper than the superficial coherence of much Impressionist painting, which tended to decompose forms and dissolve structure. Indeed, as time passed, there emerged a tendency towards abstraction in his work.

Although the successors of Morrice and Cullen, who were soon to become identified as the Group of Seven, began by adapting Impressionist techniques to Canadian landscapes, the most creative spirits among them, aware of newer Parisian and

Scandinavian conceptions began more and more to conceive their world in a post-impressionist manner which in a tentative way, and united with other influences, had actually not been absent from their earlier work.

Their impulsion to seek the eternal symbolic forms found expression in their renderings of the scarred rock and rugged forest land, the myriad lakes and rivers, of the great arc of the Canadian Shield, at a time when that country had just commenced to yield a harvest of mineral wealth, as it had already yielded fur and timber, and thus for the third time to capture the imagination of Canadians. It seems to have appeared to the artists themselves, in their fervour of creation, and to a host of enthusiastic journalists and critics, that for the first time in the nation's history a contribution was being made that was, to use the time-worn expression, "distinctively Canadian." The idea that the early immigrant Krieghoff had painted in "the European manner", whereas these more recent artists painted in a Canadian manner, provided the popular formula and the almost universally accepted canon of the nineteen-twenties when the movement was gaining its wide popularity. Few, if any, of them seemed to be conscious of the fact that in their statements they revealed themselves to be the victims of what might be called the illusion of contemporaneity. Once they had grown used to the new technique, the Canadian landscape began to look like the pictures that had been painted of it, and consequently not at all like the scenes made by Krieghoff half a century before when the vogue of romantic naturalism was widespread. It was agreed that the post-impressionist technique was congenial to the new subject matter, and that this technique had somehow provided each of our artists with the product of a cultural mutation in the form of a pair of Canadian eyes. If this was true at all, it was true within far narrower limits than was popularly supposed, and in a way that requires a more accurate definition than has yet been given it. It may be admitted that their exploration of this terrain imposed individual refinements of Impressionist and post-Impressionist techniques upon each of them, and that these techniques were expressive of feeling-tones that reflected the spirit in which Canadians were then addressing themselves to the aesthetic and economic actualities of the north. For the feeling of confidence and mastery that was almost ubiquitous in Canadian society during the first quarter of the twentieth century, and which was reflected in the boundless enthusiasm of the Group in its formative phase, was very different from the mood out of which Impressionism and post-

Impressionism had sprung in the region that gave birth to these movements. The philosophy of art for art's sake, of which these modes were somewhat related expressions, had represented a flight from the realities of the time, including that of a France that had been prostrated by the defeat of 1871 and profoundly depressed by the divided national purpose of the Third Republic. It might even be agreed that Cezanne's quest for the eternal forms, and the consequent emphasis on structure in his paintings, reflected a deep human need to escape out of an insecure world of flux and fleeting values into one of permanent symbolic order. But the spirit that animated Thomson and the Group of Seven was buoyant by comparison. Their brilliant decorative landscapes were characterized by rhythmic lines and brilliant colours, and even in their sombre moods a note of confidence was struck. Only later did members of the Group like Lawren Harris pass definitely over into a metaphysical conception of the cosmos that was perhaps revelatory of the mounting crisis in twentieth century Western culture. The real achievement of these artists was that they responded in full stature to the cultural formulations of their time by recreating for themselves, incidentally in regional content, the new felt world of the revolutionary age in which they lived.[15]

[15]The effects of the "brutal catastrophes of geological history," (D. G. Creighton, The Commercial Empire of the St. Lawrence (1937), p. 4, which the artists in question found in Algoma, and beyond, may be regarded as the "objective correlative" of their emerging vision of the world in which they found themselves.

11. An Adventure In Social History:

Arthur Lower's Vision of "les deux nations"

Professor Lower's new book* illustrates some of the difficulties of writing social history, and particularly of the problems that in the present state of knowledge must confront anyone who undertakes the formidable task of writing a social history of Canada. Of many of these difficulties, one may be sure, he is as fully aware as anyone who has ever worked in the field of Canadian history. He therefore rightly approaches the subject with the statement that the book is experimental. Like so many Canadians before him, in other spheres of activity, he is making a pioneering effort. "A good many types of history have been written about Canada – constitutional, economic, and political – and there have been plenty of articles and small books lighting up the life of a countryside or city. But as yet no one has tried to put things together in an effort to depict the growth of the country as a whole, and throughout its history".

The chief difficulty that faces the scholar who attempts to write a general social history of this country is that the articles and books to which Professor Lower refers have not been nearly numerous enough. Scholarship is a social product and a general work must necessarily depend upon a pre-existing number of special studies of particular aspects of the subject, if it is to achieve any great degree of success. The truth is that Canadians have hardly yet begun to mine the relatively voluminous resources of their social history. There are admirable sets of documents such as are to be found in the seventy-three volumes of Jesuit Relations edited by the American historian, Reuben Gold Thwaites, and the publications of the Champlain Society, that throw much light on the early phases of Canadian social life, but they merely serve to emphasize how much there is that still remains to be done even in bringing together the raw materials of the subject. When one contemplates the accumulated store of church and court records, the wealth of untapped

*Arthur R. M. Lower, *Canadians in the Making: A Social History of Canada* (Toronto, 1958).

source materials contained in the files of newspapers stored in libraries and archives from one ocean to the other, not to speak of the visible detritus of past ages that confronts the eye of the observer in the form of buildings, vehicles, costumes, and household "appliances," and decorations, as well as the habits and gestures of the people themselves, one gains some inkling of the magnitude of the undertaking that must present itself to the scholars of future generations. It is a measure of Professor Lower's ability as an historian that with so little already done, upon which to build, he has accomplished as much as he has in the work under review. On the other hand one cannot but reflect that some of the shortcomings of *Canadians in the Making* arise in part from the fact that there are as yet no detailed studies at all of many aspects and areas of Canadian social life.

Few writers of Canadian history have ever been concerned with the political development of their country to the total exclusion of the economic and social aspects, and yet Canadian historians like those in neighbouring and related countries, have tended to interest themselves most, at least until recently, in the political record. History as past politics, when politics were the means to a broadening of human freedom, was the theme *par excellence* of the Whig historians of the British universities. That so many Canadians should have chosen those mentors was partly determined by their own political background, for had not Howe and Baldwin and Lafontaine striven for, and prophesied, the liberalization of the Empire? The successful response to the political challenge of the nineteenth century for some time obscured the adventures and achievements of industrial enterprise, and the "homely" lives of the masses in the process of their halting and partial adjustments to life in a new continent. Perhaps this may help to explain, in part at least, why the attempt at a social history has been so long delayed in Canada.

Although Trevelyan wrote that "social history might be defined negatively as the history of a people with the politics left out," few historians have been quite so rigorous in practice as this statement would require, and Professor Lower is no exception. Are political factors more fundamental, that is to say, more influential causes of change, than social institutions and conditions? If this were so the facts of social history would be fully intelligible only within a political frame of reference. Professor Lower has certainly made some concessions to this view of the matter. His periodization is often a political one:

the British conquest, the American Revolution, the War of 1812, the Confederation of the Provinces, and the World Wars of the twentieth century have an evident meaning for social history as our author understands it. One may concede the wisdom of this method while pointing out the danger of obscuring other periodizations behind a political façade. His "social" stages, beginning with the trading post, and passing through the pioneer settlement, the colony, the province, to the nation, are certainly overshadowed by political considerations. The ethnologist who traces the diffusion of the swastika as an art motif or religious symbol, may find that its spacial distribution has been little affected by factors of a political nature. To the historian likewise it might seem preferable to name an epoch after an individual or a technological device, or in terms of a particular type of class structure. Professor Lower occasionally does this, as when he writes of "the great god CAR," or entitles a section of one of his chapters, "Rank, class and Sam Hughes." He cannot write of Bliss Carman's Canada with the same assurance as Trevelyan does of "Shakespeare's England," for obvious reasons, but he could fittingly refer to "the age of Macdonald," without falsifying Canadian achievements and values. This should serve to confirm the primacy of the political, for Canada at least, but it raises anew the general question of the locus of social history.

It is his strength as a publicist and moralist that he so frequently goes beyond a statement of what actually happened, but some will regard it as his chief weakness as an historian. He does not content himself with Ranke's declared aim of presenting "what had really happened" but presumes what the great German historian disclaimed, namely "to sit in judgment on the past." Far from banishing himself from his books, his writing is always or almost always, intensely personal. He is seldom content to let his narrative unfold in its own terms; instead he keeps telling the reader what to think about the subject with which he happens to be dealing. He lectures him, sometimes preaches to him, and even on occasion seems to be engaged in castigating him, especially if he is an English-Canadian and a Protestant, (*passim*). Fortunately the reader is likely to accept Professor Lower's strictures wherever they are deserved, for it must be understood that he does not necessarily castigate Protestantism, but only Protestants when the latter, as like others they may, sometimes prove deficient in understanding of their fellow-beings, especially in the circumstances of Canadian history, when the latter are French-speaking Catholics. In his efforts to get English-speaking Canadians to see the good in their fellow citizens he may often be preaching to the converted. But few people, particularly when already sufficiently convinced, enjoy being belaboured beyond a certain point, and it can be endured only in the thought that regrettably, it may still be needed for the good of some people's souls and because Professor Lower is engaged, as he says of others, "in burying the biggest hatchet in Canadian history."

In his chapter on the Conquest of New France by British forces, the distinction left in the reader's mind between the travail of war, and the relations between conquerors and conquered when the war was at an end, is not sufficiently clear. Perhaps this is because he is here describing the way in which later generations of French-Canadians chose to conceive of these events, carrying the idea of the barbarities of war over into their treatment of the years of peace. He does not in this chapter clearly refute or correct these conceptions. We read here largely of "les années terribles" followed by the slow revival of freedom, won by hardy French-Canadians from their tyrannical masters. This was how Jules Léger regarded the subject. The various meanings of the Conquest include what it meant to the people of England, of England's colonies, and France where "few tears were shed for the loss of Canada." The French-Canadian mind, we gather, was formed by such passages as "the bishop's stark description of the ruined colony . . . the almost total destruction of Quebec, the desolation of the countryside . . . the flight of the inhabitants . . . ." Surely, writes Professor Lower, "he would be dull of soul who could not comprehend the apprehension, the anxiety, the deep tragedy, which conquest involves."

Was it so? Were these understandable apprehensions justified by the sequel? Did the French-Canadians suffer oppression comparable to the people of the South after the War Between the States, or the Irish in their long years of subjection? Garneau, who contributed most to the formation of the mythos of the French-Canadians, "gives the impression that the conquered people were subjected to considered and cruel oppression," and our author supplies the corrective, not in this chapter on the Conquest entitled "The lilies come down!" but in subsequent pages where the kind of impression given by Garneau is dispelled. The conquered people did not groan under a tyrant's yoke. There was no considered tyranny, no arbitrary bloodshed. There were "individual friendships like that between John Fraser and Dr. Badelart, the Highlander the patient of the doctor on the actual field of battle that fateful September day of 1759, the French doctor the prisoner of the Highlander, close friends for forty years thereafter." The first Governors, Murray and Carleton "from the beginning were sympathetic with the plight of the French and did all they could to ameliorate it." Towards the French they displayed "qualities of kindness, magnanimity and justice . . . . They worked for the widest toleration and the most secure privileges for the Roman Catholic religion . . . . As a result they earned the affections of the French". Contemporary French-Canadians themselves testified to the fact. "Sir Guy Carleton is justly beloved of all classes of the people," writes the annalist of the Ursuline nuns. "His mild and paternal administration, his prudence and benevolence, his personal merits and kindness have rendered him dear to all ranks . . ." This happy accord, testified to by the frequency of intermarriage in the years after the Conquest, "was to be broken only with the appearance of the Francophobe Sir James Craig in 1807." If anyone had cause to complain it was the "poor mercantile devils", those English and German families, not necessarily engaged in fur-trading, that settled in Quebec immediately after the Conquest, the progenitors of what may now be nearly the oldest families of English speech in Canada. A word on their behalf is long overdue.

But as for the French-Canadians, Professor Lower has pointed out that their nationalism stemmed from later conditions. The clash with the English under Craig, Sewell and Ryland, gave direction and cohesion to it. "Whatever the niceties of the situation – and it is impossible to say unreservedly on which side the blame for it lay, though the heavier portion would appear to rest on some of the English – the racial quarrel heightened by the transfer of power from the seigneurial to the middle class, evoked the first burst of French Canadian nationalism". It was a reaction against seventeenth-century French orthodoxy and nineteenth century English commercialism (p. 223). It drew some inspiration from the French revolution, but in the end reacted against what that revolution stood for, thus strengthening the conservative tendency of Canadian life. The Loyalists, we may add, children of unsuccessful counter-revolution, had already done so. ". . . Canada was becoming the home of lost causes." The cause of French-Canadian nationalism was sometimes served by projecting the early nineteenth-century clash with "the English" back into the eighteenth century. Hence the origin of the mistaken idea that early British rule had been harsh.

In reality, if the French-Canadian survived, it was partly a result of the benignity of British rule. The continuance of their Church, that foundation-stone of their national culture, stemmed from what Professor Lower modestly calls "a typical untidy English arrangement." That the English would have been wrong not to have made that arrangement we can now see; but that it was made at a time when such liberality was rare, deserves to be commended for its excess, however slight, over mere expediency. Such commendation could not detract from Professor Lower's sympathetic treatment of French-Canadian institutions. For what other Canadian writer, French or English, has ever sought in equal reverence and humility to understand another's culture? The best, he writes, that the non-Catholic can do "is to describe as objectively as he can, well-knowing that whereas he may comprehend those areas which the two branches of the Christian faith have in common, he cannot penetrate the inner mysteries of the other, its nuances, the puzzles which make what seem irrational or erroneous to him, rational and holy for another. And yet, what historian of Canada worthy of his salt can fail to make this effort?"

Professor Lower has certainly made it. He contrasts St. Thomas' "splendidly logical collection of categories" with the "pragmatic, testing experimentation of later Protestantism . . ." "What Protestant," he asks, "can systematically discuss, say, the 'cardinal virtues', name them, and enumerate the qualities of each? Yet when St. Thomas discusses *prudence* as one of them, he does it logically, sanely, and in admirably orderly fashion. It would do no one any harm to put his ideas together about prudence. This to Roman Catholics, especially to the educated French-Canadian, has been the stuff of instruction for centuries." Its value may be conceded. Its faults may be noted. Even Professor Lower does not accept the *Summa* in its entirety (p. 59). But, as it happens, it is not the exclusive possession of the French-Canadians, since "our own English system of law, and through it, our other public institutions" are in a measure founded on it. "The modern English-speaking world finds underneath itself an embarrassing amount of Thomist foundation, and woe to it if it ever discards that for sheer expediency, for its liberties will disappear with its absolutes." Contrast this praise of the Thomist tradition with the admission that even the "Protestant Mammon" may serve a worthy end. Here is virtue of another order, without grandeur.

If there is a conscious bias in this comparison of the two dominant Canadian cultures, there is another, largely unconscious, which may account for the chief defect of the work under review. The original Dominion of 1867 resulted from a fusion of two areas, the Province of Canada as constituted by the Act of Union of 1840, and the Maritime Provinces. The latter had a long and separate history as a settled area. The three provinces by the sea had their own stops and pauses, their own conditions and determinants, which cannot always be fitted into the framework of the province on the St. Lawrence, nor can social conditions in that province be regarded as "representing" conditions on the seaboard. Professor Lower's book is an improvement on another which, in its day, was regarded as a major contribution to Canadian historical writing, namely W. P. M. Kennedy's *Constitution of Canada*, for in that work the Maritimes are referred to only fleetingly, and when the circumstances of their development happen to resemble those of the province on the St. Lawrence, or when they momentarily impinge upon the course of events in that area. The reader would never suspect that they had a constitutional history of their own, which was in significant detail different, and worthy of record.

One is prepared to admit that history happens in some places more than in others, and also that professionally written histories of phases of Maritime social life and institutions, that our author could have used in the preparation of his general work, are few in number. But there are many books of travel and description that provide much pertinent matter, and the above-mentioned conditions cannot be responsible for the scanty references to the second of the two constituent areas of the original Dominion. One can only conclude that these provinces are not really present in the foreground of our author's consciousness. As in another of his works, *Colony to Nation*, he pays a tribute to Nova Scotia for making much of itself in the early decades of the nineteenth century, and he has discerning things to say about the metropolitanism of Halifax, its class structure, and the convictions of its social élite. Nevertheless, the impression grows on the reader that when the Maritimes are referred to, it is by conscious effort to round out the story.

Sometimes the effort is not made. The title of chapter seventeen, "The height of prosperity: British North America during the eighteen-fifties," leads the reader to expect an account of British North America as a whole until on the first page he is brought up short with a reference to "the two provinces," and suddenly realizes that British North America means the areas that became Quebec and Ontario. Two passing references to other areas do not invalidate the criticism that the work cannot be considered as an adequate treatment of the social history of the whole country. When in the same chapter the reader comes upon the title of the sub-section, "The first provincial university" he find himself reading, not about the College of New Brunswick, which had been functioning as a school from 1786, and which was accorded the style and privileges of a university in its charter of February 12th, 1800, but of the University of Toronto decades later. Since the problem of the "separate watercourses" of each of the provinces has not been successfully met, the convergence of various colonial streams, wide and varied as the result may be, imposes no really new task upon the author (p. 240).

The remarks on the Maritimes, when they are made, show discernment. Nova Scotia's surviving examples of eighteenth century architecture are rightly appreciated. "Of its nineteenth century, or romantic architecture, possibly the less said the better," a remark which applies equally to Quebec where "church after church from the previous great age of building was either pulled down completely or disastrously reconstructed." These observations, and the admirable description of Kingston, illustrate the transition from an aristocratic to a middle-class society, but there is no systematic treatment of architectural styles, nor of any aspects of the social scene. He seems to move forward as material comes to hand, and as interest and fancy dictate, rather than to present an orderly progression of types under such headings as food, clothing and shelter, tools and utensils, means and amenities of travel and transportation, marriage and family life, amusements and associations, kinship and class distinctions, rituals, and beliefs. His task, the historian's task, in some sense lies midway between the categorization of the ethnolognical monograph and the imaginative reconstruction of the novelist who makes a world that might have been, but never was. His intuitive grasp of the changing patterns of time reveal the essential artistry of historical presentation, but his centres of reference may vary, and Professor Lower's is more nearly political than is, say, Trevelyan's in the latter's *English Social History*. Professor Lower has cast his subject in a wider mould than is customary with the social historian.

Nevertheless it is to some extent for his treatment of social data, traditionally conceived, this his book will appeal alike to the general reader and to the professional student. These data are drawn from many sources by an author whose eye is quick to catch the colourful, the variegated, the sometimes tragic, and the occasionally ludicrous elements of the human scene. Conclusions concerning the material conditions of life in New France may be drawn from the fact that by the mid-eighteenth century good town houses had glass windows, while farmer's houses still had paper panes. The use of forks by the upper class as early as 1662 was indicative of new standards of polite behaviour. That mediaeval ways, by contrast, persisted in the country districts is revealed by the story of the brawl between two parishes over the possession of the arm-bone of St. Paul. And how thankful were the Scottish settlers, in Cape Breton, to be divided from the unregenerate mainland is evident from the Presbyterian prayer: "And more especially do we thank Thee, O Lord, for the Gut of Canso, Thine own body of water, which separates us from the wickedness that lieth on the other side thereof" (p. 145). The Catholic and the Calvinist were no more zealous in the Faith, than the Anglican Senator Gowan of Barrie who, when a popish cross on the altar of Trinity Church met his astonished eyes, "shook the dust from the accursed spot from his feet in anger, and built his own church across the way; . . . ."

The incidents are colourful, but whether they are also typical is more difficult to say. The question must be posed in attempting to assess the value of a history of "conditions." Here norms are important and in many cases could only be fully established after a much more thorough canvass of the subject than could be attempted in the preparation of a general work such as this. Some of them are undoubtedly "far-fetched," but in the main the informed reader may sense their representative character, as in the accounts of the changing class structure and class attitudes of the country, each coloured by social origin, church affiliation, inherited and acquired wealth, and educational conditions. Generally it was the Tories and Anglicans who made most of their complex imperialism, but at one point it became general. "At the turn of the century the Canadian public school was not making young Canadians but young Englishmen. It is not surprising that fourteen years later, those boys rushed off across the seas to fight for a country they had never seen – to fight as perhaps men never fought before." There were exceptions: Canadians of French descent could not have been expected to feel this impulse in like measure, if at all. And neither could those immigrant groups, the New Canadians of whom Professor Lower gives a good account in his chapters on Canadian society in the twentieth century. What offering each element in the Canadian population will eventually leave on the altar of "the god, Equality" it is at this time impossible to say. The story is necessarily unfinished. Canadians are still "in the making." But few can any longer doubt that a new nationality is now emerging. Though Professor Lower seems to be one of the sceptics (p. xx) his own book is surely evidence of the fact.

12. On the Nature of The Distinction Between The French and the English In Canada: An Anthropological Inquiry

Anthropological investigations have long since revealed the frequency with which the names used by primitive tribes to designate themselves are, on being translated, found to mean "the people" in the sense that the users are the only "true" or "real" people and that their neighbours are scarcely to be regarded as fully qualified members of the human species. Although divine authority has not always been claimed in support of this view, the virtual universality of the conception of the chosen people, in some form or other, is generally recognized. Readers of Green and Freeman will recall the inherent virtues which they attributed to the so-called "Anglo-Saxon" element in the British population, whatever that element may be. Although the distressing history of the spurious ideas of race and racial superiority, from Gobineau through Houston Stuart Chamberlain to Hitler, has long been recognized for what it is worth, and has within the last few years been exposed in widely circulated books and pamphlets,[1] it is astonishing how much confusion reigns and how doggedly popular misconceptions of the subject persist. Barring catastrophes, shocking to think of, it is always easier to go on thinking in the habitual wrong-headed way. It conserves energy, and perhaps a general recognition of the truth would be repugnant to those self-regarding emotions that give collective coherence to large masses of men.

These misconceptions concerning the nature of race and

[1]For example, Julian Huxley, 'Race' in Europe, Oxford Pamphlets on World Affairs, no. 5 (Oxford, 1929); and Ruth Benedict and Gene Weltfish, The Races of Mankind, Public Affairs Pamphlet, no. 85 (1943).

nationality, and of the relationship between them, are not merely of academic interest. They underlie persistent mass attitudes and serve as either the springs of action, or the verbal ammunition directed against some group which is primarily an object of attack for economic or ideological reasons, far removed from the group's alleged inherent inferiority or undesirability. If these misconceptions underlie semitism, they also underlie anti-semitism. They serve to fortify the suspicions and hatred of one group for another. They nourish and add flesh to the delusions of the more virulent "racists" of Ontario and Quebec.

That the average citizen who has not made a special study of the subject often confuses the effects of nature and nurture in attribtuing certain mental endowment and temperament to particular racial stocks is perhaps not surprising in view of the fact that even scholars of eminence appear to have done so. Professor Trevelyan suggests that the sources of Shakespeare's poetic genius may be sought in the fact that he sprang from an area that was near an old borderland of Welsh and Saxon conflict. How "wild Celtic fancy" could be regarded as a cultural endowment as late as the sixteenth century, and in England at that, is hard to conceive. It is evident however that this is not how Professor Trevelyan thinks of the influence as having been handed down, for he speculates on the possible influence of the inheritance of Celtic "blood" upon the English temper.[2] We know well enough that blood is not inherited, and that even if it were, there would be no reason to suppose that it bore any relationship whatsoever to either intelligence or temperament. The statement is all the more inadmissible when it is remembered that there is not and never has been any such thing as Celtic blood. Although the four distinct blood groups recognized by scientists appear to have somewhat uneven distribution, most populations seem to have some representation from each group. Nevertheless, the fact has not yet been proved to have any significance in distinguishing between racial stocks or nationalities, for the differences in blood type do not appear to be co-ordinated with other variations in physical characteristics.[3] To include them among the factors that may distinguish one type of mentality from another would be quite fanciful in the light of present knowledge of the subject. As

[2] G. M. Trevelyan, *History of England* (London, New York, 1932), p. 45.

[3] J. S. Huxley and A. C. Haddon, *We Europeans, A Survey of "Racial" Problems* (New York and London, 1936), p. 100.

for the Celts, they may or may not have possessed so high a degree of physical uniformity as to be regarded as racially distinctive. That problem is quite irrelevant, however, for the term properly denotes a group of peoples who spoke languages which were variants of a discernible linguistic stock, and about whom there has clustered, owning to the contingencies of historic circumstances, certain cultural traits which, by association with particular peoples and the languages which they spoke, have also become commonly identified as Celtic. It is clear from the context that Professor Trevelyan does not employ the term "Celtic blood" figuratively to mean culture in accordance with common usage, but is speculating as to the reality of the biological transmission of mental and emotional characteristics throughout long periods of time. Such speculation is without scientific foundation.

Professor Toynbee does not appear to have taken the same view in his search for the origins of Egyptian civilization. Having exposed the fallacy of concomitant variations in physical and psychical characteristics with masterful irony directed against modern western racists, in what must stand as one of the finest pieces of writing on the subject, he goes on to observe that the creative contributions of more than one racial stock are necessary to the geneses of civilizations.[4] The unwary reader might suppose that what Professor Toynbee is asserting is that the mental and emotional endowment required for cultural advancement must derive from a mingling of racial stocks through miscegenation and the consequent production of a superior biological type. A closer reading, however, surely will reveal that what he intends is that there must be a mingling, not necessarily of races, but of the cultural features that they bear with them in migration, and that these cultures become creative in the moment of contact through interaction and mutual stimulation. Although the fusion of cultural strains into a richer and more vital amalgam would no doubt be hastened by the greater intimacy resulting from intermarriage between members of the converging peoples, yet the production of a hybrid physical type is incidental and irrelevant, since the association of a particular racial structure with a particular mentality is fortuitous and does not stand in the relation of cause and effect. For, as Dr. Jenness argued so convincingly some years ago, the degree of cultural advancement of any

[4]Arnold J. Toynbee, A Study of History (London, 1934), Vol. I, p. 240.

given people, and the style and content of their culture, are not
in any way related to their physique by virtue of its relative
purity or as the product of racial mixture.[5] Culture has its own
dynamic, and cultural phenomena are sufficiently explained in
their own terms. Advancement in the stages of civilization has
been enjoyed by those people who have been situated at strategic crossroads and have thus been in a position to receive and
react to the fertilizing waves of cultural influence that have
flowed in upon them from several quarters, shattering the
pattern of use and wont, setting old attitudes and old techniques at nought, issuing successive challenges to their ingenuity
and at the same time augmenting and refining their capacity
to respond creatively and effect novel integrations on ever and
ever higher levels as long as the process remains undisturbed.
There comes a time when such people become a "world in
themselves," when, as it were, the pot "comes to a boil" and
they begin to give back more than they receive. It seems likely
that in some such way as this, cultural nuclei were often formed
from which subsequently emanations have been carried out-
wards to peripheral areas. By contrast those peoples whose lot
has been cast in isolated places have remained backward. These
processes, as well as the type of culture existing in any area,
are to be defined and explained in terms of the complex inter-
actions within the cultural environment, and between it and
the physical environment, and are entirely irrespective of the
racial features of the people involved, except in so far as people
may be influenced to approve or disapprove of certain physical
types in their social relations in which case cultural processes
will be modified thereby.

The foregoing observations may serve as a sketch of the
larger setting within which the question of the nature of the
distinction between the French and the English in Canada may
be considered. We have been speaking of culture in the sense
in which it was defined by Tylor, as "that complex whole which
includes knowledge, belief, art, morals, law, custom and other
capabilities and habits acquired by man as a member of
society." We have employed the term "race" in its biological
sense as a hereditary subdivision of the species homo sapiens,
corresponding to a breed in domestic animals, or, in Professor
Ginsberg's words as "a group of individuals who, within given

[5]Diamond Jenness, *The Indian Background of Canadian History*,
Bull. no. 86, Anthropological Series no. 21 (National Museum of
Canada, Ottawa, 1937).

limits of variation, possess in common a combination of hereditary traits sufficient to mark them off from other groups."[6] He
adds that if they are to be used as criteria of race, traits must
be hereditary and remain relatively constant despite changes
in the environment, and that they must be common to a fairly
large group. It is to be inferred that he is referring to physical
and not to mental traits.

We are now in a position to apply our criteria to the problem in hand, as to the terms in which the two major Canadian
peoples are to be distinguished from each other. Our submission
is simply that the differences between them as French and as
English are not differences of racial inheritance but of cultural
acquisition, have not arisen as a result of a biological diversity,
are not in any way a reflection of unlike blood, but on the
contrary are no more and no less than very limited differences
between the cultural traits and configurations that they have
acquired through the social interaction of mind and mind, and
through which their common psychic endowment as human
beings finds a degree of expression and fulfillment. This means
that the terms French and English denote acquired mental
variations, and do not denote, either significant or relevant
variations in physique, or inherited differences in mentality.
One man is not born to think in a certain way because his
headshape is dolichocephalic, and another man differently
because he is brachycephalic. No man is born to think in a
particular way at all, or if he is, that way may not be labelled
either French or English; and no man ever had or ever will
have dolichocephalic thoughts. A man may think in a way that
can be described as English; but if he does he has learned to
think that way through his social contacts with persons of
English culture in some of its various manifestations. His doing
so is thus a cultural and not a biological phenomenon.

One would anticipate an inquiry at this point as to whether
it is here contended that the average of the physique of people
of French culture was exactly similar to the norm about which
persons of English culture vary with respect to racial traits. An
answer to this question as to whether the English and French
Canadians are racially diverse may be approached first by
making some observations on the racial composition of European peoples.

It is a well-known fact that there is a greater physical
resemblance between the Germans of the Rhineland and the

[6]Morris Ginsberg, *Sociology* (London, 1934), p. 56.

neighbouring French than there is between those same Germans and their fellow nationals in eastern Germany who resemble the Poles more closely than they resemble the western Germans. In addition to this racial diversity between east and west in Germany, it is also a well-known fact that the racial composition of Europe is characterized roughly by broad belts running east and west so that the dominant variation is between north and south. Consequently the people in the southern part of France resemble those of south Germany more than they do their own compatriots in northern France. There is considerable racial diversity in France and it is quite inaccurate to speak of a French race. The same thing may be said of England.

The populations of both places are racially mixed as are all populations, but is the same mixture to be found in France as in England? We are told that of the three so-called basic races of Europe the English exhibit more Mediterranean and Nordic traits whereas the populations of France appear to have more of the Alpine ingredient than do those of England.

It is perhaps premature to speculate on the significance of Boas's investigations into the alleged changes wrought in the anatomical structure of certain European stocks resulting from their migration to the new environment of the United States, and on the implications of the possible racial variations in the behaviour of the endocrine glands or as a result of them, which may also, if true, be reactive to environmental conditions and changes. But if there is anything in these contentions it would simply mean that racial characteristics are less stable than ethnologists have hitherto supposed. It might also add weight to the supposition that the so-called primary European races, the Alpine, Mediterranean, and Nordic, are not and never have been races at all, but are simply ideal types invented by man in his attempt to establish frames of reference with which to gauge variations in physique. If this were so we might still seek for a comparison between the norms for England and France, but we would now employ such a label as Alpine not with the idea that it designates a race that once inhabited a part of France, but only as a convenient way of describing a tendency towards stockiness in combination with dark-hairedness and round headedness. We might thus be no nearer than we were before to determining the historic affinity between the peoples of England and France whether in Europe or in North America.

Even if we shift our attention for a moment from racial groupings to those identifiable by tribal and linguistic designations, we may not be in a much better position to determine precise distinctions. But we can be reasonably sure that the affinity between Gaul and Britain, Saxon and Frank, Dane and Norman was not remote, racially mixed as these peoples must have been. The prehistoric peoples in these areas were not as distinct as night is from day,[7] and later migrations brought Huguenots into England and Celts to Britanny, to mention only two noteworthy movements of peoples. It is therefore not surprising that there are many individuals in France who resemble individuals in England far more closely in physique than they do their own compatriots. The same statement can be made with confidence about French and English Canada, in spite of the selective process involved in migration to North America.

If there are any racial differences as between the English-speaking and the French-speaking populations they are very slight. It may be that certain physical types are more commonly found in the area where English is spoken than where French is the prevailing language, or that the average tendencies towards certain types of physique are not exactly the same in the two populations. They are not exactly alike in any two selected populations. They are not alike as between Rivière du Loup and Chicoutimi, or as between Moose Jaw and Regina. And yet these facts, even if recognized by the people themselves, would not make the people of Rivière du Loup regard themselves as any more or any less truly French than the people of Chicoutimi, nor would they develop a sense of distinctive nationality on the bases of such recognition. If it were claimed that the English exhibited a stronger tendency towards blondness than the French, the same might conceivably be said of Hamilton as compared with Toronto, but we could only add that the difference, if such exists, would be totally lacking in significance. If all other marks of identification were lacking how could a pathologist decide from the physical characteristics alone whether a body recovered from the St. Lawrence River at Montreal were that of an English or a French person? What, one might well ask, does an English Canadian look like? We cannot answer that question. Many varieties are found among English Canadians, and much the same varieties are found in French Canada. If there were a general notion among the English that the French Canadians were overwhelmingly brunette, how would they account for the frequency with which blue-eyed and flaxen-haired children may be observed on the

7R. Munro, *Prehistoric Britain* (London, n.d.), p. 228.

roadways of Les Escoumains, Baie Milles Vaches, and the Saguenay villages, to mention only a remote and isolated part of the Province of Quebec. We may conclude therefore that much the same range of variation is found among both peoples, that it is impossible to identify an individual with absolute certainty from his racial features alone as belonging to either one or the other group, while admitting at the same time that certain physical types may be found more frequently among the English than among the French, or that the tendency towards certain physical characteristics may be found more pronounced and more widely diffused in the one than in the other.

But when we have said this we have said very little, for we cannot claim that any very slight differences in average tendency that there may be are of any greater significance as a basis for distinction between French and English than are the slight racial differences between any two English-Canadian communities, which means that they are no real bases at all. Such differences as there are between the French and the English are national, not racial, cultural and acquired, not inherited. It is conceivable that there might be a people possessing a high degree of racial uniformity, as among themselves, and a considerable divergence in appearance between themselves and their neighbours, the recognition of which might form an ingredient of their sense of distinctive nationality. But no such uniformity within, nor marked divergence between, the French and the English may be said to exist. Such differences as exist are popularly exaggerated and are generally misconstrued as meaning an inherited difference in mentality as between the two. There is no predisposition of a child born to English-speaking parents to speak English also. The child could as easily acquire any other language as English, in the way that all languages are acquired. That child could be taken at birth and reared in a French-Canadian household, and it would be just as truly a French Canadian as any other child, because it would acquire from its social environment those traits which would make it a French Canadian in the way in which all French Canadians come to be what they are. The reverse procedure would be exactly the same.

The complete lack of significance of the racial factor as a mark of distinctiveness between the French-Canadian and English-Canadian nationalities may be accepted more readily than the view that these groups are not to be divided from each other on the basis of hereditary temperamental differences. The question of the nature and method of transmission of temperament is an important but vexing one, since much scientific investigation remains to be carried out before positive statements can be made. Nevertheless what seem to the writer to be rational inferences may be drawn from what is now known or hypothetical, and we may profitably apply our surmises to the question which we have here been considering.

We should mention also the claims that have been made in recent years for what is in fact a new kind of climatic determinism and which must be received with definite and specific reservations. Even if we accepted the view that temperament varies between groups for physiological reasons derived from the character of diet, and in the last analysis because of climatically determined soil constituents, we should still be inclined to reject Lieutenant Commander J. R. de la H. Marett's explanation in physiological terms of such cultural differences as may distinguish one nationality from another.[8] At best the theory would require that the given population, whose temperament was to be explained, should be socially undifferentiated, immobile over a long period of time, uniform in its dietary habits, completely dependent for its subsistence upon the immediate environment, and entirely cut off from cultural contacts. If any people were so situated they must have lived out their narrow lives in a time not far removed from the dawn of the human race. Their area of distribution would conceivably have been in a large measure ecological, and their culture closely conditioned by the ecological factor. But not completely so, for the status of humanity postulates social communication (that is to say, the interaction of minds through the medium of language) and thus the existence of primary diffusion within the group, making for cultural elaboration transcending the dictates of the physical environment. The operation of physiological determinants would thus be limited on even the most primitive cultural levels. As the transcendence of such dictates by modern advanced cultures, with their technological mastery of the physical world, is so much the greater, no such condition as those adumbrated by the climatic determinists can be accepted in explanation of the difference in temperament between modern nationalities. Even if these

[8] J. R. de la H. Marett, *Race, Sex and Environment, A Study of Mineral Deficiency in Human Evolution* (London, 1936). The theory is summarized by T. K. Penniman in *A Hundred Years of Anthropology* (New York, 1936), pp. 258-63.

conditions were applicable to modern populations there would be no reason to suppose that the ecological area of a distinctive temperament would at all coincide with the area inhabited by a particular nationality. Furthermore the cultural distinction between modern nationalities is uninfluenced by the fact that they sometimes live in practically identical climatic conditions. A further objection is grounded in the fact that, with rapid and efficient transportation, large numbers of people now vary their habitat, and even if they remain where they are most of the time, they draw the constituents of their diet from many different climatic regions. The French and English Canadians of Montreal or Ottawa will both habitually eat oranges from California, drink coffee from Brazil, and even sometimes consume butter from New Zealand.

Before raising the most serious objection to this climatic theory, it might be well to dispose of the idea that the French and English Canadians are distinguished, as such, by inherited temperamental differences. We may begin by admitting that individual differences in intelligence and temperament obviously exist, and that to a limited extent they are certainly transmitted in family lines. But it is a far cry from this to the contention that whole nations have norms of inherited temperamental factors that diverge from each other.[9] A moment's reflection will reveal that such inherited mental differences cannot be attributed to a numerous population, whether that population constitutes a nationality or not. Instead of one nationality being, metaphorically, all of one colour, and the other being all of another colour, we would suggest that many and similar colours pepper each of the national areas in about equal measure. Just as there are fat men and thin men, in varying degrees, everywhere, so temperamental types probably have much the same frequency in every population, as far as the inherited element is concerned. The merging of lineages through intermarriage would certainly occur with greater frequency within one than between two nationalities, and with the passage of time the hereditary element in temperament might be expected to become more uniformly distributed throughout the population of a particular nationality, but to use this as an argument for a distinctive national temperament stemming from hereditary factors would be dangerous in view of the probability that the range of variations in temperament as between the two nationalities would appear to be much the

[9]Ruth Benedict, *Patterns of Culture* (London, 1935), p. 15.

same, with the types occuring with equal frequency in both peoples. Our argument is here hypothetical but we are not indulging in sheer speculation since the results of research appear to point towards the conclusion we have suggested. For although we have been speaking of temperamental or, more broadly, personality types as though they existed in fact, they are really abstractions in the sense that a pure racial type is an abstraction. No individual is truly representative of any of the ideal types, and there is support for the inference that the same assortment of hereditary elements possesses the same frequency regardless of differences in language and social tradition. The concomitant variation of temperament with racial traits remains to be proved. The attempt to link Kretschmer's constitutional types with particular races has not succeeded, and it is thought that all of them are found in every population.[10] Hence it may be said that nationalities, even if one allows for a possible clumping in some localities, would also appear to possess them all in much the same measure. Finally we cannot surmise what effects the blending of lineages through intermarriage would have upon temperament. There appears to be no evidence that it produces a levelling out in the population, since the characters may react in such a way as to produce perpetual differences as marked and varied as were the originals.

We may now state the most serious objection to both the environmentalist theory and that purporting to explain such temperamental characteristics as rapidity and intensity of response to stimuli, aggressiveness, sense of humour, and the like in physiological terms. If carried too far they leave little or no room for the operations of the cultural environment. Temperament is actually compounded of the interaction of physiological and cultural processes, and that the latter are not negligible could be proved from a host of examples, among which is the fact that worry sometimes causes gastric ulcers. The cultural processes react upon the physiological, and temperament is in large part a product of the social environment. It is itself to some extent an aspect of culture played upon and developed by other cultural aspects. It is acquired by man in the course of his responses, not to the physical environment alone but also to the cultural configuration of the group in which he becomes a member. Although generalizations are difficult to make in such cases, we would expect temperamental

[10]Ginsberg, *Sociology*, p. 75; Otto Klineberg, *Race Differences* (New York, 1935), p. 61.

differences to be more marked as between occupational groups in the highly differentiated society of modern Canada than we would between the French and English inhabitants of the country. In so far as temperament is an aspect of culture we are ready to agree that temperamental differences may exist as a cultural diversity exists, but this is no more than saying that the French and English represent partially diverse variants of the Western European cultural complex as modified by habituation to new world conditions. The difference between them is acquired and not inherited.

The disentanglement and clarification of the basic human categories of race, language, and culture is one of the major contributions of the science of anthropology. There was a time when it was thought that there was an organic relationship between the shape of a man's skull and the language he spoke, instead, as is now clearly realized, of an association which is really fortuitous. It was like saying that a green apple tastes green when there is no such thing as a green taste. Although language is replete with such metaphors it is essentially the language of poetry, not the language of science. As Confucius said, only social confusion and disorder can be expected to result from not calling things by their right names. To speak of an English race is to employ a cultural adjective to describe a physical noun. The effect is almost as meaningless as to reverse the order and use a physical adjective to qualify a cultural noun. The absurdity of speaking of a blue-eyed language or of a dolichocephalic religion is evident enough. As Professor Kroeber wrote a quarter of a century ago, it represents a confusion between the organic and the superorganic, between inherited and acquired characteristics.[11] Nor is it a harmless confusion, for it attributes to nature what is in reality a product of society. The widespread belief that the French and the English in Canada are distinguished from each other as are two breeds of domestic animals imposes a barrier where none in reality exists. From attributing to nature the distinction between the two peoples, it is only a step to the belief that intimacy between them is contrary to divine ordinance. The eradication of such notions should lead to an improvement of the mutual relations of the French and the English in Canada. It would represent a victory of science and rational inference from ascertained facts over the prejudice to which selfishness and ignorance give rise. One could go further than the Spanish

[11]A. L. Kroeber, *Anthropology* (New York, 1923), p. 57.

ambassador to the court of Louis XIV, and say that, as far as a barrier in nature is concerned, the Pyrenees never did exist..

Acknowledgements

The documentary poem, "Confederation Debate," which serves as a sort of frontispiece, was published in the *Dalhousie Review*, Winter, 1968-69, pp. 521-2.

Four of the papers contained in this volume have not been previously published. The first, "Vanished Iroquoians," began as an attempt to rewrite "The Significance of the Identity and Disappearance of Laurentian Iroquois" which appeared in the *Transactions of the Royal Society of Canada*, third series, section II, Vol. XXVIII (1933), pp. 97-108.

The paper entitled, "Evidences of Culture Considered as Colonial," appears in print for the first time, as do "William Alexander Foster and the Genesis of English-Canadian Nationalism," and "Canada First: the Dissident Press and the Public Image."

The second paper entitled "The Ordeal of the Eastern Algonkians" appeared under the title, "Social Revolution in Early Eastern Canada" in the *Canadian Historical Review*, Vol. XIX, (Sept., 1938), pp. 264-276.

"Creative Moments in the Culture of the Maritime Provinces" was published in the *Dalhousie Review*, Vol. 29, (Oct. 1949), pp. 231-244 and was re-printed and distributed by the Canadian Humanities Research Council in pamphlet form. It was included by Dr. George Rawlyk in his *Historical Essays on the Atlantic Provinces*, in 1967, published by McClelland and Stewart in the Carleton Library Series as Number 35. It was also included in part in *Atlantic Anthology*, published by McClelland and Stewart, in 1959.

"Literature and Nationalism in the Aftermath of Confederation" was published under a slightly different title in the *University of Toronto Quarterly*, Vol. 25, (July, 1956), pp. 409-424.

"Railways and the Confederation Issue in New Brunswick" was published in the *Canadian Historical Review*, Vol. 21, (Dec. 1940), pp. 367-383. "The Basis and Persistence of Opposition to Confederation in New Brunswick" was also published in the *Canadian Historical Review*, Vol. 23, (Dec. 1942), pp. 374-397, and was republished in *Confederation* (Canadian History Readings, 3) ed. Ramsey Cook/Craig Brown/Carl Berger, (Toronto, 1967), pp. 70-93. "Keystone of the Arch" appeared in the *Atlantic Advocate*, (April, 1964), pp. 40-41, 43-46.

Number 11, "An Adventure in Social History: Arthur Lower's Vision of *'les Deux Nations'*" was published in the *Queen's Quarterly*, Vol. LXVI, (1959), pp. 312-319 under the title of "Sitting in Judgement on the Past."

The paper entitled "On the Nature of the Distinction between the French and the English in Canada: An Anthropological Enquiry," was published in the *Annual Report of the Canadian Historical Association* in 1947, pp. 63-71. This paper was republished, but in abbreviated form, with sections left out, in *Social Problems/A Canadian Profile*, Richard Laskin, ed., (Toronto, 1964), pp. 30-35.

Permission to re-print these papers is gratefully acknowledged.

NOTE ON THE AUTHOR

Alfred Goldsworthy Bailey was born in Quebec and educated at the universities of New Brunswick, Toronto and the London School of Economics. After a spell in journalism he became Assistant Director and Curator of the New Brunswick Museum in 1935, going to the University of New Brunswick in 1938 as Professor of History and head of the department, later holding concurrently a professorship in Anthropology. From 1946 he served as Dean of Arts and in 1965 he became Academic Vice-President of the University. He is now retired from administrative duties but continues in a teaching capacity. He is a Fellow of the Royal Society of Canada and was H. A. Innis Visiting Professor at the University of Toronto in 1955-56.

A scholar of many interests, his most important work is *The Conflict of European and Eastern Algonkian Cultures, 1504-1700. A Study in Canadian Civilization*. Originally published by the New Brunswick Museum in 1937, this work has now been revised and reissued (Toronto, 1969). He is the author of several volumes of poetry: *Songs of the Saguenay and other Poems* (Quebec, 1927); *Tâo*, reflecting his interest in Chinese philosophy (Toronto, 1930); and *Border River* (Toronto, 1952).

THE CARLETON LIBRARY